BEYOND THE STATUS QUO

BEYOND THE STATUS QUO

POLICY PROPOSALS FOR AMERICA

edited by
David Boaz and Edward H. Crane

CATO
INSTITUTE

Library of Congress Cataloging in Publication Data
Main entry under title:

Beyond the status quo.

   1. United States—Economic policy—1981–   —
Addresses, essays, lectures.   2. United States—Politics
and government—1981–   —Addresses, essays, lectures.
I. Boaz, David, 1953–   .   II. Crane, Edward H.,
1944–   .   III. Cato Institute.
HC106.8. B48   1985   338.973   84-29324
ISBN 0-932790-46-1
ISBN 0-932790-49-6 (pbk.)

Printed in the United States of America.

CATO INSTITUTE
224 Second Street SE
Washington, DC 20003

Contents

I. Introduction

David Boaz and Edward H. Crane

The Potomac Fever that afflicts so many residents of the nation's capital takes many forms: the tendency to place reelection ahead of the public interest, the reluctance to "go home again" after defeat or retirement, the propensity to get so caught up in Washington that one forgets the views or even the existence of the rest of the country.

One less-remarked symptom of Potomac Fever is the policy myopia that so many policy analysts fall prey to. Analysts, especially those based in Washington, focus their attention on the White House and the legislative process to such an extent that they ignore fundamental problems and solutions. Caught up in the attempt to make incremental changes in inherently flawed programs, they miss the forest for the trees.

Consider the nature of policy debates in Washington over the past generation or more. A new program is proposed—social security, airline regulation, farm subsidies, food stamps. When it moves onto the political agenda, there is heated debate in Congress and in the larger policy community. After a few legislative failures it is finally passed by Congress, probably by a narrow margin. At the time, analysts and policymakers are closely divided as to whether or not the program is a good idea. The next year, however, when its appropriation comes up for renewal, the program is passed without debate, or with some debate over whether its budget should be increased by, say, 7 percent or 12 percent. From then on the program becomes part of the permanent governmental structure, beyond political debate. Is that because each and every program of the last 50 years has worked out so well? Obviously not. Rather, policy myopia has set in. With the establishment of a program, policy debate comes to be restricted to matters of fine-tuning; whether or not a program should continue to exist is rarely questioned.

Recently this pattern was broken in one area—airline regulation—when Congress ordered the Civil Aeronautics Board to go

1

out of existence at the end of 1984. As the end approached, bureaucrats were floundering. How do you close down an agency? they wondered. No one had any experience in it. The only previous example was the termination of the Community Services Agency in 1981—and the only precedent CSA had been able to find was the court-ordered closing of the National Recovery Administration in 1935. In other words, three significant agencies have been closed in 50 years, hardly a sign of close, regular examination of the federal government's programs.

The problem was recognized a few years ago at the state level, and several states passed "sunset laws" providing for various agencies to go out of existence at some definite time unless the legislature specifically reauthorized them. However, in most cases the agencies in question have managed to rouse themselves from lethargy to create constituencies for themselves, causing the legislature to grant them continued existence.

This experience highlights the general tendency of government agencies to perpetuate themselves and to grow. Thomas Jefferson said 200 years ago, "The natural progress of things is for liberty to yield and government to gain ground." More recently, the public choice economists have looked carefully at the nature of government and have found that Jefferson was entirely right. The concentrated benefits and diffused costs of any government action in a mixed-economy democracy mean that every program and agency will have its steadfast defenders who, in the words of Vilfredo Pareto, "know no rest by day or night" in the attempt to defend their privileges. The average consumer or taxpayer, however, paying a few cents or a few dollars for each program, never finds it in his interest to lobby against any one program. Thus the tendency is for programs and agencies to proliferate—so much so that each individual in society is a net loser regardless of what benefit he might gain from a particular program, be it trucking regulation, automobile import quotas, or Urban Development Action Grants.

Besides the influence of outside special interests, of course, there is the natural tendency of politicians and bureaucrats to expand their own power. Once we recognize that people in government are as self-interested as those in the private sector, we realize that they will try to increase their own bureaucracies, budgets, and authority. The system is sometimes called the "iron triangle": a particular agency, the congressional committees that oversee it, and the interest groups that benefit from it form a barrier impermeable

2

to outside criticism. Perhaps we should call it the "iron quadrangle," including as well the outside policy analysts who specialize in critiquing it—generally at the behest of agency, congressional committee, or interest group. Even independent policy analysts may become so mired in the details of a current program that they become unable or unwilling to look at its underlying problems.

We can be sure that the case *for* any particular program or agency will be well articulated by the agency itself and by its allied interest groups and policy analysts. In a free society, it is incumbent on independent analysts and private research organizations to counter this trend, to consider carefully whether a particular program is serving the public interest. If an analyst determines that the public good is in fact not well served, he should present his findings forthrightly, calling for fundamental change or abolition (if appropriate) and not simply for another round of fine-tuning. It is his responsibility to recommend the right course of action, not what he thinks may be "politically feasible."

The Cato Institute sees its mission in this light. It is the purpose of the institute to widen the parameters of public debate, both to involve more Americans in the debate over the direction of public policy and to illuminate policy options that are consistent with the traditional American principles of peace, limited government, and the free market.

The present volume is inspired by that sense of purpose. Though its authors range from experienced public officials to creative young analysts, they share a common concern for the values of individual liberty and economic opportunity and maintain a willingness to move beyond policy myopia to view the larger picture. Of course, no author necessarily agrees with the proposals of any other author, but their essays are bound together by this shared perspective.

As Jefferson warned, government has grown dramatically in the United States. Though we remain a free society by any standard of human history and contemporary alternatives, the growth of government has restricted our freedom in many ways. It has also, inevitably, slowed down economic growth, closed off opportunities, and shut many people out of the economic mainstream. The essays in this book point the way toward reducing the size of government and restoring growth and opportunity in a manner fully consistent with the values upon which America was founded.

Many of the problems brought about by the growth of government could be alleviated by a three-pronged attack on the tax and

3

spending process, that is, by income tax indexing, a balanced budget amendment, and tax simplification. Such a program would prevent the government from profiting from inflation through the tax system, tame the soaring budget deficits, and eliminate the distorting effects of high tax rates and complex exemptions.

The first of these objectives, of course, has been realized; but we must work to preserve indexing against those who would impose new tax increases on the middle class in the name of fiscal responsibility.

The second goal, that of requiring a balanced federal budget, is the subject of the first essay presented here. James Dale Davidson, founder and chairman of the National Taxpayers Union, has been involved in the battle for a balanced budget amendment since it began more than a decade ago. Davidson argues that current constitutional rules have allowed the political authorities to increase spending dramatically and to create a political business cycle by manipulating the monetary system. Only constitutional change, like the Balanced Budget Amendment, can constrain the power of narrow interest groups and produce fiscal responsibility. The Balanced Budget Amendment, Davidson says, is a marginal reform—not because its effects would be trivial, but because it would increase the marginal costs of additional government spending.

A third, crucial fiscal reform is tax simplification and rate reduction. Jule R. Herbert Jr. addresses the complex questions involved in tax policy, pointing out that while economic growth alone may not eliminate the federal deficit, it is certainly true that sustained growth must play some part in deficit reduction. The best way to encourage economic growth is to reduce the huge economic distortions caused by our present tax system. Herbert offers some plausible principles on which tax reform should be based, ranging from the familiar concepts of equity, economic efficiency, and simplicity to some equally important but less often noted principles: tax consciousness, the idea that taxpayers should know just how much they are paying in taxes, so hidden taxes should be avoided; taxpayer solidarity, resulting from a tax system that puts all taxpayers in the same position relative to the tax level rather than pitting them against one another; and neutrality, the idea that taxes should do "as little as possible to interfere with the marketplace decisions that would be made if taxes were actually market-generated prices." He concludes that an appropriate tax reform plan would increase personal exemptions, lower maximum rates, and eliminate at least some special interest deductions.

As we endeavor to reduce the size of government and to promote economic prosperity, it is important to evaluate specific government programs while bearing in mind that government cannot produce prosperity; it can only allow people to create it. The largest domestic program by far is social security, for almost 50 years the cornerstone of the American welfare state. Social security now stands as a monument to the welfare-state concept: teetering at the edge of bankruptcy, inflexible, and increasingly a bad deal. Peter J. Ferrara, whose 1980 book *Social Security: The Inherent Contradiction* was the most detailed fundamental critique of the system's problems ever written, contends that the 1983 tax increase package cannot save social security. The program, he argues, still faces short-term economic vulnerability and long-term bankruptcy. Rejecting both benefit cuts and additional tax increases, Ferrara calls for a reform that would gradually allow young workers to opt out of the system. The reform would begin by guaranteeing benefits to current retirees and by creating a new Super IRA program into which workers could invest part of their social security taxes. Eventually workers would be allowed to transfer all their payroll taxes to private retirement plans, which would give them a much better return on their investment. Ferrara's proposal would protect the elderly from a future tax revolt, prevent staggering tax burdens on younger workers, inject hundreds of billions of dollars into the private economy, and avert the economic and social catastrophe of a social security collapse. It would eventually reduce the size of government dramatically, while guaranteeing American workers a more secure and comfortable retirement.

All of these proposals—the Balanced Budget Amendment, tax reform, and social security privatization—would reduce the burden of government on the economy and encourage economic growth. But these policies are not the only reforms required for an economic environment conducive to prosperity. Bruce Bartlett argues that a renewed appreciation of the role of the entrepreneur is essential. He cites the benefits of competition and entrepreneurship in the high-technology field and the results of deregulation in such areas as air travel. He warns that "the cost to society of . . . restrictions on freedom is measured in products not produced, inventions not invented, innovations not pursued, savings not achieved, and

5

advances not made." To encourage entrepreneurship, he recommends such reforms as eliminating the double taxation of corporate dividends, replacing income taxation with consumption taxes, reducing the estate and gift tax, and deregulating in many areas.

One of the most important ways government interferes with the market process and discourages economic growth is protectionism. Since the time of Adam Smith, economists have agreed that the general interest is well served by free trade. But since before Smith's time businessmen have sought protection from the rigors of international competition, and governments have given it to them. Murray L. Weidenbaum decries the costs of current American trade barriers and proposes several strategies for moving toward free trade: sound macroeconomic policy, limits on trade-adjustment assistance, resistance to international regulation, and a "reciprocity" program under which the United States would simultaneously remove specific barriers to imports and to U.S. exports. If the Reagan administration is truly committed to free enterprise—and not just to helping business—it will move to reduce U.S. trade barriers. No other program would so clearly serve the public interest and impart greater health to our economy.

International affairs, of course, are not limited to economic matters. In a penetrating essay, Earl Ravenal warns about the costs and dangers associated with our commitment to the defense of Western Europe. He points out that American and European interests are increasingly divergent, making the Atlantic alliance less stable and perhaps untenable. Our commitment explicitly involves a willingness to use nuclear weapons to respond to a Soviet attack on Europe, clearly heightening the risk of nuclear war for Americans. Ravenal also points out that the United States will spend on NATO some $129 billion this year and some $2 trillion over the next decade, a cost that American taxpayers may be increasingly unwilling to bear in a time of $200 billion deficits. American disengagement from Europe, Ravenal argues, would not mean European defeat. Our allies would no doubt pursue several courses, possibly including national nuclear forces, improved conventional defenses, or a new European military community. When we contemplate European discontent with American policies, and the costs and risks to Americans of our NATO commitment, disengagement seems the most plausible solution for both parties to the alliance.

Moving back to domestic issues, Thomas Gale Moore discusses some regulatory reforms that the Reagan administration has so far failed to take up. Moore has been urging deregulation for more than a decade in such books as *Freight Transportation Regulation: Surface Freight and the Interstate Commerce Commission* and *Trucking Regulation: Lessons from Europe*. In his present essay, he urges the administration to make congressional action on regulatory reform a high priority. He identifies two particular reforms as most important: a more cost-effective approach to the Clean Air Act and the abolition of natural gas regulations. These are not the only instances in which regulation restricts consumer sovereignty or raises costs, however, and Moore also urges reform in such areas as emissions control, surface transportation, communications, banking, food and drugs, and the like. If Moore's proposals were implemented during the next four years, consumers would save tens of billions of dollars, economic growth would increase, and jobs would be created.

Focusing on a specific regulatory area, Catherine England urges sweeping reforms of the antitrust laws, criticizing them for favoring competitors over the competitive process and for discouraging vigorous competition. Antitrust is based on the naive economic theory of "perfect competition"—in which virtually all the processes one normally associates with competition are absent. This theory leads regulators to penalize firms for such consumer-oriented activities as price-cutting, economies of scale, and new product introduction. While abolition of the antitrust laws might well serve consumers best by allowing vigorous competition, several reforms short of abolition could be undertaken immediately to reduce the costs of antitrust. Ultimately, England argues, "the only sources of permanent monopoly power are governments," and those who want to root out monopolies would be well advised to direct their scrutiny toward such government activities as marketing orders, licensing laws, and exclusive franchises.

Milton Mueller examines deregulation in an industry where regulation has implications far beyond those pertaining to economic efficiency—the information industry. The information revolution, he argues, is not just deregulation but the extension of the capitalist revolution of the Renaissance to the information economy. At long last information is slipping out of the control of governments, with far-reaching consequences—not just for economics but for civil liberties. Mueller urges a move toward private property and free markets in communications as the best means to protect First Amendment rights, and warns of a reaction against the free flow

7

of information by governments and ideologues of both left and right.

Clint Bolick takes up another form of information transmittal—education. Concerned about the rising costs and declining quality of public schools, he places the blame squarely on the fundamental problem: the monopoly nature of public schooling. Public education is a political process and as such is susceptible to control by special interests. Monopoly schooling requires homogenization, thus severely limiting educational diversity. Most fundamentally, monopolies are subject to little or no competitive pressure and hence do not have to produce a quality product. Bolick, an attorney who has been involved in both legislative and judicial efforts for education tax credits, urges a federal tax credit program to give educational choice to parents who cannot now afford it. He points out that many poor families already scrape up the money to send their children to private schools; more children should have the opportunity to escape the trap that an inferior education creates for them. A meaningful tax credit program, with credits large enough to cover the full cost of schooling at an average private school, would give millions of parents and students new options. In addition to tax credits, Bolick urges such "trust-busting" reforms as legalizing home schooling, relaxing private school regulations, and eliminating teacher certification requirements. Ultimately, "America's educational crisis can be solved only by freeing the market for education."

Low-quality education traps many poor children, but it is not the only trap we have created for the poor. In a wide-ranging and provocative analysis of poverty and the public policy reaction to it, Joan Kennedy Taylor argues persuasively for what she calls "deregulating the poor." After reviewing English and American treatment of the poor throughout recent history, she argues that we have now created a welfare system that tremendously distorts incentives. The Great Society did not reduce poverty; it increased it, and today we need a new approach to help restore a more personal and compassionate society. Taylor urges that we start by exempting people below the poverty level from income taxes and by deregulating the poor—repealing the minimum wage law and the hundreds of licensing laws that prevent the most industrious poor from working. Then, she says, we should consider Charles Murray's suggestion of scrapping all welfare support for working-aged persons in order to radically change the dismal incentive structure we have established for lower-income people. In the final analysis, she suggests, it is not kind to encourage able people not to work; instead of helping them, welfare policies make work an irrational choice for the poor, trapping them in a web of dependency.

Besides poverty, the area where people most believe that government action to change market outcomes is needed is the environment. But here, too, Terry Anderson says that government solutions have failed. One of the leading figures in the "new resource economics," Anderson charges that pollution and the misuse of natural resources are caused not by market failure but by a failure to establish markets. The failure to define property rights in resources leads to the tragedy of the commons, where every user tries to get his share of resources ahead of everyone else. Turning resources over to government makes resources subject to political decision making, a process in which politicians and interest groups combine to produce results that are rarely in the public interest. Pointing to such problems as the misuse of federal land, the approaching water crisis, and air and water pollution, Anderson offers solutions based on private property and free markets. He argues that these market-oriented policies would result in greater economic efficiency and a cleaner environment. Anderson calls for a coalition between environmentalists and fiscal conservatives on such issues as water pricing, deficit timber sales, synthetic fuels, and natural gas deregulation.

The previous authors offer proposals that could be implemented by legislative or, in a few cases, executive action. In the book's final chapter legal scholar Bernard H. Siegan suggests some guidelines for the Supreme Court, a particularly relevant topic in view of the likelihood that President Reagan will be making several Court appointments in his second term. Siegan argues that the Court's responsibility is to protect two things: the constitutional structure of government and the liberties of the people. Perhaps the Court's greatest failing in recent years has been its unwillingness to protect economic liberties from the depredations of legislative bodies, and indeed its own enthusiasm for mandating restrictions on economic freedom. Siegan offers much evidence to prove that the Framers of the Constitution, as well as those who wrote the Fourteenth Amendment, intended to protect the rights of life, liberty, and property. The Fourteenth Amendment effectively incorporated into the Constitution the Civil Rights Act of 1866, which guaranteed the rights of citizens "to make and enforce contracts . . . [and] to inherit, purchase, lease, sell, hold and convey real and personal property." Supreme Court justices can play a major role in reaffirming our commitment to the traditional American values of individual liberty and limited government if they remember, first, that their role is not to legislate, but to enforce the Constitution; and second, that the purpose of the Constitution was—and is—to "secure the blessings of liberty."

There is much talk these days about the need for new ideas. Younger voters in particular seem to be searching for a party or a movement that offers a new approach to public policy. In 1984 a solid majority of them seemed to decide that President Reagan's ideas were fresher than those of Walter Mondale, despite their concern over the president's views on social issues and foreign intervention. In the future, however, they will demand candidates who offer more of what they want: economic growth and opportunity, a commitment to the economy of the future rather than that of the past, social tolerance, clean air and water, a compassionate and realistic approach to the less fortunate in society, a solution to the arms race, and a peaceful foreign policy.

The ideas found in the pages of *Beyond the Status Quo* fit this profile well. As the tired liberal-conservative debates of the past become increasingly less relevant, we need to move forward in new directions with new agendas: constitutional restrictions on interest-group spending policies; fundamental tax reform; a secure retirement for today's young workers; a clearing away of the morass of taxes, subsidies, tariffs, and regulations that prevent the economy from growing and creating jobs; a real solution to the nuclear threat; educational choice; deregulation of the poor; and improved environmental protection. We have no doubt that if these proposals were adopted, 10 years from now the United States would be a freer, more prosperous, and more secure society. They would not solve all our public policy problems, but each is a major step in that direction.

Some of the proposals presented here seem radical in the context of today's legislative stalemate and interest-group politics. But ideas have consequences, and ideas that make sense will get a hearing. When the Cato Institute published Peter Ferrara's *Social Security: The Inherent Contradiction* in 1980, the conventional wisdom was that privatizing social security was a pipe dream, thoroughly outside the parameters of policy debate. But five years later, after yet another social security crisis, the proposal appeared on the front pages of America's leading newspapers. Two or three or five years from now, when the *next* social security crisis occurs, privatization may be seen not as a radical idea but as the only way out. In a like manner, as the interests of the United States and our European allies become increasingly divergent, U.S. withdrawal from NATO may come to be seen as proper and even necessary.

Despite the recent economic recovery and the more general "good feeling" about the direction of the country, we still face some major problems. Government continues to get bigger, the threat of nuclear war continues to haunt us, too many people are unemployed or trapped in poverty. Fundamental problems require fundamental solutions, not just the fine-tuning produced by Washington's policy myopia. It is in this belief that we offer these proposals for moving public policy beyond the status quo.

II. The Balanced Budget Amendment: A Truly Marginal Reform

James Dale Davidson

Thirty-two state legislatures have officially called for a constitutional convention to propose a Balanced Budget Amendment. Thirty-four are needed to trigger a convention. In a majority of the remaining legislatures, convention call resolutions have passed one or both houses. In California and Montana, voter initiatives aimed at precipitating convention calls were canceled by state courts in 1984. Without judicial intervention, both states would probably have joined the convention call. Opinion polls showed overwhelming support for both measures. Indeed, polls around the country show broad and deep support for the Balanced Budget Amendment itself. For as long as the question has been asked, super majorities, sometimes exceeding 80 percent, have favored the amendment.

These sentiments mirror a general belief among persons of all walks of life that federal spending is careening out of control. They also reflect an abiding opposition to deficit spending. In spite of all that economists have tried to teach us about the wisdom and occasional virtue of federal deficits, the American people still believe the old injunction: "live within your means." As individuals, they must do this in their household economies. They do it in their businesses and in the lower levels of government. And they would have the federal government do it. Today, as throughout U.S. history, Americans believe the words spoken by Franklin D. Roosevelt in a radio address in July 1932: "Let us have the courage to stop borrowing to meet continuing deficits. Stop the deficits. . . . Revenues must cover expenditures by one means or another. Any government, like any family, can, for a year, spend a little more than it earns. But you and I know that a continuation of that habit means the poorhouse."[1]

---

[1]Cited in William Breit, "Starving the Leviathan," in *Fiscal Responsibility in Constitutional Democracy*, eds. James M. Buchanan and Richard E. Wagner (Leiden: Martinus Nijhoff, 1978), p. 17. This article by Breit discusses the enduring American belief in balanced budgets.

A good deal of the support for balancing the budget arises from this simple appeal to simple principles. Yet it would be wrong to conclude that the amendment itself is therefore a simple-minded proposition. In fact, the Balanced Budget Amendment is probably the most complicated item on the American political agenda. It involves two separate orders of constitutional complexity, as well as a tangle of overlapping issues of policy preference and political partisanship. Hidden behind these questions is a higher and more abstract level of confusion over the relative importance of goodwill versus determinism in shaping outcomes in government. This confusion is at least partly a matter of choice, for reasons I explore below. It is also a matter of genuine intellectual difficulty, which helps account for the rather low incidence of discussion of situational determinism in the news media and in political patter at the local bar.

For whatever reason, most people have very little conception of the extent to which situational incentives vie with judgments of right and wrong in forming decisions. Where one does find interest in the role of incentives in forming behavior, such as in management textbooks or articles in the *Harvard Business Review*, the context of the discussion is likely to be non-political. And very seldom is the implied tension between the two notions of human behavior brought into the open. But proponents of the Balanced Budget Amendment must bring it into the open. The essence of the issue is whether fiscal outcomes should be left solely to goodwill. For proponents, at least, the case for a Balanced Budget Amendment must also be an argument that situational incentives play a large role in shaping the budgetary choices that politicians make.

The Balanced Budget Amendment and the
Equal Rights Amendment

Consider, by way of comparison, the complexities involved in the debate over the Equal Rights Amendment (ERA). It, too, involves the enactment of a constitutional rule. In the case of the ERA, however, the amendment was proposed in the Congress by a well-understood procedure. By contrast, the Balanced Budget Amendment is being sought through the convening of a constitutional convention, a procedure that is unrehearsed and less well understood and accepted. Consequently, the debate over the Balanced Budget Amendment has been confused by debate over the desirability of a convention, a debate that never sidetracked the proponents of the ERA.

To take the comparison a little further, proponents of the ERA were able to make the case, though perhaps not successfully enough, that their amendment had far-reaching symbolic effect, quite apart from its likely impact in objectively altering laws. A similar claim has been made by advocates of the Balanced Budget Amendment. At this level, both proposals operate on nearly equal footing, with the budget proposal being slightly more difficult in that it involves a procedural restraint on government rather than establishing or clarifying a right of individuals.

It is possible that the failure of the ERA to win ratification had as much to do with the rejection of the amendment at the symbolic level by women and men of more traditional outlook as it did with any practical consideration of the amendment's effect in altering particular laws. Indeed, advocates of the ERA often argued that the amendment would not be interpreted literally. It would not, they said, require the integrating of toilets in public places or the sending of women into combat.

To the extent that economics entered into the arguments over the ERA, it was in the debate over how the amendment would shift income among women. On the one side, professional women with significant human capital investment expected to gain by the amendment. On the other, those without marketable skills probably expected to lose from the ERA's effect in voiding state laws that protect them in matters of divorce, child care, and so forth. While not every professional woman supported the ERA and not every traditional housewife opposed it, the divergence along economic lines was broadly congruent with the debate over the issues at a symbolic level. The economic debate, if it had been taken further, would not have elucidated many divisions that were not fairly well canvassed and understood.

By contrast, the Balanced Budget Amendment would undoubtedly shift income, but its effects are harder to predict. It would operate at the procedural level by altering the constraints on governmental expenditure. By making these constraints tighter, it would presumably produce a smaller government sector. There is no particular distribution of skills or talents, however, that would be unambiguously harmed by smaller government. Outside government employees, among whom there is a wide variety of skills and talents, practically any group could end up a winner.

15

The distribution of gains would become evident only in the actual event. There is certainly no consensus in forecasts of the amendment's effect. The assessment by older industrial unions, for example, that their members would be harmed by a balanced budget rule seems to be derived from a symbolic commitment to fiscal demand management rather than from an analysis of the effect that eliminating deficits would have on income distribution. A strong case could be made that industrial union members are among the foremost losers from a regimen of continuous deficit spending. High interest rates, engendered by strong government credit demands, drive up the exchange value of the dollar, placing individuals in the unionized manufacturing sector at a competitive disadvantage with workers overseas. This squeezes wage rates. It also reduces employment levels, both by encouraging the migration of industry to low-wage areas and by accelerating the pressure for automation. Furthermore, high interest rates also reduce the capitalization of rents, thereby shortening the investment horizon. This diminishes the demand for long-lived goods of the sort produced in the heavy industrial sector.

It is quite possible, therefore, that the greatest beneficiaries of a Balanced Budget Amendment would be members of the industrial unions that are its most vigorous opponents in the present political circumstances.

The Economics of Politics

This is all by way of illustrating that the complexities surrounding the Balanced Budget Amendment are of a much higher order than those of practically any other policy question. By far the greatest of these complexities involves not the strictly economic effects of such an amendment, but the economics of its political effect. These are obscure, not only because they involve a fairly lengthy chain of cause and effect but also because the very context in which they operate is one that is largely disreputable and therefore hidden.

The strongest argument for a balanced budget rule is that it would alter the costs and rewards of decision making in the political process. The amendment would raise the costs to politicians of imposing additional spending, and it would lower the costs of curtailing or reducing spending. Economists agree that when one raises the cost of something, one generally gets less of it. Therefore, if deficits at ever-higher levels are irresponsible, the Balanced Budget Amendment would produce less irresponsibility. A difficulty arises, however, because there is a consensus in modern society that budgetary and other choices by political leaders ought not to be determined by the costs and rewards of each choice to those decision makers. Rather, such choices should be decided by good judgments about what makes for the well-being of everyone.

Close analysis, such as that pioneered by the public choice school of economists, offers scant support for the public-spirited or "goodwill" model of the way politics works. Such authors as Gordon Tullock, James Buchanan, Mancur Olson, and others have developed robust models of political decision making determined according to a cost-reward framework.

The difficulty with the public choice models is not that they are misleading or less informative than the conventional goodwill model. To the contrary, the problem that inhibits their acceptance is altogether different: it arises from their effect in laying bare a tension between morality and convenience. This tension is one that practically everybody assiduously avoids confronting. When it is confronted and its implications analysed, it involves costs that are not only psychological but practical.

The nature of these tensions and costs can be understood by considering more closely the two conflicting models of decision making. The predominant, though often misleading, model is essentially a value-driven model. It proposes that choices are informed by what the decision maker deems to be right. Therefore, efforts to reform a pattern of unsatisfactory decisions rest largely on moral suasion: an attempt to inform the decision maker of facts he may be overlooking or, more ambitiously, to altogether reform his notion of what is right.

It is evident that practically all political discourse is carried on within these terms. By contrast, the cost-reward framework is a determinist one. It holds that people generally and routinely make choices so as to optimize their surplus of reward over cost. If one could accurately identify what those costs and rewards are, one could practically predict what choices would be made. This is what many public choice models have done—usually, but not always, with good results.

The Weakness of the Goodwill View

It is rather easy to show that the consensus goodwill view of politics is a defective one. Anyone who really believes that political outcomes are not determined within a cost-reward framework ought

17

to find the opposite view at many points irrelevant. If budget decisions, for example, are really determined by what is held to be right rather than by the individual incentives facing decision makers, there should be no predictable effect from changing these incentives. For example, if the Constitution said that the pay of congressmen would be cut to zero in any year in which the budget was in deficit, the goodwill school ought to predict that this would produce no change in the tendency to incur deficits. Of course, no one would be so silly. That such incentives would bite is too obvious to be denied.

The deficiency of the goodwill school, so clearly evidenced in the counterfactual example above, is ignored for what are largely emotional rather that intellectual reasons. It is not difficult to see why. The dictionary definition of a cynic is "a person who believes that people are motivated in all their actions entirely by selfishness."[2] "Cynical" is defined as being "inclined to question the sincerity and goodness of people's motives and actions, or the value of living."[3] These definitions are not exhaustive, but they do suggest that in common usage the economic point of view and cynicism are more or less synonymous. It is equally enlightening that the adjectival form implies a denigration of human goodness and even calls into question the value of living.

Ideas Themselves Have Different Utilities

Economists and others who analyze the flow of ideas have a tendency to treat the process as though it were "unbiased."[4] I believe that this is mistaken on two levels. It is mistaken on the social level because it ignores the differential incentives that some groups have to cultivate and publicize perceptions that facilitate rent seeking on their part.[5] The view is also mistaken on the individual level. There is no reason to believe that all ideas are equally pleasing and that the only thing that differentiates them is the

---

[2]*Webster's New World Dictionary* (1966).

[3]Ibid.

[4]Hansen and Prince define an "unbiased society" as "any situation in which the probability of any specific preference ordering occurring is equal to that of any other specific preference ordering." Thomas J. Hansen and Barry L. Prince, "The Paradox of Voting: An Elementary Solution for the Case of Three Alternatives," *Public Choice* 15 (Summer 1973) :103.

[5]James Davidson, "The Political Economy of Ideological Change," paper delivered to the Public Choice Society, 1982.

18

degree to which they are likely to be true. In fact, it would be astonishing if there were no differential utility among ideas. That would imply that an individual would get quite as much utility from the belief that his soul would cease to exist upon his death as from the notion that he would continue to survive in immortal bliss. Quite apart from the truth of the matter, it must be obvious from the axiom that human beings prefer more to less that they will prefer ideas that offer the promise of more over those that promise nothing, let alone those that promise less than nothing.

If ideas had no practical consequences and the only utility derived from them came from what they suggest about life, then everyone would believe nothing but illusions. For practically every circumstance there is an illusion more pleasing than reality. It also happens, however, that some of the more pleasing potential realities are within the reach of human effort. Individuals, therefore, face a choice of either adopting ideas, attitudes, and evaluations that are instrumentally useful or of adopting those that may be pleasing in themselves, but nonetheless counterproductive. It seems apparent that almost the whole process by which human understanding has progressed, to the degree that it has, has been informed by the practical necessity of utilizing ideas in an instrumental way.

Minimal Practical Value of Political Ideas

From this perspective, it is not surprising that the areas of greatest confusion and malfunction in modern life are the areas of political and social choice. These are precisely the areas in which most of the understanding one gains is largely a public good with few appropriable benefits. If it were possible for a citizen to thoroughly grasp the defects of current political decision making, for example, it is not evident that he would be any better positioned to profit from this sorry situation than one whose political evaluations are largely rooted in illusion.[6]

Into such an environment there comes the economic analysis of

---

[6]Ironically, to the extent that individuals with superior insight into the malfunction of the political process seek to capitalize on it, such as by purchasing gold bars to protect themselves against inflation, or Treasury bonds to protect themselves against deflation, they probably have a perverse incentive to see that the malfunctioning of the process continues. In effect, they would be in the same category in which Buchanan places constitutional lawyers. James M. Buchanan, "Sources of Opposition to Constitutional Reform," paper prepared for Heritage Foundation Conference on Constitutional Economics, November 1982.

politics. The scholars who use this form of analysis employ models of rational behavior that generate a prediction of unsatisfactory outcomes. Because these first-order choices are unsatisfactory, they seek to move the debate to a second-order choice "of the rules or institutions which will govern the former."[7] This reform promises, if it works, to provide what would be for most citizens a public good. This public good, however large, will be shared only to a small extent by any given citizen.

If there were no other source of opposition, this public-goods dilemma alone would inhibit the success of the cost-reward analysis of politics. In how many cases will an individual's share of the gain from acting on this analysis seem to outweigh the disutility of adopting a cynical or dismal economic view of the actions of his national leaders? The apparent unpopularity of constitutional economics as a line of analysis (as opposed to the clear popularity of specific reforms such as the Balanced Budget Amendment) suggests that this formula works out in an unfavorable way. Thomas Gray's often-quoted lines probably apply here:

> . . . why should they know their fate,
> Since sorrow never comes too late,
> And happiness too swiftly flies?
> Thought would destroy their paradise.
> No more; where ignorance is bliss,
> 'Tis folly to be wise.[8]

In short, our happiness in many areas of life may depend in some measure on our own illusions. Otto von Bismarck was on to this when he said that "no people should know how their laws or their sausages are made."

It is not surprising, therefore, that many people do not seem to know how their laws are made. To return the discussion directly to the question of the Balanced Budget Amendment, it is less surprising than it may seem that some people are willing to face runaway fiscal chaos rather than confront the way their laws are actually made.

The Right/Wrong–Reward/Cost Tension

In most areas of life, moral choices and practical choices tend to coincide. There are cases, though, in which a contradiction exists

[7]Ibid.

[8]Thomas Gray, "Ode on a Distant Prospect of Eton College."

20

between what is "right" and what is rewarding. In these cases, there is less likelihood that the "virtuous" choice will be taken as the reward rises. Because choices in one's career tend to involve higher rewards than in other areas of life, most contradictions of the sort being considered here occur in careers. They tend to be resolved in the indicated way. This is why good Christian merchants today all offer installment credit, in spite of the biblical injunctions against usury. This is why politicians usually, although not always, obey situational constraints rather than "do what is right."

Politicians differ from most people in that their careers involve a large number of high-reward choices that conflict with judgments about what is "right." This distinguishes most politicians from most of their constituents, not in a qualitative sense but in a marginal sense. For most of the public, from farmers to shipping clerks to ditch diggers, there are few opportunities in which practical considerations provide high reward or cost avoidance for doing what is "wrong." In the few occupations in which such temptations are significant, as in the sale of used cars, public attitudes reflect that fact. Used-car salesmen have reputations similar to those of politicians. Individuals in such careers may or may not be more dishonest than others, but they certainly face more high-value situations in which practical considerations make it attractive to cheat than do other people. For the rest of us, temptations are of relatively low value and are more likely to be overriden by moral considerations.

This bears directly on the question of the Balanced Budget Amendment because it bears on the strength of the objection to the strongest argument for that amendment. While there are many cases, of course, in which morality and practicality coincide, it is also true that there are circumstances, millions every day, in which individuals could increase their material rewards by some niggling little act that imposes on the rights of others. If every individual who could commit fraud undetected or steal something and get away with it did so, we would live in a meaner world.

Conflicting Micro-Macro Requirements

It is to the general advantage, therefore, that moral considerations, right thinking, fellow-feeling, and old-fashioned goodwill be given prominent emphasis in considerations of conduct, even political conduct. However, this creates a problem: such emphasis, which is necessary to reduce mischief, thievery, and other misery committed by individuals on a micro level, runs quite contrary to what is required on the macro level. There, as we have seen, moral considerations are less likely to predominate over time where persistently high costs are involved in doing "what is right."

That is the case with the federal budgetary process: a pattern of unhappy outcomes is traceable to perverse incentives. The indicated step, therefore, is a change in constraints—not merely an effort at moral suasion. Where the margin is too great to be swayed on the basis of morality alone, incentives must be changed to change outcomes.

A Fallacy of Composition

The frequently heard objection that a balanced budget amendment is unnecessary because "Congress has the power to balance the budget" is plausible only within the goodwill frame of analysis. The moment incentives are considered, it becomes simply a fallacy of composition. One may argue with equal plausibility that restrictions on pollution are unnecessary because "people have the power not to pollute." Both statements are equally true in the trivial sense— and equally misleading. What people have the "power to do," either as congressmen or industrialists, is not always a guide to what they are likely to do. Just as industrialists operating under a defective system of property rights will tend to pollute because the rewards to them for doing so exceed the costs, so the Congress will continue to be fiscally irresponsible as long as the rewards for doing so exceed costs.

High Costs for Spending in the Past

In times past, government budgets were smaller and better balanced against resources.[9] A variety of explanations for this is possible. James Buchanan, among others, argues that there was once a de facto constitutional requirement for a balanced budget.[10] The more conventional view, argued in many forms by opponents of the Balanced Budget Amendment, turns on two variables: first, the macroeconomic case for the deficits or surpluses; and second, the "responsibility" of political leaders in implementing the policy recommended by the best thinking of well-meaning people. I would

[9]See Breit, pp. 9–24.

[10]See James Buchanan and Richard E. Wagner, *Democracy and Deficit: The Political Legacy of Lord Keynes* (New York: Academic Press, 1977).

focus an explanation of the change on two entirely different factors, both of which relate to the costs and rewards of making budgetary decisions.

Money and the Business Cycle

The first factor is the change in world monetary arrangements that has eliminated the commodity linkage of the currency. The dollar is now a purely fiat money that can be issued at will by political authorities to finance any deficit. There are undoubtedly long-term costs of excessive debt finance through a system of fiat currency. But the time required for these to take effect seems to exceed the length of the political cycle. Under the gold system, when excessive debt creation fueled an expectation of inflation to come, that expectation immediately set in motion a countervailing reaction: the monetary base was contracted as paper dollars were redeemed for gold. Such a contraction would have immediate effect in contracting real economic activity. Even in the days before the political business cycle had been studied academically, there was wide understanding among politicians that reelection prospects dimmed as the economy declined. The chain of cause and effect that led from runaway spending to electoral defeat tended to keep federal spending under control, except in times of war, when a shared sense of emergency obviated the otherwise crippling political costs of incurring deficits.

The Growing Strength of Interest Groups

The second factor involved in increasing the political payoff from deficits arises from the increasing number and effectiveness of narrow-interest groups. These groups have the ability to impose costs upon politicians who resist their demands for appropriations from the public coffers. A politician who angers too many of these groups will be unable to stay in office.

In effect, therefore, the politician's decision to deficit spend is now encouraged from both directions. Not only has the *cost* of spending decreased, but the *demand* for such spending is more acutely felt because there are more narrow-interest groups that have organized and achieved political effectiveness.

Mancur Olson has shown why narrow groups have a fundamental advantage in pressing their claims at the expense of larger groups.[11]

[11]See Mancur Olson, *The Logic of Collective Action* (Cambridge, Mass.: Harvard University Press, 1965).

23

Olson proved that however much members of a large group would benefit as a group by political action, it is rarely rational for them to pursue it. As individuals, they have no incentive to act in their group interest, so they will continue to act in their personal interests, even if this makes them all worse off.

For example, most citizens of the United States today have every reason to hope that a stable price level will be maintained. By and large, most citizens would benefit greatly if that happened. Yet only a very few individuals will actually work politically for the good of eliminating inflation and preventing deflation; most will not. The reason is clear: In our society, the benefits of stable economic policy would be shared by about 230 million citizens—citizens who know that (1) no effort that is within their reach is likely to be decisive in stabilizing the price level, and (2) if inflation or deflation is to be avoided by the efforts of others, they will necessarily enjoy all of the benefits, whether they have contributed to achieving them or not. In short, the old adage is true: "Everybody's business is nobody's business."

A Political Prisoner's Dilemma

If individuals were willing to undertake collective action to halt inflation, it would be quite as rational, Olson has pointed out, to expect citizens to voluntarily tear up their own money or repay loans without employing the proceeds to reduce the money supply. He writes:

> Why would the people of this (or any other) country organize politically to prevent inflation when they could serve their common interests in price stability just as well if they all spent less as individuals? Virtually no one would be so absurd as to expect that the individuals in an economic system would voluntarily curtail their spending to halt an inflation, however much they would, as a group, gain from doing this. Yet it is typically taken for granted that the same individuals in a political or social context will organize and act to further their collective interests. The rational individual in the economic system does not curtail his spending to prevent inflation (or increase it to prevent depression).[12]

Olson's argument demonstrates that political self-interest is against any concerted effort to promote a genuinely public interest in

[12]Ibid.

government. Rather, political outcomes are likely to depend upon a confluence of private interests matched only by coincidence, if at all, with what would be required to promote the interests of everyone. Policies such as effective stewardship of public funds, maintenance of a sound economic climate, and balancing the budget are seldom achieved because they have nothing but conscience to recommend them. What is involved is a "political prisoner's dilemma."

Once this dilemma is grasped, it becomes clear why government must continue to grow in the absence of constitutional change (or some purely accidental meandering in the structure of the economy) that substantially raises the costs of employing politics to reward special interests. As long as this division of labor breaks up the population into greater numbers of small groups, these groups will achieve political strength. This does not happen all at once, but it does happen. In time, more and more groups form to change the terms of competition in the market—at the expense of the remaining members of society.

There is scarcely an existing group that cannot think of some policy to be undertaken by government, usually at substantial fiscal cost, to make that group better off. Even the imposition of trivial costs on each member of the taxpaying public could finance substantial benefits for a rent-seeking group. A subsidy that would take just one dollar from the pockets of 100 million taxpayers would bring $100 million in additional revenue to a politically active industry. Many people will spend a great deal of their time and energy to achieve $100 million. On the other hand, few taxpayers would be willing to work hard to save a dollar. It is from this imbalance of incentives that ever-increasing government spending has resulted.

Perverse Incentives in Congress

Of course, the money to pay for this spending must come from somewhere. Even small sums add up. The people who are asked to pay through ever-increasing taxes do not wish to do so. The Congress has attempted to resolve this hopeless contradiction by resorting to deficits. That is why we have a national debt measured in the trillions of dollars, with direct federal borrowing in recent years absorbing the lion's share of new savings.

The fact that a continuation of such a policy would drive the nation toward backruptcy will not in any great measure alter the perverse nature of the system. To see why, consider an analogy.

Pick any 435 people off the street and give each an American

Express card with the same account number. Each cardholder would be liable for ¹⁄₄₃₅th of the total bill each month. Under such circumstances, how would the rational person behave? Answer: he would spend like a congressman. He would buy everything in sight on credit, even if he recognized that the whole group was headed for the poorhouse. The reason is that any cardholder would receive 100 percent of the value of his purchases. If he declined to spend, he would save only ¹⁄₄₃₅th of the total bill due at the end of the month. In short, anyone who refrained from spending would gain practically nothing. He would be no less bankrupt than the others. He would simply enjoy fewer benefits along the way.

So it is in Congress. Even if a representative opposed every expenditure, it is highly improbable that he would succeed in cutting the federal budget by as much as one penny. Rarely does a major appropriation turn on a single vote. This is not to say that a determined effort to reduce the budget deficit by an individual congressman would be without effect. Quite the contrary, it would have a real and immediate effect. By consistently voting to reduce the budget, a member of Congress would reduce the income of his own constituents. His colleagues would soon learn that they could not gain his vote for their own pet projects by lending their votes to him. Consequently, special appropriations to benefit his district would be scratched. There would be no new public works projects, no new dams, no new funding for sewage treatment plants. If the farmers in his district were unlucky enough to grow a special crop, that crop could be removed from the list of agricultural subsidies. Small Business Administration loans would go elsewhere. Failing businesses in his district would have little hope of getting extraordinary relief. Even ordinary citizens, baffled by bureaucracy and needing a permit for a project or help in finding a lost social security check, could find their economizing congressman of less help than his more free-spending colleagues. And for obvious reasons: A congressman who will not repay the bureaucracy with what it wants—money—will not be well positioned to get what he wants from the bureaucracy.

While the constituents of the economizing congressman would gain as little as possible of the bounty of federal spending, they would be no less obliged to absorb all the costs of government. Taxes would be just as high as ever. The financing of the deficit, with its inflationary or deflationary effects, would reach them no less than it would have done had they voted for a candidate who supported every single appropriation. So if voters are rational, they will defeat the economizing congressman and replace him with someone who will follow Washington's motto, "To get along you go along."

This is the logic of the system. As long as congressmen respond rationally to incentives, overspending is the only outcome to be expected, with deficits mounting to disastrous levels.

Only Constitutional Reform Will Work

The solution, if there is to be a solution, will not come from "the better breed of candidate" recommended by advocates of the good-will school of government. The only way fiscal order can be restored is by constitutional reform that changes incentives at the margin, raising the costs to congressmen of spending and borrowing money. The higher these costs go, the less government will spend.

The Balanced Budget Amendment is truly a marginal reform, not because it would be likely to have a trivial effect if enacted, but because it would reform the margins upon which far-reaching decisions are made. By raising the costs of additional government spending, the amendment would reduce the growth of government even if the immediate desire for additional spending were in no way affected.

Small changes in marginal costs often have large long-run effects. For example, a man who eats at a smorgasbord will consume more calories than he would by ordering a la carte (where each additional helping involves an additional cost). Over a lifetime, the difference in outcomes can be striking. A one percent increase in body weight each year caused by overeating could make someone grossly fat by the end of his life. Just as higher costs will reduce the amount he consumes, in time they may also reduce his desire to consume. For example, if the cost of eating at a smorgasbord is raised, say, by the knowledge that obesity could shorten life, then the man's desire to eat more may decline.

Over time, the Balanced Budget Amendment, which increases the costs of additional government spending, may also create feedback effects that lessen the demand for such spending. The more difficult it is to forage in the public purse, the more attention and effort will be devoted to alternative channels of enrichment. In a sense, therefore, a nation's constitution may help determine not only the extent to which individuals are able to exploit one another through the political process, but their desire to pursue such gains in the first place.

The debate on budgetary breakdown should focus on the constitutional level. Ultimately, the choice of situational constraints determines the choice of outcomes. Although not everyone is prepared to recognize this, those who are concerned with sound policy should be. We have already learned that the way to stop pollution is not to plead with polluters, but to recognize that their behavior is rational and impose costs sufficiently high to make them stop. The same is true with deficits. They are the acid rain of politics. Their long-term effects will do for our economy what long-term pollution does for our lungs. The Balanced Budget Amendment provides a reasoned solution to a problem that will otherwise not be solved. Although the issues involved are more complicated than perhaps any other on the political horizon, the solution is ultimately simple—as are the solutions to many of our problems. But as Harry Johnson once said, "The hard part is to recognize simplicity when you see it."[13]

[13]Harry G. Johnson, "The Study of Theory," A. E. R. Papers and Proc. 64 (May 1974): 324.

III. An Agenda for Tax Reform

Jule R. Herbert Jr.

"Taxes are frequently so much more burdensome to the people than they are beneficial to the sovereign."

> Adam Smith,
> *The Wealth of Nations*, 1776

To even the casual observer there appears evidence of a growing interest in the public, in the halls of Congress, and in the scholarly literature for a fundamental and drastic reform of the federal tax system. This interest has taken many forms. Tax reform means different things to different people, depending on their views about the level and substance of government programs requiring tax dollars and, in addition, what role, if any, the government should take in directing the path and redirecting the outcome of private economic activities.

In the discussion that follows, "tax reform" does not directly mean "tax relief," nor does it mean either an increase or a decrease in total tax revenues. Moreover, in these days of runaway budget deficits, it should be noted that tax reform here likewise does not mean an increase or a decrease in total tax revenues relative to the total level of government expenditures.

However, any tax reform worth pursuing will obviously have an impact on these and other matters, and one's opinion or special interest can be presumed to influence the way one feels about any specific proposal to "reform" the tax system.

Indeed, it may well be that only a tax reform proposal that (1) gives "tax relief" (the reduction of effective tax rates) to a substantial number of current taxpayers and (2) shows substantial promise of both *decreasing* the total burden of taxes relative to total private income and *increasing* (or at least not decreasing) tax revenues relative to total government expenditures (i.e. reducing the budget deficit) can attract sufficient support from the coincidence of interests required to secure its passage by Congress.

29

The possibility of tax reform along these lines is, of course, precisely what Adam Smith meant to suggest by his observation that taxes are often imposed in such a way that they are more burdensome to the private sector as a whole than they would be under another tax system able to raise the same or even a greater amount of revenue. From this viewpoint, which is adopted for the present discussion, "tax reform" should refer to the "how" rather than directly to the "how much" of taxation. *The goal of tax reform should be to reduce, as far as practicable, the total burden of taxes relative to the total level of private income.* Therefore, not only those structural reforms that reduce tax rates directly, but those that tend to increase private income or rearrange the tax system to make it more tolerable to the private sector can be seen as potential elements of a tax reform agenda.

The present federal personal and corporate income tax system—which together account for 53 percent of total federal revenues and 84 percent of federal revenues outside of social security and medicare—can be fairly characterized as nominally imposing a steeply progressive schedule of tax rates on annual incomes, ranging from 11 to 50 percent on personal taxable income and 16 to 46 percent on corporate taxable income. These schedules comprise only a few pages of the tax code. The balance of the code is taken up with detailing the exclusions, credits, deductions, exemptions, and other "tax preferences" that reduce the income base to which a schedule is applied. Given the nominal rate structure, much of this has been considered necessary to protect taxpayers from what otherwise would be confiscatory tax rates.

Is Tax Reform Possible?

As nominal incomes rose in the years since the basic tax structure was enacted, more and more taxpayers fell into income brackets originally put in place to apply only to the "excessive" income of the very wealthy. Most piecemeal tax reform legislation in recent years has stemmed from a recognition of this trend and a desire to lessen its impact on taxpayers and the private economy.

The income tax law passed by Congress in 1913 as part of an "Act to Reduce Duties" had a maximum rate of 7 percent. It was not a tax levied on the working class. A rate of 2 percent was assessed on incomes of $20,000 to $50,000, gradually increasing to a 7 percent marginal rate on $500,000 or more.

When World War II served to justify raising maximum rates as high as 94 percent, still only a very few paid taxes at rates even approaching the maximum level. In 1947, 80 percent of the families in the United States had an annual income of less than $5,000. The effective tax rate was about 8.4 percent. For these Americans taxes had doubled between 1939 and 1941 and doubled again between 1941 and 1947. Even so, a worker making $5,000 who was married and had two children paid around $420 in income tax plus $30 in social security taxes. However, he now faced a marginal tax rate of 20 percent. Only 2.8 percent of the families in America had incomes greater than $20,000, which then carried a 56 percent marginal rate. Of course, today's dollar is worth only about one-fourth of the 1947 dollar, but the point is that in 1947, after the biggest war in history, few people were in high marginal tax brackets.

As a result of inflation and economic growth, by the late 1970s 80 percent of the families in the United States had incomes over $10,000, and 50 percent made more than $20,000. As a consequence, the average worker was confronted with tax rates many times higher than those that were originally legislated.

Additionally, maximum employee social security payroll taxes have risen from a mere $30 annually in 1947 to $2,532 in 1984, an 8,340 percent increase in this tax. For the first 20 years of social security, from 1937 to 1956, nobody contributed more in a year than today's worker is expected to pay every other week. In the ten years prior to 1981, total federal tax liabilities rose twice as fast as income for the average worker.

If it had not been for periodic changes in the income tax law, including frequent reductions in nominal tax rates, effective levels of taxation would have increased even faster. For example, the maximum marginal tax rate imposed on the filers of a joint return with $20,000 in taxable income has fluctuated over the years, first rising rapidly and then falling gradually. The maximum marginal rate on $20,000 of taxable income grew from 2 percent in 1913 to a high of 59 percent in 1948 when the joint return was introduced. It had been cut to 28 percent by 1977. Because of the 1981 Economic Recovery Tax Act (ERTA) reforms, the maximum marginal tax rate on this income has now been cut to 22 percent. The indexing provisions of this important tax reform ensure that the rate will continue to decline each year in the future so that inflation will not result in tax increases for those moving up to this nominal income level.

The effect of these changes, as far as the federal income tax is concerned, is that the tax burden on a family of median income has been reduced to roughly what it was in 1960, undoing the constant increases that occurred in the high-inflation years between 1970 and 1981.

In 1960 the median income for all families with one earner employed full-time, year-round was $5,847. A married couple with two children filing a joint return at this level paid income taxes of $475, an effective rate of 8.12 percent and a marginal rate of 26 percent. In 1984 a median family's income had risen in nominal dollars to $25,700, and it owed taxes of some $2,400, an effective rate of 9.33 percent and a marginal rate of 25 percent. This compares with effective rates of over 10 percent and marginal rates of 28 percent and 32 percent in the early 1980s. It should be clear not only that tax reform is possible, but that tremendous progress and groundwork have already been accomplished.

These significant gains were, however, more than offset by the substantial increases in social security taxes that have occurred since 1965. During this period, social security taxes have grown from accounting for less than 20 percent to over 35 percent of total federal taxation. Social security payroll taxes on a median family's income have increased from $144 in 1960 to $1,721 in 1984.

But the enormity and apparent intractability of the problems surrounding social security should not obscure the fact that modest tax reform (in the sense of reducing the economic burden from what it would otherwise be) *has* in fact occurred in recent years. This progress has been further hidden by the fact that the reforms generally took place in a piecemeal, haphazard manner, thereby ignoring one of the generally accepted criteria of tax reform—simplification. Further, the effect of the chief reform—the indexing of rate brackets—has yet to be felt.

With maximum marginal income tax rates now frozen for the first time in terms of real income—barring a specific congressional vote to raise tax rates—the stage is set to change the course of previous attempts to ameliorate the negative economic effects of high taxes. Piecemeal, after-the-fact efforts to undo the effects of "bracket creep," and industry-by-industry attempts to mitigate the negative consequences of the tax system on the economy are no longer considered to be enough. A substantial consensus, evidenced by growing numbers of advocates in both parties all along the political spectrum, has concluded that the time for a fundamental restructuring of the tax system has come.

On the other hand, however surprising it may be to some, the Internal Revenue Code of 1954—which repealed the 1939 Code and, as it is amended with increasing frequency, is presently published in eight volumes containing over 5,000 pages—was not the product of pure accident. Each section of the tax code has its supporters. Even if it is almost universally admitted that the current tax system fails every imaginable criteria of sound tax policy, reform will not come easily.

Only a broad coalition of interests committed to the passage of a comprehensive tax reform program will have a chance to overcome the special pleadings of those who will oppose it. But only a proposal offering benefits that outweigh those of the current tax structure can attract the support of such a broad coalition. Of course, this is how all legislation is passed, and it is precisely how the substantial, if piecemeal, tax reform legislation of recent years was enacted. Fundamental tax reform will require an unusual commitment both to a legislative strategy and to certain principles of institutional reform that should not be compromised.

Principles of Tax Reform

According to Adam Smith, the "subjects of every state ought to contribute towards the support of the government, as nearly as possible, in proportion to their respective abilities; that is, in proportion to the revenue which they respectively enjoy under the protection of the state."[1] This is a common assertion, and it may appear to most to be merely common sense.

While Smith is clearly not making a serious attempt here to justify taxation as the most appropriate means of financing all governmental activities, his dictum is an attempt to restate the traditional thinking on how to most equitably distribute the burden of taxation. It is, of course, theoretically possible to conceive of other institutional arrangements to take the place of those that in the present day are believed to require compulsory tax levies.

Beyond this issue, however, it is obvious that all taxes serve as penalties on private economic activity, and that all taxes must ultimately be borne by the incomes of specific individuals. Every tax alters economic costs and income from what they would otherwise be. Every tax abrogates certain property rights belonging to the

---

[1] Adam Smith, *Wealth of Nations* (1776; reprint ed., Indianapolis: Liberty Press, 1982), p. 825.

individuals who are forced to pay it. To the extent that various government functions can be integrated into the market process, or "privatized," both the economic distortions and the injustices to property rights brought about by taxation are minimized. In the marketplace people pay for what they get, deciding how much they want and whether the product or service is worth the asking price.

Assuming, however, that the rationale for some given level of taxation is either granted, glossed over, or accepted on the grounds of tradition or convenience, then a rational basis for its allocation may be sought to lessen its negative impact on the economy and society as a whole.

For years the economic literature has been filled with heated discussions over the appropriate criteria for the fair imposition of taxes. While no definitive consensus has been reached, a brief review of the generally accepted principles of tax policy should prove useful in developing a pragmatic program for tax reform.

Equity

It is often asserted that taxes should be straightforward assessments, apportioning the necessary costs of government according to each taxpayer's "ability to pay." Presumably the easiest application of this principle is that taxpayers in the same circumstances should pay an equal amount of taxes. This is called "horizontal" equity and is summed up in the phrase, "Like to be treated alike."

But, even for this apparently simple extension of the rule of "equality before the law," it is necessary to *measure* each taxpayer's "ability to pay" to determine if, in fact, two taxpayers are in the same circumstances relative to their ability to pay an equal amount of taxes. Additionally, when, by whatever measure is chosen, it is determined that one taxpayer has a greater ability to pay than another, a second standard must still be applied to determine the amount of additional taxes that can be equitably extracted from the more able taxpayer. This complicating factor is generally called "vertical" equity.

The debate over what is the appropriate measure of a taxpayer's ability to pay has taken a prominent role in the discussions over competing proposals for tax reform. While these proposals will be summarized below, here it can be pointed out that the *tax base* of any tax system is the chosen measure of a taxpayer's presumed ability to pay. The possible measures are an individual's (or family's) income, consumption, or wealth. These tax bases chiefly differ only

34

in the treatment of savings. Since it is now quite clear that a direct tax on accumulated wealth—a pure tax on capital—would promote rapid capital consumption and a consequent rapid decline in general standards of living, a wealth-based tax is no longer seriously considered to be a viable alternative to either an income or a consumption-based (consumed-income) tax.

Once a tax base or measure of ability to pay is chosen, the concepts of horizontal and vertical equity must still be applied. Assuming that income is the tax base chosen, the horizontal-equity considerations introduce questions over what deductions, if any, should be allowed against gross receipts to determine a taxpayer's actual ability to pay. Among economists there is general agreement that deductions for the costs of earning income should be allowed, but there is little additional consensus. Should, for example, deductions for medical expenses or housing costs, which arguably are costs of maintaining health and physical well-being and are therefore necessary to earn an income, be allowed?

Even more controversial are the policy implications that are asserted to follow from the concept of vertical equity. Taxpayers who have clearly different levels of resources obviously have different abilities to pay taxes. But there does not seem to be any accepted way to measure these differences. The progressive income tax is based in part on the premise that it is equitable for the percentage of income taken in taxes to increase as the tax base rises. Proponents of proportional taxation, on the other hand, argue that fairness requires that the ratio of taxes to the tax base remain constant. Which of the following tax systems, for example, is more "fair"?

The table below illustrates three possible tax regimes. Tax plan 1 reflects the effective average rates prevailing under the current federal income tax law. Taxpayer B earns 6.67 times the income of A, but he must pay 17 times more income tax. Theoretically, of course, the progressive nature of a single tax, such as the federal income tax, should be distinguished from the nature of the tax system as a whole. It is possible that a specific progressive tax could be used merely to offset an otherwise regressive tax system, leaving overall tax burdens roughly proportional. However, this is not the case with the current tax system in the United States.

Another equitable argument that could be made in favor of the progressive tax plan rests on the assumption that about $24,350 in tax revenue must somehow be apportioned between these taxpayers A and B. It might then be argued that the progressive structure

Tax Plans

1. Progressive Income Tax

Taxpayer	Taxable Income	Tax	Percentage Rate
A	$ 15,000	$ 1,350	9
B	$100,000	$23,000	23

2. Proportional Income Tax (a)

Taxpayer	Taxable Income	Tax	Percentage Rate
A	$ 15,000	$ 1,800	12
B	$100,000	$12,000	12

3. Proportional Income Tax (b)

Taxpayer	Taxable Income	Tax	Percentage Rate
A	$ 15,000	$ 3,150	21
B	$100,000	$21,000	21

found in plan 1 would be more fair than the proportional system that would be required in order to raise the same amount of revenue (plan 3), on the assumption that Taxpayer B has a greater ability to pay an extra $2,000 in taxes under plan 1 than Taxpayer A has of paying an additional $1,800 under plan 3. Unfortunately, this "soak the rich" fallacy is based on the mistaken notion that A and B represent a more or less equal number of taxpayers in the tax system.

Given the fact that in the United States in 1981 there were 21 taxpayers paying at the A rate for every taxpayer paying at the B rate, it can be seen that, even ignoring possible incentive effects, plan 2 is the proportional income-tax system that would raise roughly the same amount of total tax revenue as plan 1.

In spite of this, it is equally difficult to make a convincing *equitable* argument in favor of plan 2 over plan 1. Under either plan some taxpayers are worse off than under the other plan. The concept of "ability to pay" is simply too fuzzy a notion to be of help here. While "horizontal" equity clearly appeals to our sense of fair play, it is doubtful that "vertical" equity can ever amount to more than mere subjective opinion. Other criteria of tax policy must be considered.

Economic Efficiency

A second commonly accepted goal of tax policy is that taxes should, as much as possible, be "neutral." In other words, they should not unnecessarily interfere with the private economic decisions, especially those regarding how much to consume or save, that would be made in the absence of taxation or, more precisely, if taxes were market-generated prices willingly paid by the citizens of a government. This goal recognizes the fact that voluntary market activities tend to maximize the social utilities of those who participate. Resources are channeled into their most profitable uses. Decisions about work, savings, and consumption are based on choices made by those who know best what combinations will result in the greatest personal satisfaction—the individual decision makers involved.

Taxes reduce the incentives for saving, investment, capital formation, and productive work. Additionally, many, if not all, of the government expenditures allowed by taxation further reduce these incentives and consequently distort the entire market process still more.

The impact of taxation on the structure of the marketplace is most clear in the case of partial or selective excise taxes by which some specific economic activity is penalized. An excise tax on cigarettes, for example, penalizes the economic activity involved in the production and marketing of cigarettes. The stock of cigarettes becomes lower than what it otherwise would be, the market price increases, the economic returns (incomes) of both the specific factors and (to a lesser degree) the nonspecific factors of production are reduced. Marginal firms are forced out.

Now, while a general excise tax may reduce this sort of distortion in resource allocation, it remains a penalty on economic activity both by reducing the amount of economic factors available to the private sector and by necessarily falling more heavily on work and saving/investment than on leisure and consumption. Consumption and leisure (being, after all, the *end* of prior economizing) require no future economic activity. On the other hand, work and saving/investment themselves *comprise* future economic activity. A tax drives a "wedge" between the economic value of the work performed or capital accumulated and the return allowed to the factor's owner. This wedge changes the relative costs and prices that guide economic activity.

Consider an economy in which there were no taxes. Then introduce an income tax of, say, 50 percent. If Jones had $1,000 when taxes were zero, he could have spent it on immediate consumption or he could have bought a bond paying, say, 5 percent per annum for ten years—$50—plus return of his principal at the end. Each alternative is the opportunity cost for the other. If Jones "buys" $1,000 worth of consumption, the opportunity cost is the $50 in additional annual income not received. On the other hand, the cost of $50 in additional annual income is $1,000 in foregone consumption.

But a new tax of 50 percent changes things. While $2,000 of income is now required to enjoy $1,000 of present consumption, $4,000 is now required to generate the equivalent after-tax benefits of the bond (assuming interest rates remain at 5 percent). Relative costs have been distorted. This doubles the cost of saving relative to consumption. A progressive tax, which would impose still higher tax rates on additional income, would greatly exacerbate the problem and disproportionately increase the cost of saving relative to consumption for those who have saved the most or have made the most productive investment decisions.

A proportional income tax would lessen such distortion and would thus be a more appropriate tax from the standpoint of economic efficiency. Proportional taxation leaves the relationship between the net return for different kinds of work and saving/investment decisions unchanged, within those classifications. Since the net economic returns received for the use of resources determine their allocations, a tax that leaves these relationships unchanged relative to one another will be less damaging to the market. On the other hand, a progressive tax will not only especially penalize saving/investment returns—as will any tax—but the taxation on a given amount earned will additionally vary according to the time rate at which the income is earned.

Many people argue that a proportional income tax is just as arbitrary a principle of taxation as is a progressive system. Indeed, it was shown that from the perspective of equity or "ability to pay" neither a proportional nor a progressive tax was clearly preferable over the other, and that choices between the two would likely come down to arguments over subjective value judgments. It is important to note that we are not here talking about the total incomes of individuals and whether or not a proportional or progressive tax would leave the relative total incomes of any two of them unchanged.

38

That is precisely the "ability to pay" criterion that has been proven incapable of application to taxpayers of different levels of income. The economically relevant factor is not total income but the relationship between net returns for specific work or resources. "This," according to F. A. Hayek,

> . . . is the crucial issue with regard to which the effects of progressive taxation are fundamentally different from that of proportional taxation. It is, of course, the reward received for the use of particular resources which determines their allocation, and what is important is that taxation should leave these relative rewards unchanged. Progressive taxation, however, alters them very considerably by making the net reward received by the owner dependent on what else he has earned during some arbitrary period, such as a year. If, before taxation, a surgeon gets as much for an operation as an architect for planning a house, or a salesman selling ten refrigerators as much as a photographer for making forty portraits, this will still be true if equal proportional deductions are made from these payments. But with progressive taxation of incomes this relation may be violently changed. Not only will services which before taxation receive the same reward leave very different net rewards to those who rendered them; a much larger payment for one service may indeed leave less to him who rendered it than a smaller payment to another person.[2]

Of course, since any tax necessarily distorts the economy, the fact that a proportional tax is less damaging than a progressive tax of similar dimensions should not obscure the overriding truth that it is the total burden of taxes relative to private income that should receive the greatest consideration. Better a progressive tax at low rates than a proportional tax at high rates.

Additional Institutional Constraints

It is often stated that a third goal of tax policy, along with equity and economic efficiency, ought to be simplicity. However, simplicity per se is likely to represent tax policy characteristics that can be subsumed under the criteria of equity and economic efficiency. And, to the extent that a tax system is either unnecessarily inequitable or inefficient, simplicity has little to offer. The more

---

[2]"Progressive Taxation Reconsidered" in *On Freedom and Free Enterprise: Essays in Honor of Ludwig von Mises*, ed. Mary Sennholz (New York: Van Nostrand, 1956), pp. 276–77.

complicated a really bad tax is, the greater the likelihood that many taxpayers will be able to partially avoid it. Of course, this means that similarly situated taxpayers will have different tax liabilities, violating the goal of horizontal equity. But if the tax is grossly inequitable in the first place, the whole notion of an equal apportionment of the tax burden loses its equitable appeal.

A similar institutional constraint for which a case is sometimes made is known as tax consciousness: the awareness of taxpayers of the level and burden of the taxes they are paying. Hidden taxes are wrong, the argument goes, for if taxes are perceived as the "price" paid for government, the electorate will be better able to judge how much government it desires and is willing to pay for.

But this is a particularly optimistic and naive view of how governments operate and how the total level of taxation is actually determined. Taxation is but one side of a larger *tax and expenditure process*. It is in fact the spending of government that ultimately constitutes the fundamental burden on taxpayers. Bad tax policy simply adds to the burden in a way that hurts taxpayers without helping either the government or the tax-consumers who benefit from the expenditure side of the process.

However, a tax structure that would tend to give more political cohesion to taxpayers could serve as a valuable institutional constraint. It is for a constraint of this sort that those who call for simplicity and a heightened tax consciousness are generally searching.

Since specific government expenditures greatly benefit specific groups of tax-consumers, and the costs of such benefits are diffused among a much larger number of taxpayers, it is easy to see why there is so much clamor from special interests for government spending projects and so little effort made by individual taxpayers to stop specific spending proposals. The reason is that the government adopts its budget in a piecemeal manner, with no limit on the total amount to be spent. Since each program adopted provides a substantial benefit to a well-defined group while imposing small relative costs on individual taxpayers, the system is prejudiced toward increasingly higher spending. In short, benefits are particularized; costs are generalized.

It is virtually impossible for an individual taxpayer to determine his taxed share of any government project and, even if he could, he would find his share very small and not worth fighting over. But the value of a project to a bureaucrat (it is his career) and to government contractors (their livelihoods depend on it) *can* be determined and certainly explains their support for the project. These people can be expected to spend a great deal of time and money lobbying on its behalf. The average taxpayer thus remains ignorant of the whole affair and would not get involved even if he knew the facts of the matter. Such is the case for every budget item, year after year. As long as concentrated spending interests are pitted against diffused taxpayer interests, it is likely that spending and taxing will increase.

It is suggested that a broad-based, indexed, proportional income tax would put all taxpayers in the same position relative to the taxing side of the tax and expenditure process. The resultant political cohesion may be termed "taxpayer solidarity." Such a tax system would also meet more closely than does the current tax system other appropriate criteria of tax policy: equity and economic efficiency.

One of the effects of pitting taxpayers against one another in a progressive tax system is that all of them, including the majority middle-income classes, end up paying tax rates higher than those they would pay if a single tax rate—the rate chosen voluntarily by a political majority—had been established in the first place.

Taxpayer solidarity can be expected only if taxpayers perceive a common interest, such as reducing or maintaining a tax rate they all face. The experience of the current taxpayers movement bears this out. The two dramatic examples of an undercurrent of popular sentiment for a modern American tax revolt were the passage of Proposition 13 in California in 1978 and Proposition 2½ in Massachusetts in 1980. Both involved widespread popular taxpayer support for the reduction of an existing flat-rate tax. (*Ad valorem* property taxes are uniformly flat-rate taxes.)

On the other hand, the period between those two votes saw the overwhelming and disastrous defeat in June 1980 of California's Proposition 9, which according to most analysts "marked the end of the tax revolt" in California at that time. Known also as "Jarvis II," this initiative would have cut the state's progressive income-tax rates in half, from a range of 1 to 11 percent to 0.5 to 5.5 percent. When it was pointed out that 50 percent of the tax reductions would go to only 10 percent of the taxpayers, the proposal was immediately branded and perceived as "unfair." Polls showed that fully two-thirds of those who cast a negative vote did so apparently on that basis. Fully 41 percent of those who had voted *for* Proposition 13 voted *against* Proposition 9 (while, of course, virtually everyone who voted "no" in 1978 did so again in 1980). Polls further revealed that over half of this 41 percent felt that other taxes would be raised if Proposition 9 passed. In other words, because of the perception of skewed benefits and the risk of new, alternative taxes, taxpayer solidarity broke down.

If progressive tax rates within a democratic system have an inherent bias resulting in higher taxes than would otherwise be the case, then it must be admitted that changing the rate structure to flatten it or to institute a proportional tax system will result in increased political pressure to reduce overall tax burdens. In other words, moving toward a flat-rate tax system, which is "revenue neutral" initially, will also reverse the institutional tendency in favor of higher taxes. Under that system, if the majority in society desires to enlarge the "public sector," they must be willing to impose on themselves a proportionate share of the increased taxes required.

The Tax Base

We have discussed the principles of tax policy based on the requirements of equity, economic efficiency, and institutional constraints. Income—all a person's gains, after meeting the expenses needed to generate them, over some period of time—was selected as the most generally accepted, if necessarily ambiguous, measure of a taxpayer's "ability to pay" in assessing horizontal equity. But we also noted how taxes necessarily penalize saving and investment relative to consumption and leisure.

Because of this distortion many economists—especially conservatives—argue that the individual income tax should be replaced by a tax on consumed-income or consumption expenditures. Under these proposals the level of actual consumption of goods and services, rather than potential consumption, would be used to measure an individual's tax liability. Either progressive or proportional rates could be applied to this narrower tax base, depending on the plan selected. Both the value-added tax (VAT) and the consumed-income tax (and its variation, the "cash flow" tax) are consumption-based taxes.

While the tax consequences of any of these proposals are roughly the same, the consumed-income tax is the most straightforward and most consistent with the subsidiary goal of increased tax visibility or tax consciousness.

A consumed-income tax would allow the deduction of saving

from gross income with the inclusion of all returns from previous savings. Thus, the taxpayer would be taxed on income minus net savings.

Arguments over whether income or consumption is the more appropriate tax base tend to boil down to an apparent conflict between the goals of equity and economic efficiency (or tax neutrality). Advocates of the income tax base do not generally dispute the contention that the income tax—by taxing both the income destined for saving and then the returns received from saving—encourages taxpayers to consume rather than save. They argue, however, that the lower tax rates that can be levied on the broader income base minimizes such distortion. They also argue that income itself, not personal decisions about how much income should be consumed or saved, is in any event the more equitable measure of a person's actual ability to pay taxes.

But is, in actuality, a consumed-income tax more "neutral" than a straightforward income tax? Proponents of a consumed-income tax claim that the principle of economic efficiency implies that economic actors—in spite of the fact that their real wealth is reduced by taxation—*ought* to make their decisions as to how to use the resources left under their control *as if* they were not being taxed at all.

A more appropriate goal of tax policy would comply with the more straightforward notion of economic efficiency defined earlier. This goal is a tax system that does as little as possible to interfere with the marketplace decisions that would be made if taxes were actually market-generated prices and taxpayers were voluntarily reducing their wealth by the amount of the total tax. Taxes are not, of course, market-generated prices. If they were, they would be voluntary and "neutral" as to market allocations. But the point is, taxes in that event would not be "zero"—the things currently "bought" by taxes would still have costs and prices. Thus it is pointless to think of "neutrality" in the terms adopted by proponents of a consumed-income tax.

Further, tax payments can be viewed as *savings* in the sense that every taxpayer must save—not consume—that part of his income required by the tax collector. The fact that the subsequent government expenditures are likely to squander his tax money on immediate consumption or even on wealth-destroying activities does not alter the fact that the taxpayer does not consume that money himself.

Even if it were desirable to set the ratio of private consumption and saving where it would be if there were no taxes, neither the consumed-income tax nor any tax supposedly based on consumption does this. A tax on any tax base will have an impact on income. Since a taxpayer controls only his after-tax income, he must necessarily make his decisions about how he allocates his saving and consumption based on his real, disposable income and not on his nominal income. No one should be either surprised or upset, therefore, when the taxpayer voluntarily allocates the income left to him in a way that takes the fact of taxation into account.

Further, decisions about the allocation of a given amount of income between present and future consumption (the latter represented by present saving plus the return it earns over time) are determined fundamentally by a taxpayer's value scale, which ranks alternative uses of resources, and specifically by the degree to which he would prefer to have something now rather than later. Thus a flat-rate consumed-income tax would be translated into an income tax, and the actual effective tax rates would vary wildly depending on a taxpayer's time preferences. Those with low incomes and who might therefore desire to spend a greater proportion of income on immediate needs would, in effect, face higher tax rates on income than would those who were relatively better off. Similarly, those with identical incomes but with different time preferences would face different effective income tax rates. Of course, rewarding taxpayers for saving is precisely the effect intended by consumed-income tax advocates who feel that taxpayers would otherwise choose a below-optimal level of savings.

Finally, the present income tax is largely income-based. Pragmatically, it would likely be easier to amend the current system by lowering rates and broadening the base than to substitute a new tax in its place, especially one that lessens rather than increases taxpayer cohesion.

Current Tax Reform Proposals—A Comparison

The Bradley-Gephardt "Fair" Tax

The intent of this proposal, introduced by Sen. Bill Bradley (D-N.J.) and Rep. Richard Gephardt (D-Mo.), is to reduce tax rates and broaden the tax base by eliminating many existing deductions, exclusions, and credits. Its proponents claim that it would raise approximately the same revenue as the current system without changing the average tax burden of any income class.

The Bradley-Gephardt proposal would provide for a progressive income-based tax with three marginal rates for individuals—14, 26, and 30 percent—and a single tax rate of 30 percent for corporations. Most taxpayers would pay only the 14 percent rate. The 26 percent rate would apply only to individuals with adjusted gross incomes exceeding $25,000 and to couples with adjusted gross incomes exceeding $40,000. The top rate of 30 percent would apply only to individuals with adjusted gross incomes over $37,500 and couples with adjusted gross incomes over $65,000.

The proposal would provide an increase in the personal exemption from $1,000 to $1,600 for taxpayers and spouses ($1,800 for a single head of household) and an increase in the standard deduction from $2,300 to $3,000 for single returns and from $3,400 to $6,000 for joint returns. A family of four could earn up to $11,200 before being subject to the tax. It would repeal most itemized deductions, credits, and exclusions. Retained would be the $1,000 exemptions for dependents, the elderly, and the blind; and deductions for home mortgage interest, charitable contributions, state and local income and real property taxes, payments to IRAs and Keogh plans, and employee business expenses. Exclusions would be retained for veteran benefits, social security benefits for low and moderate income persons, and the interest on general obligation bonds. The personal exemptions and itemized deductions would apply only against the 14 percent rate.

The present deduction for 60 percent of net long-term capital gains would be repealed, raising the maximum marginal tax rate on capital gains from the current 20 percent to 30 percent. The present law requiring indexing of the tax rates and personal exemptions for inflation would also be repealed. As nominal incomes rose, an increasing number of taxpayers would be paying at the 26 and 30 percent rates.

The Kemp-Kasten "Fair and Simple" Tax (FAST)

This proposal, introduced by Rep. Jack Kemp (R-N.Y.) and Sen. Robert Kasten (R-Wi.), is broadly similar to Bradley-Gephardt and appears to be modeled after it. It too reduces tax rates and broadens the tax base by eliminating many existing deductions, exclusions, and credits, while retaining such politically popular ones as interest deductions. Again, its proponents claim it would raise approximately the same amount of revenue as the current system without changing the average tax burden of any income class.

Kemp-Kasten would provide for a flat-rate, income-based tax. Income would be taxed at a flat 25 percent rate, and that tax would be coordinated with the social security payroll tax. To do this, 20 percent of the wage income that is subject to the payroll tax would be excluded from the income tax.

The wage base for the social security tax is currently $37,800 and is scheduled to rise to $39,300 in 1985. The effective marginal tax rate on this income would thus be 20 percent plus the 7 percent payroll tax. Above that point, Kemp-Kasten would reduce the 20 percent exclusion by 12.5 percent of the income in excess of the social security wage base. This would result in smooth, virtually flat total (income plus payroll) marginal tax rates for all income levels.

Kemp-Kasten would increase the personal exemption from $1,000 to $2,000. The zero bracket would also be increased. Consequently, a family of four could earn $14,375 before being subject to the tax.

Like Bradley-Gephardt, this proposal would repeal most itemized deductions, credits, and exclusions. Both plans allow deductions for charitable contributions, mortgage interest, property taxes, and medical exenses in excess of 10 percent of adjusted gross income. However, under Bradley-Gephardt these apply only to the 14 percent "normal" tax rate, not to the additional 26 percent and 30 percent marginal rate brackets. Unlike Bradley-Gephardt, Kemp-Kasten neither permits a deduction for state and local income taxes, nor taxes employees for the value of employer-contributed life and health insurance premiums in addition to compensation actually received.

The Kemp-Kasten proposal would provide for full taxation of net capital gains at the 25 percent rate. It would, however, index the basis of a capital asset; alternatively, for a 10-year transition period, a taxpayer could choose instead a 25 percent exclusion of his capital gain.

Kemp-Kasten retains the inflation-indexation provisions found in the current law with regard to the zero-bracket amount and the personal deduction.

For corporations, the proposal would eliminate most tax preferences, including the investment tax credit. It would lower the corporate tax rate from a maximum 46 percent to 30 percent. The business capital gains tax rate would be lowered from 28 percent to

20 percent, with indexing, in contrast to Bradley-Gephardt's proposed elevation of that rate to 30 percent, without indexing. While Bradley-Gephardt would institute a system approximating the pre-1981 depreciation schedules, Kemp-Kasten would retain the 1981 capital cost recovery schedules.

The Kemp-Kasten proposal would also retain two special provisions for small business: a reduced, 15 percent tax rate on the first $50,000 of income, and the ability to expense up to $10,000 per year of business property. Bradley-Gephardt would eliminate both of these.

Consumed-Income Tax Proposals

Economists Robert Hall and Alvin Rabushka have devised a flat-rate expenditure tax as a substitute for the current income-based tax system. It would have the same impact as a consumed-income tax since both would exclude saving/investment from the tax base. A consumed-income tax excludes the amount of net saving in the taxable year. For individuals, Hall-Rabushka would exclude the returns on savings realized in the taxable year, while for business it would exclude net saving. This proposal has been introduced in Congress by Sen. Dennis DeConcini (D-Ariz.) and Sen. Steven Symms (R-Idaho).

A pure consumed-income tax has been proposed by economists at the Brookings Institution. A similar "progressive consumption tax" with rates on consumed income ranging from 10 to 50 percent has been introduced by Rep. Cecil Heftel (D-Hawaii). Sen. William Roth (R-Del.) has announced that he will introduce an income tax reform proposal providing for "super savings accounts" that would allow individuals filing a joint return to deduct net savings of up to $20,000 per year from taxable income. These accounts would be a major step toward a consumed-income tax.

The Hall-Rabushka proposal would impose a flat 19 percent tax on the wages of individuals. Standard deductions of $4,100 for single taxpayers, $6,700 for married persons, and $810 per dependent would be allowed. No further deductions, including interest payments, would be allowed. A family of four could earn up to $8,320 in wages before becoming subject to the tax, as compared with $8,936 under current law. Dividends, capital gains, returns from saving, and other income received by individuals would not be taxed.

All other income taxes would be collected through the "business tax," a flat 19 percent tax on business revenue less expenditures on goods, services, and materials, whether resold or not. Capital equipment, structures, and land would be expensed just like other costs. By taxing all net business income—corporate and non-corporate—at a single uniform rate on the business unit, and then by taxing only wages at the individual level, Hall-Rabushka completely integrates the corporate and personal income tax.

By thus eliminating the current practice of double taxation of corporate dividends, the proposal resolves one of the fundamental biases of the present tax system against capital formation and growth. Such features could also be drafted onto a straightforward income-based tax, which would have a broader base and a lower rate or rates than are required under Hall-Rabushka.

The proponents of all these reform proposals, both income- and consumption-based, claim that their plans are revenue-neutral. It is highly unlikely that this is the case. Additionally, Hall and Rabushka admit that, while middle-income taxpayers would face lower marginal rates under their proposal, their effective tax rates would be increased, and they would pay much higher taxes than at present. Increases as high as 46 percent for a range of incomes from $15,000 to $45,000 would be felt. For this reason alone it is not, in its present form, a politically acceptable substitute for the current income tax system.

The question of what to do about the federal deficit will remain. Tax increases, in the straightforward sense of raising the nominal rates found in the tax schedules, have never had much political appeal, and fortunately the advent of tax indexing has now shut the door on the tempting yet counterproductive strategy of inflation-induced "bracket creep." The most that advocates of higher taxes are willing to claim is that increased economic growth is not likely to be sufficient to reduce future deficits to a manageable level. They do not deny that if the current modest and fragile economic recovery is prematurely cut off on account of tax increases or other political miscalculations, then it will likely be absolutely impossible to develop a constituency for needed reforms, of whatever sort, on the spending side.

Thus, while it may be perfectly true that economic growth alone cannot resolve the deficit question, it is equally true that the question will never be resolved without a sustained period of renewed prosperity. In the short run, it seems that those who are serious about reducing the deficit have few alternatives but to work to rectify the admittedly huge economic distortions and inefficiencies institutionalized in the present tax code. A simple compromise plan—based on the Bradley-Gephardt and Kemp-Kasten bills—to increase personal exemptions, lower maximum rates, and eliminate at least some of the current special interest deductions is likely to receive growing support as it becomes increasingly clear that little else of a constructive nature stands a chance of legislative passage.

IV. Social Security Reform: The Super IRA

Peter J. Ferrara

Despite social security's increasingly inadequate service to the elderly and incredible tax burdens on the young, establishment Washington refuses to consider any fundamental changes in the program. But public awareness of the overwhelming and rapidly worsening problems of social security is spreading. These severe problems make fundamental reform of the program politically possible as well as pragmatically necessary.

The key to turning this possibility into reality is to design reform proposals which do not threaten the elderly, but rather enlist their support by making changes which benefit them as well as today's workers. With such proposals, fundamental social security reform can in fact become a widely popular issue, with important benefits for everyone. This chapter will explain how to structure reform proposals that benefit both the elderly and today's workers and solve the serious problems now facing social security.

The Current System: Reason for Despair

Financing Problems

Though costly rescue legislation—harmful both to the elderly and the young—was passed in 1983 to save social security from bankruptcy, the program still faces serious short-term and long-term financing problems.

In the short run, the program remains vulnerable to the cycles of inflation and recession that have dominated the American economy for the last 20 years. Inflation causes social security expenditures to rise, because benefits are indexed. Recession causes social security income to fall from expected levels, because unemployment rises, wage and employment growth slow down, and payroll taxes consequently produce less revenue. Without a large trust fund to back

51

the system up, social security cannot survive periodic sharp inflation and steep recession.

The inflation of the early 1970s and the subsequent 1974–75 recession caused a social security crisis requiring a legislative rescue in 1977, which involved the largest peacetime tax increase in U.S. history. The inflation of the late 1970s followed by steep recessions from 1979 to 1982 caused the crisis requiring the 1983 rescue legislation.

The 1984 annual social security trustees report[1] projects that the trust funds for the predominant Old-Age, Survivors and Disability Insurance (OASDI) portion of social security—the entire program except Hospital Insurance (HI)[2]— will be about the same size relative to social security expenditures for the rest of this decade, as was projected for the years immediately following the 1977 bailout. This means that just as social security was not able to survive inflation and recession after 1977, without emergency measures, so it will not be able to survive further rounds of sharp inflation or serious recession in the next few years. The 1984 trustees report itself repeatedly warns of the program's vulnerability to a sharp recession at least until 1987.

Even without another inflation/recession cycle in the short run, social security will remain vulnerable. The financial rescue plan passed in 1983 relied on massive payroll tax increases scheduled for 1988 and 1990 to move the program out of the range of vulnerability. But these tax increases will slow the economy, with particularly harsh effects on employment, resulting in less new revenues than expected.

Other elements in the 1983 rescue plan are also likely to fail to meet expectations. The plan makes social security benefits subject to income taxation for recipients above certain income thresholds,[3] with the resulting revenues to be used for social security. But many

---

[1]*1984 Annual Report of the Board of Trustees of the Federal Old-Age and Survivors Insurance and Disability Insurance Trust Funds* (Washington, D.C., April 5, 1984). (hereafter cited as *1984 OASDI Report*)

[2]Social security includes Old-Age and Survivors Insurance (OASI), Disability Insurance (DI), and Hospital Insurance (HI). OASI plus DI is OASDI. OASDI plus HI is OASDHI. OASI currently accounts for about 72 percent of social security expenditures, DI about 8 percent, and HI about 20 percent. HI financing problems are discussed in more detail below.

[3]The income thresholds are $25,000 for single recipients and $32,000 for married recipients filing jointly.

retirees are likely to shelter their incomes to fall below these thresholds, reducing expected revenues. In addition, the plan sharply increases payroll tax rates for the self-employed.[4] This is likely to result in fewer self-employed workers, earning less income than expected, resulting again in less than projected new revenues.

Moreover, the HI portion of the program is expected to run short of funds by the end of the decade in any event.[5] If any surpluses from the rest of the program are used to bail out HI, the entire social security system will at best remain vulnerable to inflation and recession. Indeed, the 1984 trustees report indicates that the entire, combined social security program would run short of funds by the mid-1990s under the so-called pessimistic (Alternative III) assumptions.[6] Historically, the "pessimistic" assumptions have always been closest to reality.

Over the long run—the next 75 years—the 1984 trustees report projects that OASDI would run a negligible deficit of 0.06 percent of taxable payroll under the widely cited Alternative IIB assumptions. But this summary statistic hides a serious long-term financing problem for this portion of social security alone, even under these assumptions. The year-by-year projections under Alternative IIB assumptions show large annual surpluses in OASDI beginning at the end of this decade and continuing until 2015–2020, leading to the accumulation of a large OASDI trust fund. After 2020, however,

---

[4]Under the 1983 legislation, the self-employed social security tax rate will be increased by 1990 to the total combined employer/employee rate, an increase of over 40 percent. Though half the tax will be deductible for federal income tax purposes, this will only offset a small proportion of the payroll tax increase for most workers.

[5]*1984 Annual Report of the Board of Trustees of the Federal Hospital Insurance Trust Funds* (Washington, D.C., April 5, 1984). (hereafter cited as *1984 HI Report*)

[6]Buried in Appendix F of the *1984 OASDI Report* are projections under Alternative III assumptions showing that the combined trust funds for the entire program as a percentage of all social security expenditures are projected to decline from 23 percent in 1984 to 11 percent in 1993, when the projections stop. Given that a minimum of about 9 percent of one year's expenditures is needed to maintain the cash flow to pay benefits on time, the strong and steady downward trend indicates that the entire, combined program would be unable to pay timely benefits soon after 1993. Calculations based on data in Harry C. Ballantyne, Chief Actuary, Social Security Administration, "Long-Range Projections of Social Security Trust Fund operations in Dollars" (Actuarial Note 120, Social Security Administration, U.S. Department of Health and Human Services, May 1984) confirm that the combined program would be unable to pay full promised benefits by 1995 under the Alternative III assumptions.

large annual deficits in OASDI appear, continuing throughout the remaining 40 years of the projection period. By 2060, OASDI expenditures are running almost 20 percent higher than revenues each year, and the OASDI trust funds have just been exhausted. Clearly, the program will be unable to pay promised benefits after that point.

Adding in HI, the long-run financial problems for the entire, combined program are staggering, even under Alternative IIB projections. Assuming assets from any of the program's trust funds would be used to pay any of the program's benefits when necessary, social security as a whole would become unable to pay promised benefits under Alternative IIB projections by 2020, before those entering the work force today will have retired.[7] By 2060, social security expenditures would be running 55 percent higher than revenues each year.[8] Over the entire 75-year projection period, the program as a whole runs a cumulative deficit under the Alternative IIB assumptions about twice as large as the total amount raised in new revenue or cut in benefits over the same period by the 1983 social security rescue legislation.[9]

Moreover, even the Alternative IIB assumptions appear broadly overoptimistic. Inflation is assumed to stabilize over the next few years at 4 percent and remain at that level every year until 2060. Unemployment is assumed to stabilize at 6 percent likewise remaining at that level every year until 2060. Other key economic variables are assumed to follow a similar pattern. These assumptions are reasonable for individual, good, economic years, but not as averages over 75 years, when periodic bouts of substantial inflation and sharp recession may still be expected. The Alternative IIB assumptions assume, in effect, that there will not be a single serious recession or major burst of inflation for the next 75 years.

Alternative IIB assumptions also include a significant and permanent increase in fertility (lifetime births per woman) over current levels. Yet, U.S. fertility has fallen steadily over the last 200 years, except for the relatively brief postwar baby boom produced by

[7]Calculated from *1984 OASDI Report*.

[8]Calculated from *1984 OASDI Report*.

[9]The 1983 legislation reduced the financing gap for the next 75 years by 2.09 percent of taxable payroll under 1983 Alternative IIB assumptions, which are basically the same as 1984 Alternative IIB assumptions. But the 75-year deficit for the entire program under 1984 Alternative IIB assumptions is still 4.09 percent of taxable payroll. See *1983 OASDI Report* and *1984 OASDI Report*.

the back-to-back cataclysms of the Great Depression and World War II.[10]

The potentially most wildly inaccurate Alternative IIB assumptions of all are those relating to mortality. Alternative IIB assumes that the rate of increase in life expectancy will slow substantially over the next 75 years. But with the promising potential for major technological breakthroughs in health care over the next 75 years, this surely seems unrealistic. Indeed, major and unforeseen extensions in life expectancy in the next century could become the new primary cause of financial disaster for social security, as the elderly would live and draw benefits for many more years than now expected.

The so-called pessimistic Alternative III set of assumptions seems far more realistic. Inflation is assumed to stabilize at 5 percent and unemployment at 7 percent. Fertility is assumed to fall and then stabilize consistently with long-standing trends. Life expectancy is projected to increase at historical rates. In the past, as noted, reality has always followed most closely the Alternative III assumptions.

Under Alternative III projections, the combined social security program would be unable to pay full benefits by 1995.[11] Based on the published data, one can estimate that under these assumptions social security expenditures by 2055 would be 2⅓ times as large as revenues each year.[12] The cumulative deficit over the 75-year projection period would be almost four times as large as the financial

[10]See Peter J. Ferrara, *Social Security: The Inherent Contradiction* (Washington, D.C.: Cato Institute, 1980), table 33. Fertility in the U.S. has fallen from a rate of 7.04 in 1800 to 1.86 in 1982. The fertility rate has increased over the last six years, apparently because of increased births among older women who had much fewer children at younger ages than in the past. But this development is likely to stabilize. Based on historical trends and social attitudes favoring fewer children, it still seems most likely that the fertility rate will eventually resume its long-standing downward trend.

[11]Calculated from Ballantyne; *1984 OASDI Report; 1984 HI Report.*

[12]Under Alternative III projections, OASDI expenditures in 2055 would equal 25.43 percent of taxable payroll. HI expenditures, under Alternative IIB, in that year would equal 9.46 percent of payroll. Though Alternative III projections for HI extend only until 2005, in that year HI expenditures under Alternative III are already running 2.53 percent of taxable payroll higher than under Alternative IIB. If one assumes that at least this margin is present in 2055 (it would surely be greater than this), then expenditures for the entire program in that year would be at least 37.42 percent of taxable payroll. Total revenue in that year would be approximately 16 percent of payroll. See *1984 OASDI Report, 1984 HI Report.*

gap addressed by the 1983 legislation.[13] In order to pay the benefits promised to those entering the work force today, the combined employer/employee social security payroll tax rate under these projections would have to be raised to at least 33 percent, compared with the current 14 percent.[14] This would mean a total, annual social security tax of $6,700 for a worker making $20,000. Former social security chief actuary A. Haeworth Robertson suggests that payroll tax rates may have to climb to over 40 percent to pay all the benefits promised to these workers.[15]

Bad Deal for Young Workers

What is truly devastating, however, is that even if all the benefits promised to today's young workers are somehow paid, the program will still represent a miserable deal for these workers. The rate of return paid by social security has been falling steadily for years, and by the time those entering the work force retire, this return will be well below market levels. This is true even though today's retirees are still getting a good deal from the program.

The developing problem is a natural consequence of social security's "pay-as-you-go" method of operation whereby the taxes paid

[13]The 1983 legislation reduced the financing gap over the next 75 years by about 2.7 percent of taxable payroll under 1983 Alternative III projections, which are basically the same as 1984 Alternative III projections. The 75-year deficit for OASDI under Alternative III projections is 4.12 percent of taxable payroll. HI under Alternative IIB projections would offer a 75-year deficit of 4.03 percent of taxable payroll. As noted in footnote 12, though Alternative III projections for HI are not published past 2005, by that year HI expenditures under Alternative III are already running 2.5 percent of taxable payroll higher than under Alternative IIB. This differential could only be expected to widen further over the following 55 years, so that over the entire 75-year period the deficit would probably be at least another 2 percent of payroll higher under Alternative III than under Alternative IIB. Consequently, the 75-year deficit for the entire program under Alternative III would be at least 10.15 percent of taxable payroll. See 1983 and 1984 trustees reports for the OASDI and HI programs.

[14]Under Alternative III assumptions, by 2035 OASDI will cost 21.33 percent of taxable payroll. HI under Alternative IIB assumptions would cost 9.14 percent of payroll in 2035. Since the increased cost of HI under Alternative III in 2035 should be at least 2.53 percent of payroll higher than under Alternative IIB (see footnotes 12 and 13), costs for all of social security in 2035 should be at least 33 percent of payroll. See *1984 OASDI Report; 1984 HI Report* (HI).

[15]A. Haeworth Robertson, *The Coming Revolution in Social Security* (Reston, Virginia: Reston Publishing Company, 1981). Robertson states that he still believes tax rates have to climb to 40 percent even with the 1983 legislative changes.

into the program are not saved and invested to pay the future benefits of today's workers, but are instead immediately paid out to finance the benefits of current beneficiaries. Similarly, the taxes of the next generation of workers are to be used to finance the benefits of today's workers.

We can trace from the beginning of social security how this method of operation has led to an inevitable collapse of returns. Workers retiring in the early years of the program had to pay social security taxes only for part of their working careers. The tax burden in those years was also quite low: The maximum annual social security tax, including both the employer and employee shares, was $189 as late as 1958 and $348 as late as 1965. But because the program is run on a pay-as-you-go basis, the benefits paid to these early retirees were not limited to what could be paid based on their own past taxes. These retirees were instead paid full benefits out of the taxes of those still working. Their benefits consequently represented a high return on the taxes they did pay.

Over time, however, the rate of return paid by social security naturally began to fall as workers began paying higher taxes for more of their working careers. For today's retirees, as noted, the program's benefits still represent an above market return on the taxes they and their employers paid into the system. But those entering the work force today must pay taxes of several thousand dollars a year for their entire working careers. The maximum annual tax, including employer and employee payments, is today almost $5,300 and will be almost $8,000 by the end of the decade.[16] For most of these young workers, the real rate of return paid by social security will be 1 percent or less.[17] For two-earner couples or maximum income workers—a large proportion of this rising generation—the real return will be practically zero, or even negative in many cases.[18]

These workers could earn much higher returns if they could use their social security tax money to invest in the private sector through an Individual Retirement Account (IRA). Addressing the issue of possible private-sector returns on retirement investments, Martin

[16]Calculated from *1984 OASDI Report.*

[17]Calculated from the Alternative IIB assumptions in the 1983 trustees reports for OASDI and HI. These calculations will be published in a forthcoming Cato Institute study.

[18]Ibid.

Feldstein, former chairman of the Council of Economic Advisors and now professor of economics at Harvard University, wrote in 1976,

> Over the past twenty-five years, the real annual yield after adjusting for inflation was 8 percent for common stocks and 3 percent for corporate bonds. A conservative portfolio with half of each would have yielded 5.5 percent.[19]

In fact, if half the annual payments into an IRA were invested each year in common stocks with an 8 percent real return and half in corporate bonds with a 3 percent real return, and the return on each half were reinvested in stocks and bonds respectively, then the average real annual yield after 41 years would be 6.3 percent.

During the entire postwar period, 1946 to 1983, the average combined real rate of return on all stocks on the New York Stock Exchange was 6.9 percent.[20] If we go all the way back to include the Great Depression, taking the period 1926 to 1983, the real return is still 6.4 percent.[21] Simple, long-term, diversified retirement investments—basically buying a piece of the economy as a whole rather than trying to pick individual winners—would regularly earn such returns. Indeed, mutual funds over the last 10 years have averaged even higher real returns.[22] Workers with such simple but broadly diversified retirement investments would face only the risk of general economic collapse, a risk faced by social security as well.

If young workers entering the work force today could invest all their social security tax money, including the employer's share, in IRAs, then at no more than a 6 percent real return most would receive *three to six times the retirement benefits promised them under social security,* while at least matching the other types of benefits provided by the program.[23] Career minimum wage earners would receive about twice the retirement benefits of social security, while

---

[19]Martin Feldstein, "Facing the Social Security Crisis," Harvard Institute of Economic Research, Discussion Paper No. 492, July 1976, p. 5.

[20]Roger G. Ibbotson and Rex A. Sinquefeld, *Stocks, Bonds, Bills and Inflation Quarterly Service* 1, no. 2 (July 1983).

[21]Ibid.

[22]Phone interview, Investment Company Institute, Washington, D.C.

[23]Ferrara, *Social Security: The Inherent Contradiction,* chapter 4; Peter J. Ferrara, *Social Security: Averting the Crisis* (Washington, D.C.: Cato Institute, 1982), chapter 4.

families with both spouses earning maximum taxable incomes would receive at least eight times the benefits.[24]

Moreover, the investment returns cited above are actually after-tax returns received after the corporate income tax and other taxes have been paid. Since the social security returns discussed above are the full, untaxed returns provided by the program, a truly fair comparison between social security and private alternatives would have to include the real, *before-tax* returns under the private system as well. By taxation of these returns—which represent the full benefits produced by the private system—the government would merely be appropriating part of them for other uses. These increased resources available to the government would go either to provide government services that voters have chosen through the political process or to reduce other taxes. Either way, individuals would still be receiving the full, before-tax benefits of the private system.

Studies by Martin Feldstein and others indicate that the before-tax real rate of return on capital in the American economy is at least 12 percent.[25] Of course, this figure would be relevant only to what individuals could earn if they could invest IRA funds without any taxation on the returns at any point, unlike the current IRA system. But the structure for such a reformed, totally untaxed IRA has been proposed.[26] In any event, as indicated above, even if some of the before-tax returns were taken in taxes, the revenues thus generated would still have to be considered an additional benefit produced by the private system.

There is simply no sense in requiring today's young workers to pay so much into social security as a retirement investment when that investment promises to pay such a low rate of return, zero or even negative in many cases. Now that the start-up windfall of social security's pay-as-you-go system has passed, this problem of low returns will plague all future generations as well.

---

[24]Ibid.

[25]Martin Feldstein, "National Savings in the United States," Harvard Institute of Economic Research, Discussion Paper No. 566, October 1976; Martin Feldstein, "Toward a Reform of Social Security," *The Public Interest* (Summer 1975): 75–95; Martin Feldstein, "The Optimal Financing of Social Security," Harvard Institute of Economic Research, Discussion Paper No. 338, 1974; Alicia H. Munnell, *The Future of Social Security* (Washington, D.C.: Brookings Institution, 1977), p. 128.

[26]Ferrara, *Social Security: The Inherent Contradiction*, chapter 13; Ferrara, *Social Security: Averting the Crisis*, chapter 10.

Destroying Jobs and Economic Growth

As presently structured, social security also severely damages the economy, destroying jobs and economic growth. A primary agent of this destruction is the social security payroll tax.

To the extent that the tax is borne by employers, it discourages them from hiring. To the extent that the tax is borne by employees, it discourages them from working. Though economic analysis indicates that the tax is in fact borne fully by employees,[27] in either case the result is less employment and, consequently, less output. The payroll tax is nothing more than a tax on employment, and here, as elsewhere, the result of taxing something is that there is less of it.

As noted, the maximum annual payroll tax is already almost $5,300 and is scheduled to rise to *almost* $8,000 by the end of the decade. For at least half of all workers covered by social security, the combined payroll tax is more than they pay in federal income tax.[28] In 1983 payroll tax revenues, drawn primarily from low and moderate income workers, were over 70 percent greater than total federal corporate and business tax revenues.[29] In a society deeply concerned about employment opportunities, this incredible tax burden on labor is ludicrous. Yet, without fundamental reform, the future holds in store only dramatic payroll tax increases.

Social security also tends to discourage saving because to many workers paying into the program appears to be the same, in effect, as saving for retirement. They will consequently tend to reduce their retirement savings by roughly the amounts paid into social security. Since social security operates on a pay-as-you-go basis, however, no offsetting savings are actually made through the program, and the result is a net loss of savings.

This loss could be quite enormous, potentially reducing national savings and capital by 40 to 50 percent.[30] The result of less savings is less capital for investment and hence lower economic growth and

---

[27]See Ferrara, *Social Security: The Inherent Contradiction,* chapter 2.

[28]Benjamin Bridges, Jr., "Family Social Security Taxes Compared with Federal Income Taxes, 1979," *Social Security Bulletin* 44, no. 12 (December 1981).

[29]President's Council of Economic Advisors, *1984 Economic Report of the President,* (Washington, D.C.: U.S. Government Printing Office, 1984).

[30]See discussion in Ferrara, *Social Security: The Inherent Contradiction,* chapter 3; Ferrara, *Social Security: Averting the Crisis,* chapter 3.

GNP. It has been estimated that a savings loss of this magnitude causes a loss of almost one-sixth of GNP.[31]

Economists generally recognize this effect of social security in reducing national savings. But many try to explain it away by arguing that the program has countervailing effects tending to increase savings. Unfortunately, these supposed countervailing effects are all based on highly implausible rationales and are likely to have little if any significant impact in producing savings increases today.[32] The fact is, apart from social security most workers today are providing for retirement through private savings vehicles. Social security, however, *forces* workers to provide for the bulk of their retirement through a system that creates no savings. In essence, social security is a form of *forced non-saving* for retirement. It would be truly remarkable if such an anti-savings constraint were not today substantially reducing private savings.

Inequities, Discrimination, and the Poor

Social security's benefit structure is also highly inequitable. Two workers who pay exactly the same taxes into social security throughout their working careers may receive widely different benefit amounts. For example, larger benefits are paid to workers with non-working spouses or with dependent children, even though they may have paid precisely the same taxes as workers without such relations. A two-earner couple may pay twice the taxes of a single-earner couple, yet receive only one-third more in benefits. Single workers without young children must pay for social security survivors insurance, even though no survivors benefits can ever be paid on their behalf. The same is true for many two-earner couples: Survivors benefits will not be paid before retirement for working widows or widowers without children.

The program's benefit structure also seriously discriminates against blacks and other minorities. For example, because the life expectancy of blacks is significantly less than that of whites, blacks can expect to receive less in benefits than whites for the same taxes. According to a study by the National Center for Policy Analysis,[33]

---

[31]Martin Feldstein, "Social Insurance," Harvard Institute of Economic Research, Discussion Paper No. 477, May 1976, p. 33.

[32]For a more thorough discussion see Ferrara, *Social Security: The Inherent Contradiction*, chapter 3; Ferrara, *Social Security: Averting the Crisis*, chapter 3.

[33]National Center for Policy Analysis, *The Effect of the Social Security System on Black Americans* (Dallas: National Center for Policy Analysis, 1983).

a black male born today has a life expectancy of 64 years, and therefore on average he will not live long enough to receive social security retirement benefits for even a single day. A black male at age 25 today can expect to receive full social security retirement benefits for only five months, while a white male age 25 can expect six years of full benefits—about 15 times as much. The NCPA study also points out that blacks are, on the whole, significantly younger than whites. Thus, since the program offers a worse deal the younger one is, it discriminates against blacks on this account, too.

The poor in general are hurt by the program in many other important ways as well. Lower-income workers tend to have left school and started working earlier than those with higher incomes. Yet social security credits these workers with little, if any, additional benefits for their early years of work and tax payments. Although single workers are statistically much more likely to be poor than are married couples, the program pays additional benefits to married workers not available to single workers.

A significant proportion of the benefits paid through social security are really based on a welfare rationale: They are not justified by past taxes paid into the program but are paid instead to help those who may be in need. But since the program's benefits are paid without a means test, such welfare assistance ends up going to too many who are not in need. Consequently, resources available to help the poor are wasted on the non-poor. In addition, the poor are naturally the people most hurt by both the negative effects of the program on the general economy and the loss of higher benefits in the private sector.

While social security contains important welfare elements that help the poor, these same resources could be devoted to the poor through an alternative vehicle without the negative effects of the current system.

A Populist Proposal for Reform

The solution to the many serious problems plaguing social security does not in any way require imposing sacrifices on the elderly. Quite the contrary, appropriate reform would strengthen social security and assure today's elderly their benefits, while providing new opportunities to today's young workers so that they may look forward to a secure and prosperous retirement.

Guaranteeing the Elderly

In fact, the first element of any legislative package embodying fundamental social security reform should be an ironclad guarantee that the elderly will continue to receive their promised social security benefits in full. A truly meaningful guarantee can be provided by fundamentally upgrading the legal status of social security benefits.

The Supreme Court held in a 1960 decision, *Flemming* v. *Nestor*,[34] that Congress has the power to reduce or cut off social security benefits to any or all of the elderly at any time. Congress has the authority to reverse this statutorily based decision, and should do so as follows.

At the time that a worker retires in reliance on his future, promised social security benefits, he should receive a U.S. government bond stating his contractual entitlement to those benefits. All those already retired at the time of the reform would receive such a bond as well. The bond would not change the amount of the retiree's promised benefits in any way. It would simply embody a contract with the government promising that the retiree will receive his monthly benefit amount each month for the rest of his life, plus COLA increases, calculated under the law in effect at the time he retired (or, for those already retired when the reform is adopted, when the bond is received).

Congress would statutorily express its intent that the retiree would have the same legal status in regard to his social security benefits, as promised by his government-backed bond, as a U.S. treasury bond holder has in regard to the payment of the interest and principal on his bond. The Constitution prohibits the federal government from reneging on the payment of interest and/or principal on any U.S. government bond. Similarly, under the proposed social security bond system, it would be unconstitutional to cut the expected social security benefits of workers once they retired. Such a guarantee for the elderly would calm the political atmosphere and allow consideration of more fundamental reform.

The Super IRA Option

A second element of a fundamental reform package would be to allow workers the option of beginning to rely on an expanded "super" IRA in place of some of their social security benefits. To

[34]363 U.S. 610.

63

accomplish this, starting on, say, January 1, 1986, workers would be allowed to contribute to their IRAs each year an amount up to 20 percent of their social security retirement taxes (OASI) in addition to any other amounts they may contribute under current law.[35] Instead of the usual IRA income tax deduction for these contributions, however, workers would instead receive a dollar-for-dollar income tax credit. Workers would also be allowed to direct their employers to contribute up to 20 percent of the employer share of the tax to the workers' IRAs, with each employer again receiving a full income tax credit for these amounts.

Workers who utilize this tax credit option would then have their future social security benefits reduced to the extent they did so. A worker who opted for the full credit during his entire working career would have his social security benefits reduced by 20 percent. A worker who took half the tax credit each year would have his future benefits reduced by 10 percent. A worker who took half the credit for half his career would have his benefits reduced by 5 percent. Of course, the expanded IRAs of these workers would pay higher benefits which would more than make up for the foregone social security benefits.

Since the tax credit is taken against income taxes rather than payroll taxes, social security revenues would not be reduced in any way, and would continue to flow into the program in full to finance benefits for today's elderly. The credit option would result only in a loss of *income tax revenue*. If the credit option were in effect in the current fiscal year (FY 1985) and workers utilized it twice as much as they currently use conventional IRAs, the income tax revenue loss for the year would be $14.5 billion.

This loss would eventually be offset completely by reduced social security expenditures, as more workers retired relying to a large extent on IRAs rather than social security. Long before that point, however, the revenue loss would be eliminated on net by taxes generated from the increased investment through IRAs. In the meantime, moreover, there would be increased savings through the IRAs at least equal to the amount of revenue lost, since the tax

---

[35]Workers would not have to contribute anything else to their IRAs before they could take advantage of this credit option. From the first dollar of contribution, workers could choose whether to take the current deduction or the new credit along with future reduced social security benefits (as described in the text), up to the maximum limit for each.

credit would be allowed only for IRA savings.[36] So even if the government had to borrow entirely to cover the revenue loss, there would be no net increase in the government borrowing drain on private savings.

A third element of the reform package would provide that starting on a later date, say January 1, 1990, workers would be allowed to contribute additional amounts to their IRAs each year, up to 10 percent of the employee's OASI taxes, for the purchase of term life insurance. Workers could also direct their employers to contribute up to this amount to their IRAs for such insurance purchases. Employer and employee would again each receive income tax credits equal to the amount of their contributions, rather than the usual IRA deduction.

An employee with no dependents who may not need such life insurance coverage would be allowed to devote these additional contributions to his retirement benefits instead. An employee with one dependent would be allowed to use half these contributions for retirement.

Social security currently pays survivors benefits on behalf of a deceased taxpayer who leaves a dependent spouse and young children, or an elderly spouse. For workers under 65, private term life insurance can perform this function entirely. Consequently, the survivors benefits of a worker who died before 65 would be reduced to the extent that he had used the tax credit option to purchase term life insurance in force when he died.

Once again, the tax credit would be taken against income taxes rather than payroll taxes, and consequently social security revenues would continue to flow into the program in full. If this credit option

[36]To avoid the danger of a mere shifting of existing savings into IRAs to obtain the credit, workers should be prohibited from withdrawing before retirement IRA contributions for which they obtained the credit, and the returns associated with those contributions. This would make the IRA savings unsuitable as a substitute for non-retirement savings, since they could not be used for non-retirement purposes. Because social security benefits would be reduced for credited IRA contributions, the IRA savings would be needed to replace those lost benefits, and therefore would not be available as a substitute for other retirement savings either. As a result of these factors, any shifting of existing savings into IRAs rather than new savings to obtain the tax credit should be negligible, because such IRA savings will no longer be able to perform the function of other savings. To enforce this withdrawal prohibition, Super IRA contributions receiving the tax credit would have to be maintained in a separate account from regular IRA contributions for which only a tax deduction is received.

were in effect in the current fiscal year and workers utilized it twice as much as they now use conventional IRAs, the income tax revenue loss for the year would be $7 billion. This loss would be offset rapidly by reduced social security expenditures, since from the first year the survivors of all who died while relying on insurance purchased through the tax credit would immediately receive private insurance rather than social security benefits. The fully funded private life insurance system would also produce new investment, savings, and tax revenues to offset the temporary income tax revenue loss.

Later legislation could expand the Super IRA option. The maximum credit for IRA contributions could be increased to 40 percent of OASI taxes, for both employees and employers, in return for further proportional social security benefit reductions in the future. Eventually this credit could be expanded to 100 percent of OASI taxes. Workers could then be allowed to purchase disability and old-age health insurance through their IRAs, with further credits allowed for these purchases in return for reduced reliance on social security. Ultimately, workers could have the complete freedom to choose how much to rely on Super IRAs or social security. But an initial reform package could begin with just the three elements described above.

Benefits of the Reform

As a result of the reform, social security itself would be greatly strengthened and any long-term financing problems likely eliminated if the Super IRA option were expanded rapidly enough. While social security revenues were maintained in full, the program's expenditures would be reduced substantially as workers relied more and more on IRAs rather than social security. With the Super IRA option eventually expanded to the maximum, social security expenditures would likely be reduced dramatically, allowing room for sharp reductions in payroll tax rates. Moreover, the elderly would have their benefits constitutionally guaranteed through the proposed social security bonds.

In addition, workers would have the complete freedom to remain in social security as is if they wished to do so. Those already in the work force who opted for the Super IRAs to whatever degree would receive full credit toward social security benefits for amounts they paid into the program in the past or might pay in the future.

Those workers who did opt for a Super IRA could expect much

higher retirement benefits. As discussed above, a fully expanded Super IRA option would give today's young workers the opportunity to earn several times the retirement benefits promised by social security. The Super IRA benefits, moreover, would be financed on a fully funded basis, thus securing them against the financing problems inherent in social security's current pay-as-you-go system. The IRA alternative would also allow workers complete freedom to choose their retirement age after the 59½ minimum age for IRA benefits under current law. Workers would not lose benefits for choosing late retirement, as is the case with social security.

The reform would also have several important benefits for the economy. The funds paid into Super IRAs could increase national savings sharply, with a fully expanded IRA option potentially producing hundreds of billions of dollars in increased savings each year. Such a savings increase would in turn produce new jobs and sharp increases in economic growth. Eventual payroll tax reductions would also stimulate job creation and economic growth.

Benefits paid through the Super IRAs would also be completely equitable, since each worker would receive in benefits what he paid in contributions, plus interest, on an actuarial basis. Workers who must pay for social security survivors insurance, which offers them no benefits, would be allowed to purchase private life insurance or devote the funds instead to their retirement, eliminating one of the grossest inequities of the current system. Minority workers with shorter life expectancies could retire earlier and/or leave their accumulated Super IRA funds to their survivors, instead of the quite limited survivors benefits offered by social security.

The poor would be particularly helped by the proposed reform. Those who start work at a younger age, like many of the poor, would receive greater benefits through Super IRAs for their early contributions, rather than less as through social security, because such early IRA contributions would accumulate interest for more years. Single workers, who on the average are more likely to be poor than are married workers, would receive the same returns as married workers through the Super IRAs, rather than the lower returns offered by social security. The higher retirement benefits available through the Super IRAs would also be most important to the poor, as would the likely improvement in economic performance resulting from the reform. Any eventual reductions in the regressive payroll tax would also benefit the poor in particular, since the tax falls most harshly on those with lower incomes.

Moreover, the proposed reform would create special new opportunities for the poor because it would give them control over some capital through their Super IRAs. If a career minimum wage earner entering the work force today could pay into a Super IRA, along with his employer, what he otherwise would be required to pay into social security, then at market returns he would accumulate almost $300,000 in today's dollars by retirement.[37] This fund could pay him, out of interest alone, more than he is currently promised under social security[38] and could be left intact to his children to serve as a sturdy foundation for their economic advancement.

The Supplemental Security Income program (SSI) would continue to provide means-tested, general revenue financed welfare benefits to the elderly poor, ensuring that their retirement income would not in any event fall below a basic minimum. The more the Super IRA, which of course pays no welfare benefits, is expanded and utilized in place of social security, the more the welfare assistance now paid through social security will instead be paid through means-tested SSI. To the extent this occurs, it would eliminate the current waste of welfare assistance paid through social security to many who are not poor, which as noted earlier occurs because social security has no means test.

In addition, the more workers across the whole economy are allowed to accumulate assets in their Super IRAs in lieu of social security, the more broadly based the national distribution of wealth will become. If all workers paid into Super IRAs rather than social security, the national concentration of wealth would be reduced by one-third.[39] Yet, this would be achieved not by redistributing wealth, but by providing an opportunity for the creation of widely distributed new wealth. Through the private IRA investments each worker would be developing a substantial ownership stake in America's business and industry. This would revolutionize political attitudes, for instead of developing a psychology of dependence on big government, as with social security, retirees would understand that their prosperity depended on private enterprise and free markets.

The proposed reform package would also allow workers more

[37]See Ferrara, *Social Security: The Inherent Contradiction*, chapter 4; and Ferrara, *Social Security: Averting the Crisis*, chapter 4.

[38]Ibid.

[39]Martin Feldstein, "Social Security and the Distribution of Wealth," *Journal of the American Statistical Association* (December 1976).

freedom and control over their own incomes. They would control the assets in their Super IRAs, choosing the investment vehicles they desired to meet their retirement and insurance needs. This greater freedom would increase still more as the Super IRAs were eventually expanded.

Fundamentally, the reform would tend to denationalize the large portion of the pension and insurance industry now represented by social security, shifting functions to the private sector that can be better performed there. It is particularly ridiculous that simple and easily available private life insurance coverage is today being displaced by social security survivors benefits. The proposed reform package would address this absurdity.

Moreover, as the reform reduced social security expenditures through reliance on Super IRAs, federal spending would be reduced. With an option to rely completely on Super IRAs, federal spending could potentially be reduced by more than one-fourth.[40]

The Politics of Reform

The problems of social security we have discussed demand fundamental reform. They cannot be ignored; the program itself will not allow it. On its present course, social security offers only the prospect of periodic financial collapses, leaving politicians with the choice of politically unacceptable benefit cuts or politically unacceptable tax increases. No politician can survive supporting either deep slashes in the incomes of the retired mothers and fathers of America or combined payroll tax rates of 30 percent and more. This is especially true when such tax increases and/or benefit cuts will only reduce further the negligible or even negative returns offered to today's young workers.

The political future belongs to those who can transcend the benefit cut/tax increase dilemma and yet still address the serious problems of the program. The proposed reform does precisely that, by offering workers the opportunity to participate in a better deal in the private sector without benefit cuts or payroll tax increases.

Such reform could solve the serious problems of social security at the cost of no more than a temporary loss of income tax revenues.

---

[40]As noted earlier, social security today accounts for almost 30 percent of the entire federal budget. With the insurance function of social security performed through Super IRAs, most of this spending would be taken out of the federal budget altogether and shifted to the private sector.

At the same time, it could provide new savings to offset any increase in government borrowing resulting from the revenue loss. Moreover, all this would be accomplished in a totally non-threatening manner. The elderly would have their benefits constitutionally guaranteed, and the financing of social security itself would be sharply strengthened. All workers would still be completely free to participate in social security as is, if they so desired.

Structured in this way, the reform would not take anything away from anybody. It would simply increase the freedom and options of workers and thus should be enormously popular. Why shouldn't workers be able to choose a better deal in the private sector if they desire? With the elderly benefiting at the same time and social security strengthened, such a question should become politically unanswerable.

One can readily see that the reform has many features that should appeal to key political constituencies. Labor and unions would have many strong reasons to support it. Workers, particularly young workers, would have the opportunity to receive higher retirement benefits and to accumulate large amounts of wealth through their Super IRAs. The reform would alleviate and could eventually eliminate the long-term financing problems of social security that threaten the future financial security of these workers. It would likely improve the economy in which these workers must earn their living today, creating more jobs and economic growth. Eventually, it could lead to a substantial reduction of the tax burden on these workers. The reform would also provide the average worker with the opportunity to acquire a large ownership stake in America's business and industry.

Labor unions in the United States in fact originally opposed social security, instead preferring labor union pension systems over which workers would have direct control and which would help build worker interest in unions. For the same reasons, British labor unions supported social security reform enacted under a Labour government in 1978, allowing industries that set up their own alternative pension systems to opt out of half of the country's social security system. Over half of Britain's workers have today so opted out. Under the proposed Super IRA system, American workers would be able to pool and invest their IRA funds through labor union pensions, as they can with IRAs today.

Business should naturally support the reform as well. The option in the proposed package allowing workers to substitute private life insurance for social security survivors insurance offers insurance companies the possibility of more than $10 billion per year in new business. A completely expanded Super IRA option would offer hundreds of billions of dollars in new business each year to banks, mutual funds, stock brokers, insurance companies, and other financial intermediaries. For business in general, there is the potential for a massive increase in new funds for capital investment through the Super IRAs, and the economic benefits of possible eventual reductions in payroll taxes.

The elderly should be among the reform's strongest supporters. The constitutional guarantee of benefits would be a quite meaningful improvement in their economic security. The strengthened financial prospects for social security would enhance this improvement in a direct, practical way. The elderly would surely also treasure the improved prospects for their children resulting from the reform.

The premier national organization for the elderly, the 15-million member American Association of Retired Persons (AARP), in fact recognizes that social security is not offering nearly as good a deal to today's young workers as to today's elderly and that prospects for the young must be improved. AARP also recognizes that the program's benefit structure is inequitable in many respects and should ultimately be rationalized so that workers will receive in benefits the actuarial equivalent of what they and their employers paid in taxes, plus fair interest. But these two problems cannot be solved within the current structure of social security. Future benefits for today's young workers cannot be raised to a fair level because it is already quite doubtful whether the benefits now promised can be paid. Moreover, simply redesigning the current benefit structure without increasing benefits overall means that some would receive significant benefit cuts while others receive benefit increases, which is likely to be politically untenable.

These problems can be solved only by turning to the private sector and Super IRAs. Today's young workers could then receive full market returns and higher benefits paid on a fair actuarial basis, related strictly to past payments into the system. This benefit restructuring becomes politically feasible because *all* workers would receive higher benefits, though some would receive bigger increases than others due to the elimination of former biases.

Young people should naturally favor the reform, since it offers increased benefits and the elimination of long-term financing threats.

The reform should be especially appealing to the politically influential young urban professionals, or "yuppies." Because of their higher-than-average incomes, and the prevalence of single workers and two-earner couples in this group, they can expect to receive especially low returns from social security. Since single, childless and two-earner-couple workers generally receive little or no benefits from social security survivors insurance, they would also benefit from the opportunity to avoid such insurance. These professional workers should also be quick to grasp the virtues of a private alternative to social security.

This analysis indicates that the Super IRA proposal should have overwhelming political appeal based on its own merits. Nevertheless, three external factors not encompassed in the structure of the reform itself do create political difficulties today that must be overcome before the reform can be adopted.

First, the temporary loss of income tax revenue resulting from the reform would, in the short run, increase the already large federal budget deficit—a prospect likely to meet with special political resistance. However, the reform has been carefully designed to avoid a large loss of income tax revenues at any one time. In normal circumstances, although the initial loss of $10–15 billion in revenues annually could definitely be considered a cost in some sense, it would not be an insurmountable political barrier as long as the benefits were worth the cost, as they seem to be here by a wide margin. Today's special circumstances of unusually large federal deficits should not prevent the reform's adoption either. The reform and its benefits are extremely important and needed now, and the magnitude of the revenue loss is still manageable. Moreover, most importantly, the reform itself as we have noted will produce new savings through the Super IRAs which should at least offset any increase in government borrowing resulting from the revenue loss. Consequently there would be no net increase in the government borrowing drain on private savings, the true concern behind worry over increased budget deficits. Given this, it would be ironic and misguided to allow concern over budget deficits today to prevent adoption of a reform which will probably reduce federal spending substantially over the long run.

In any event, if politically necessary, the reform could start more slowly and/or be phased in more gradually. The low-cost survivors insurance option could begin first, for example, or the reform's implementation could be delayed until January 1, 1988. Eventually, the special budget deficit problem of today will be resolved one way or another and will no longer pose a significant problem for the reform.

A second political challenge is the demonstrated ability of opponents of any significant change in social security to engage successfully in scaremongering. Past experience indicates that opponents of the reform may try to campaign against it on false, indeed ridiculous, charges totally unrelated to its substance. They may contend, for example, that it will "destroy social security" or demolish the economic security of the elderly. If they are allowed to indulge in such irresponsibility and abuse, without harsh counter-criticism, they may be able to foreclose public debate and consideration of the reform entirely. They would then be able to short-circuit the democratic system and prevent voters from deciding the issue.

Such tactics cannot succeed over the long run, for eventually the reform proposal will become widely understood, and the voters will reject irresponsible opposition to it. Articulate leadership on behalf of the reform would accelerate this process. But such abuse should be stopped now. The public watchdogs in the media and elsewhere should demand sharp improvements in the level of debate over social security, so that the democratic system can function properly today. The public is entitled to a full and fair debate over the proposed Super IRA reform on its own merits.

The third problem facing the reform is an absence of leadership. Many labor leaders may be too enthralled by Big Government ideology to recognize and represent the interest of their workers in such reform. Many business leaders may be too intimidated, dispirited, or unimaginative to recognize the practicality and potential of such reform. Many political leaders may be just too cautious or inarticulate to express the clear virtue of such reform effectively. If so, these leadership inadequacies will slow the momentum of the Super IRA reform. But they will not stop it. Rather, our society, as it has done so often in the past, will call forth new leaders with the vision and spirit to meet the demands and needs of the times.

V. The Entrepreneurial Imperative
Bruce Bartlett

One of the many benefits of the "high-tech" revolution sweeping the country is a renewed appreciation for the free market. In the high-tech sector people can see clearly the benefits of competition in the battle to develop and market new computers, microchips, and software. The result has been a proliferation of new products, pathbreaking technological developments, and, best of all, fierce price cutting.

In years past, the sight of such market activity would have led to calls for government regulation to stop the "cutthroat" competition. But having just experienced a decade of high inflation consumers are more sensitive to the benefits of lower prices whenever they can get them. Appreciation for the fact that such activity can lead to lower prices is not entirely theoretical, either, for recent experience in such areas as airfare decontrol has also involved fierce competition and lower prices.

Perhaps as importantly, people seem to recognize that the break-throughs in the high-tech field are principally the result of efforts of individuals and small businesses, rather than large corporations. Indeed, the history of recent high-tech developments is almost exclusively a study of individuals who took great risks and endured great hardships to develop and market their ideas.[1] This stands to reason since the major economic advantage of size is in marketing and in achieving economies of scale, not in coming up with a radical new vision of the future.

This ability to identify economic progress with individuals rather than big companies appeals to people. In his best-selling book, *Megatrends,* John Naisbitt points out how the baby boom generation, which came of age in the 1960s, developed a very negative opinion of big companies and large institutions in general as a result of the

---

[1]For examples, see George Gilder, *The Spirit of Enterprise* (New York: Simon & Schuster, 1984).

Vietnam War. Also, the slow economic growth of the 1970s forced many baby-boomers into starting their own businesses rather than working for big corporations, as their fathers probably did.[2] Hence they have a much more favorable attitude toward the small businessman and individual entrepreneur than they may have toward business in general.

In a sense, therefore, it is the glorification of the entrepreneur that is spearheading this new appreciation for the free market. People seem to feel instinctively that entrepreneurship just can't be cultivated by government programs. Besides, some people probably wouldn't trust the political process to do it right anyway.

Confirming this view is the experience of some European countries that have attempted to leap ahead in the high-tech race by using government to aid high-tech development. The problems with this approach are manifold. By the time government planners identify a fruitful idea for funding, the idea has already been eclipsed by developments elsewhere. Also, government planners inevitably tend to target projects that promise the highest political, rather than economic, return. For their part, businessmen often find that having the government for a partner is more of a hindrance than a help. Thus a recent article dealing with the European perspective on U.S. high-tech competition made this observation:

> In a period of pervasive unemployment, the natural temptation for governments across the Atlantic is to step in either individually or collectively with positive interventionist policies designed to enhance the environment for their own high-tech companies at the expense of the Americans. Today a primary brake against such actions is the widely accepted belief in Europe that the American high-tech industry has flourished in an essentially laissez-faire environment with minimal direct promotional involvement by the U.S. government. Tampering with this premise should not be undertaken lightly.
>
> From their own experience, most Europeans believe that state interference in the high-tech marketplace generally results in second-rate product performance which then impacts the international viability of their manufacturing and service industries as a whole.[3]

[2]John Naisbitt, *Megatrends* (New York: Warner Books, 1982), pp. 148–49.

[3]Harold E. Fitzgibbons, "A European Perspective on U.S. High Technology Competition," in *High Technology: Public Policies for the 1980s* (Washington: Government Research Corporation, 1983), p. 96. For details on European industrial policies toward high-tech, see *Innovation Policy: Trends and Perspectives* (Paris: OECD, 1982).

Consequently, even the socialist government of France reluctantly concluded that if France hoped to stay in the high-tech race it would have little choice but to abandon efforts to stimulate technological development directly through government programs. In hopes of stimulating entrepreneurial activity, President Mitterrand has even gone so far as to roll back some of the surtaxes imposed on the rich.[4]

The problem is, however, that socialists really don't understand what entrepreneurship is all about. While they may make halfhearted efforts to stimulate entrepreneurship, they remain wedded to the collective and to a governmental approach to all problems. Thus, although they may take some steps toward stimulating entrepreneurship, they will never surround the entrepreneur with the total environment necessary to achieve real entrepreneurial success.[5]

The critical thing to understand about entrepreneurs is that they change things. "The function of entrepreneurs," Joseph Schumpeter wrote in *Capitalism, Socialism and Democracy,*

> is to reform or revolutionize the pattern of production by exploiting an invention or, more generally, an untried technological possibility for producing a new commodity or producing an old one in a new way, by opening up a new source of supply of materials or a new outlet for products, by reorganizing an industry and so on.

Schumpeter then went on to point out how hard it is to be an entrepreneur:

> To undertake such new things is difficult and constitutes a distinct economic function, first because they lie outside of the routine tasks which everybody understands and, secondly, because the environment resists in many ways that vary, according to social conditions, from simple refusal either to finance or to buy a new thing, to physical attack on the man who tries to produce it. To act with confidence beyond the range of familiar beacons and to overcome that resistance requires aptitudes that are present in only a small fraction of the population and that define the

[4]Paul Lewis, "French Budget Curbs Outlays and Cuts Taxes," *The New York Times,* September 13, 1984; David Bell, "Supply-Side Socialism," *New Republic,* October 8, 1984, pp. 12–13.

[5]Peter Drucker, "Europe's High-Tech Delusion," *The Wall Street Journal,* September 14, 1984.

entrepreneurial function. This function does not essentially consist in either inventing anything or otherwise creating the conditions which the enterprise exploits. It consists in getting things done.[6]

For fifty years the critical role of the entrepreneur in the economic system was largely ignored.[7] Economists and policymakers tended instead to concentrate on such things as the maintenance of aggregate consumer demand via budget deficits. If demand were maintained at the proper level, the economic models all assumed, then the production of goods, the invention of new machines, the development of new products, and the establishment of new businesses would take care of themselves.[8]

Then in the 1970s economists and policymakers discovered two related problems: U.S. competitiveness in world markets was deteriorating and U.S. productivity growth was at a virtual standstill.[9] These problems finally drew attention to the long-neglected "supply side" of the economy.

While some useful things have been done in the name of "supply-side economics," such as the reduction in marginal tax rates and some modest decontrol of government regulations, concerns about productivity and competitiveness have also spawned new efforts to impose a form of centralized government planning on the economy in the name of a "national industrial policy." Fortunately, such efforts have not achieved significant support.

One reason why industrial policy has failed to ignite the imagination of the public is this: The high-tech revolution of Silicon Valley and a general disillusionment with big institutions, as in the "small is beautiful" movement, have generated new understanding and appreciation for the entrepreneur. As a famous 1960s radical, Jerry

[6]Joseph Schumpeter, *Capitalism, Socialism and Democracy*, 3d ed. (New York: Harper & Row, 1950), p. 132.

[7]This point is emphasized in Jonathan Hughes, "Entrepreneurial Activity and American Economic Progress," *Journal of Libertarian Studies* 3 (Winter 1979): 361–62.

[8]Interestingly, the father of demand management, John Maynard Keynes, was very sympathetic to the importance of preserving entrepreneurial freedom. See George Gilder, *Wealth and Poverty* (New York: Basic Books, 1981), pp. 40–44.

[9]See, for example, Edward F. Denison, *Accounting for Slower Economic Growth: The United States in the 1970s* (Washington: Brookings Institution, 1979); *Report of the President on U.S. Competitiveness* (Washington: U.S. Government Printing Office, 1980).

Rubin, recently put it: "The challenge for American capitalism in the 1980s is to bring the entrepreneurial spirit back to America. The large organizations have discouraged people's expression and ambition. America needs a revitalization of the small business spirit."[10]

When policymakers attempted to tap into this entrepreneurial spirit with the same old government programs, however, they ran into a brick wall, even among the young. The so-called Atari Democrats, like Senator Gary Hart, for example, tried desperately to attract support from high-tech entrepreneurs. But they tried to do so with government programs for picking "winners."[11] The reaction of those who were supposed to be the beneficiaries of this governmental largess was totally hostile: "I guarantee you that no government agency can target the right industry; in fact, I'll almost guarantee they'll target the wrong one," said Nolan Bushnell, founder of Atari. "The targeting role belongs to the entrepreneurs. The problem is that these Atari Democrats would never have targeted Atari."[12]

Deprived of their traditional prescription for all society's ills— more government—the Atari Democrats were left with nothing to offer the Silicon Valley crowd they so desperately wanted to attract. This is one important reason why Senator Hart's presidential bid collapsed. Though billed as the candidate of new ideas, people quickly discovered he really didn't have any.

This raises the fundamental question: If we want to encourage entrepreneurship, innovation, inventiveness, and risk-taking, how do we go about it?

Enormous research has been done on this question, correlating market structure, expenditures on research and development, and just about any other quantifiable factor.[13] About the only conclusion that can be drawn from this research with regard to the role of

[10]Quoted in Naisbitt, p. 149.

[11]Randall Rothenberg, *The Neoliberals* (New York: Simon & Schuster, 1984), pp. 147–59.

[12]Quoted in Joel Kotkin and Don Gevirtz, "Why Entrepreneurs Trust No Politician," *The Washington Post,* January 16, 1983, p. B2.

[13]Some of this literature is reviewed in F. M. Scherer, *Innovation and Growth* (Cambridge, Mass.: M.I.T. Press, 1984); Edwin Mansfield, "Industrial Organization and Technological Change: Recent Econometric Findings," in John V. Craven, ed., *Industrial Organization, Antitrust, and Public Policy* (Boston: Kluwer-Nijhoff, 1983), pp. 129–43; Morton Kamien and Nancy Schwartz, "Market Structure and Innovation: A Survey," *Journal of Economic Literature* 13 (May 1975): 1–37.

government is that it should absolutely avoid efforts to pick winners. Government can help by preserving private property and the sanctity of contract, and through education; but when it attempts to pick winners, it fails totally.[14]

Thus the best thing that can be done to stimulate entrepreneurship is to allow as much economic freedom as possible. This is because innovation, entrepreneurship and inventiveness are creative endeavors, like art and music, and cannot be programmed. One never knows where the inspiration for creativity is going to come from; hence, one must be extremely careful not to foreclose unanticipated opportunities. As F. A. Hayek put it, "Liberty is essential in order to leave room for the unforeseeable and unpredictable."[15]

A student of Hayek, Professor Israel Kirzner, elaborates on this point: "Restrictions on economic freedom," he says,

> hurt society . . . in ways far more serious than recognized by most economists. . . . The restriction of economic freedom may inhibit individuals from discovering opportunities they might have noticed had they been free to exploit them. Loss of freedom may thus lower individual and social achievement without anyone's realizing what has been lost or not achieved. A free society is fertile and creative in the sense that its freedom generates alertness to possibilities that may be of use to society; a restriction on the freedom of a society numbs such alertness and blinds society to possibilities of social improvement. By the very nature of the damage such restriction wreaks, its harmful effects on social welfare may not be able to be noticed, measured, or specified.[16]

History abounds with examples of machines, processes, and products that might never have come into existence if the views of the experts and those in authority had prevailed. Only the perseverance of a few hardy individuals and the economic freedom they

---

[14]See Richard Nelson and Richard Langlois, "Industrial Innovation Policy: Lessons from American History," *Science* 219 (February 18, 1983): 814–18; Richard Nelson, ed., *Government and Technical Progress* (New York: Pergamon Press, 1982).

[15]F. A. Hayek, *The Constitution of Liberty* (Chicago: University of Chicago Press, 1960), p. 60. See also F. A. Hayek, "The Use of Knowledge in Society," *American Economic Review* 35 (September 1945): 519–30.

[16]Israel M. Kirzner, *Perception, Opportunity, and Profit* (Chicago: University of Chicago Press, 1979), p. 239.

had for pursuing their "follies" gave us many of the products we use and depend on every day. Here are a few examples:[17]

> Well-informed people know it impossible to transmit the voice over wires and that were it possible to do so, the thing would be of no practical value. (Editorial in the *Boston Post*, 1865)

> The phonograph . . . is not of any commercial value. (Thomas A. Edison, inventor of the phonograph, 1880)

> When the Paris Exhibition closes electric light will close with it and no more will be heard of it. (Erasmus Wilson, professor at Oxford University, 1878)

> Radio has no future. (Lord Kelvin, 1897)

> While theoretically and technically television may be feasible, commercially and financially I consider it an impossibility, a development of which we need waste little time dreaming. (Lee DeForest, American radio pioneer and inventor of the audion tube, 1926)

> I think there is a world market for about five computers. (Thomas J. Watson, chairman of IBM, 1943)

> There is no reason for any individual to have a computer in the home. (Ken Olsen, president of Digital Equipment, 1977)

In short, the cost to society of allowing a few experts to place restrictions on freedom is measured in products not produced, inventions not invented, innovations not pursued, savings not achieved, and advances not made which would have been made had someone had the incentive and the means to do so. This is one of the main reasons why America depends on its small businesses so much. After all, if freedom—not merely from government, but from institutional constraints as well—is what is critical to the encouragement of entrepreneurship, then the ability to start and run one's own business is a necessary, if not sufficient, prerequisite.

The importance of small business to the national economy cannot be overestimated. There is, first, the widely cited fact that most jobs are created by small businesses. According to David Birch of M.I.T., two-thirds of the jobs created in the United States between 1969 and 1976 were in firms employing fewer than 20 workers. Eighty

---

[17]Christopher Cerf and Victor Navasky, *The Experts Speak* (New York: Pantheon, 1984), pp. 203–9.

percent of jobs were created in businesses with fewer than 100 employees.[18]

More importantly, small businesses are the major source of new inventions and innovations in our economy. Research shows that this is especially true in the case of radical innovations. Moreover, small businesses are able to market new inventions much faster than big businesses.[19] And the trend is continuing. According to the Small Business Administration, small firms now dominate those sectors of the economy that show the fastest growth.[20]

Clearly, therefore, if we want more innovation and entrepreneurship, we are going to have to remove barriers to them. From the point of view of the entrepreneur, the most important governmental barrier to success is a tax policy designed to discourage the growth of large incomes and the accumulation of personal wealth, which at the same time tends to encourage the growth and profitability of large, established firms.

The most important thing we need to understand about how tax policy affects small businesses and entrepreneurs is the fact that it is the individual income tax, not the corporate tax, that is the chief concern. When one thinks about business taxes, one tends to think mainly about the corporate tax. But the reality is that the vast majority of businesses in the United States are either sole proprietorships or partnerships, not corporations. In 1980, according to IRS data, there were 12.7 million proprietorships and 1.4 million partnerships that filed United States tax returns. By contrast, there were just 2.7 million corporations. This means that the individual income tax law is of greater significance for most businesses than the corporate income tax law.

The importance of this fact is that the personal income tax is steeply progressive, with the highest income tax rate exceeding the highest corporate tax rate. Although the gap is not as wide as it once was, it is still significant. Also, there are many features of the corporate tax that are far more generous than those available to

[18]David L. Birch, "Who Creates Jobs?" *The Public Interest* (Fall 1981): 3–14.

[19]These studies are summarized in *The State of Small Business: A Report of the President, March 1983* (Washington: U.S. Government Printing Office, 1983), pp. 121–34; *Innovation in Small and Medium Firms* (Paris: OECD, 1982); *Small Businesses Are More Active As Inventors Than As Innovators In The Innovation Process* (Washington: U.S. General Accounting Office, PAD-82-19, 31 December 1981).

[20]*The State of Small Business: A Report of the President, March 1984* (Washington: U.S. Government Printing Office, 1984), pp. 11–12, 22–32.

individuals, such as being allowed to carry back losses. The result is that the individual income tax is more punitive to entrepreneurs when they do "strike it rich."

Today's high tax rates on both individuals and corporations make it exceedingly difficult for small businesses to internally generate the capital they need in order to grow. It is no coincidence that most of the largest corporations in America got their start in a much earlier era, when taxes were not so high. They were able to grow, as the Ford Motor Company grew, by plowing profits back into the firm year after year.

When small firms cannot grow into large ones, one effect is to allow large firms to become complacent as the threat of competition diminishes. Thus the economy suffers in ways that are very hard to see, in lower quality, higher prices, and lower efficiency than would otherwise be the case. This point is made vividly by Ludwig von Mises in *Human Action:*

> Every ingenious man is free to start new business projects. He may be poor, his funds may be modest and most of them may be borrowed. But if he fills the wants of consumers in the best and cheapest way, he will succeed by means of "excessive" profits. He ploughs back the greater part of his profits into his business, thus making it grow rapidly. It is the activity of such enterprising parvenus that provides the market with its "dynamism." These nouveaux riches are the harbingers of economic improvement. Their threatening competition forces the old firms and big corporations either to adjust their conduct to the best possible service to the public or go out of business.
>
> But today taxes often absorb the greater part of the newcomer's "excessive" profits. He cannot accumulate capital; he cannot expand his own business; he will never become big business and a match for the vested interests. The old firms do not need to fear his competition; they are sheltered by the tax collector. They may with impunity indulge in routine, they may defy the wishes of the public and become conservative. . . . In this sense progressive taxation checks economic progress and makes for rigidity.[21]

Congress has not been oblivious to the tax burden on business. Over the years many special features of the tax code have been enacted specifically to aid business. Unfortunately, because it has

---

[21]Ludwig von Mises, *Human Action,* 3d ed. (Chicago: Henry Regnery, 1966), pp. 808–9.

83

not recognized the critical role of individual entrepreneurship in our economic system, Congress has tended to concentrate its tax benefits on large corporations rather than on small businesses or individual entrepreneurs. Most of the important business tax incentives in the tax code are designed to aid capital formation. The investment tax credit and accelerated depreciation are the two most important in this respect. But they really don't help small firms very much. In fact, the accelerated depreciation reforms enacted in the Economic Recovery Tax Act of 1981 actually increased the tax burden on small high-tech firms, whose capital depreciates so rapidly that anything more than immediate write-off is extremely burdensome.[22]

Moreover, large firms can more easily afford the expensive lawyers necessary to figure out other incentives in the tax code, such as DISC and the foreign tax credit, which are too complex for small firms to master and of virtually no use to individuals. Thus, although such items as the investment tax credit and the foreign tax credit are theoretically available to all businesses, in practice the major portion of their benefits go to just one-tenth of one percent of all corporations.

Generally speaking, small, entrepreneurial businesses tend to be labor intensive while large ones tend to be capital intensive. Thus measures designed to aid capital formation are inherently more valuable to large firms than to small ones. This is especially true if one considers that a business just starting out will probably not have any profits for several years and will therefore pay no taxes. If a firm is not paying any taxes, all tax incentives are essentially valueless.

At the same time, one can argue that the major effect of the investment tax credit is not to stimulate capital investment, but rather to lower the tax liability of large firms. This is because the investment tax credit is inframarginal and does not distinguish between investments that are made only because of the credit and those that would be made anyway. This is not an argument for raising taxes on big corporations. But the rationale for the investment tax credit was precisely to stimulate new investment. Since the credit cannot be used, generally speaking, by new firms or firms

[22]Charles R. Hulten and James W. Robertson, *Differential Effects of the Accelerated Cost Recovery System on Investment* (Washington: National Science Foundation, October 1983).

losing money and goes instead to firms that would have made the same investments without the tax credit, at the very least one can say it is a very inefficient method of stimulating investment, with very uneven impact on different firms.[23]

Another failure of policymakers to understand how the tax law implicitly hurts small, newly established firms is in the area of social security taxes. Since a small firm is more labor-intensive than a large firm, this tax affects the small firm's costs to a much greater extent than those of a large firm.

However, the single most important tax affecting small businesses and entrepreneurs is the capital gains tax. The impact of this tax on small firms is well-known. Small firms just starting up are not going to have profits or dividends to pay to investors for a long time. But if they are successful and have good prospects, the value of their assets may rise sharply. Thus, in terms of inducing investments in venture capital the capital gains tax is by far the most important one. It is, in short, a direct tax on risk capital—the kind entrepreneurs absolutely depend on.

The story of how the 1978 capital gains tax cut stimulated venture capital investment and entrepreneurial activity is a classic success story of supply-side economics in action. The tax had been doubled in 1969, and virtually every year thereafter less and less money went into venture capital investments. As a result, government revenue from the capital gains tax fell to virtually nothing. Then in 1978 Congress reversed itself and cut the tax rate back to its pre-1969 level.[24]

The results were astounding. In 1977 there were just two initial offerings of stock in the United States. After the capital gains tax cut, however, they skyrocketed, reaching 304 in 1983. The number of stocks listed on the over-the-counter market jumped 60 percent in two years, and the total amount of venture capital raised went from $300 million in the mid-1970s to about $13 billion in 1983. New business incorporations soared from 280,000 in 1978 to over 600,000 in 1983. There is little doubt that much of the credit for all this

---

[23]See Alan J. Aurback and Lawrence Summers, *The Investment Tax Credit: An Evaluation* (Cambridge, Mass.: National Bureau of Economic Research, Working Paper No. 404, November 1979).

[24]See Bruce Bartlett, *Reaganomics: Supply-Side Economics in Action* (New York: William Morrow, 1982), pp. 150–58.

activity goes to the 1978 capital gains tax cut.[25] Indeed, the tax cut was so stimulative that it actually paid for itself by increasing capital gains tax revenues.[26]

Another tax that has a heavy impact on small businesses and entrepreneurs is the estate and gift tax, which is a direct tax on capital. It is also more of a tax on labor and entrepreneurial activity than people imagine. Professor Richard Posner of the University of Chicago made this point well when he said, "Since the accumulation of a substantial estate is one of the motivations that drive people to work hard, a death tax is indirectly a tax on work."[27]

It takes a long time to build a small business into a large, profitable one. Many entrepreneurs know full well that most of the benefits of their efforts may not be realized until after their death. But they continue to work hard nevertheless because they want their families to be better off. If they thought, however, that the government was going to be the major beneficiary of their efforts—even were that to happen after their death—it could have a major impact on their willingness to work and sacrifice during their working lives.[28] With entrepreneurs being such a valuable resource, this is something that should concern us.

Finally, one might note that the tax treatment of interest under U.S. tax law has a tendency to aid large firms at the expense of small ones. This is because interest paid is, by and large, fully deductible, while interest earned is fully taxed. The effect—to encourage borrowing and discourage saving—is important for entrepreneurs and small businesses for two reasons. First, most small businesses do not have the same access to borrowed funds that large firms have. They must raise their capital through equity or private saving, which has no tax advantage relative to

[25]Gilder, The Spirit of Enterprise, pp. 44–47.

[26]Gerald Auten, "Capital Gains: An Evaluation of the 1978 and 1981 Tax Cuts," in Charls E. Walker and Mark Bloomfield, eds., New Directions in Federal Tax Policy for the 1980s (Cambridge, Mass.: Ballinger, 1983), pp. 121–48.

[27]Richard A. Posner, Economic Analysis of Law (Boston: Little, Brown & Co., 1972), p. 244.

[28]See Tom Persky, Mike Schuyler, and David Raboy, An Introduction To the Economics of Estate and Gift Taxes (Washington Institute for Research on the Economics of Taxation, June 1981).

borrowing.[29] Second, the burden of taxation on private savings makes it very difficult for an entrepreneur to accumulate capital through his own means. The effect this has on entrepreneurial activity was eloquently stated by British economist Lord Robbins:

> The fact that it has become so difficult to accumulate even a comparatively small fortune must have the most profound effects on the organization of business. . . . Must not the inevitable consequences of all this be that it will become more and more difficult for innovation to develop save within the ambit of established corporate enterprise, and that more and more of what accumulation takes place will take place within the large concerns which— largely as a result of individual enterprise in the past—managed to get started before the ice age descended?[30]

This is why a House Small Business Committee report concluded that "the practical effect of Federal tax policy has been the tendency to encourage the growth of large firms at the expense of the small."[31]

This is not to say, however, that there is something bad or unproductive about big companies. Indeed, the very invention of the large corporation is one of the most important innovations in history.[32] But in order to stimulate innovation and create dynamism it is generally necessary for one person in a firm to have complete authority over that firm. Firms run by professional managers simply do not have the authority, the vision, the incentive, or a sufficiently long time horizon, in many cases, to make the investments or take the risks necessary to achieve success. They must always be concerned about how the current quarter's earnings report will look to the board of directors. But someone who owns a firm outright, or at least has majority ownership, can afford to take greater risks and

---

[29]Moreover, to the extent that small businesses can borrow funds, they generally must do so at floating bank rates rather than through fixed-rate commercial paper, which large firms use. This means small businesses are more vulnerable to Federal Reserve "credit crunches" than large firms. See *Small Business Report, March 1984,* pp. 181–212.

[30]Lionel Robbins, "Notes on Public Finance," *Lloyd's Bank Review* (October 1955): 10.

[31]Quoted in Kenneth Chilton and David P. Hatfield, *Big Government and Small Business: The Changing Relationship* (St. Louis: Washington University, Center for the Study of American Business, 1981), p. 7.

[32]Alfred D. Chandler, Jr., "The Beginnings of Big Business in American History," *Business History Review* (Spring 1959): 1–31.

make investments that may not pay off for a long time because he has no one to answer to but himself. This point is confirmed by a study of high-growth companies by McKinsey and Company.[33]

One reason why large firms stratify and lose their dynamism is precisely because growth eventually requires a company to issue more and more stock to raise capital, thus diluting the influence of the founder, whose entrepreneurial genius got the company off the ground. "There is a point," Alfred P. Sloan, founder of General Motors, once said, "beyond which diffusion of stock ownership must enfeeble the corporation by depriving it of virile interest in management upon the part of some one man or group of men to whom its success is a matter of personal and vital interest."[34]

This brings us to the question of specific policies that could help encourage entrepreneurship and give people the incentive to innovate. One might start by looking at the tax reforms suggested by Joseph Schumpeter:[35]

1. Eliminate the double taxation of corporate profits—first at the corporate level and again when those profits are paid out as dividends. Almost every public finance theorist who has ever studied the subject has recommended abolition of the corporate income tax in order to eliminate this double tax. Yet many people continue to believe that the corporate tax should actually be raised.[36]

2. Eliminate the double tax on savings by allowing individuals to deduct from their taxable income the portion of their income

[33]Arthur Levitt, Jr. and Jack Albertine, "The Successful Entrepreneur: A Personality Profile," *The Wall Street Journal*, August 29, 1983. See also "Today's Innovators Are the Same—Only Different," *The Economist*, December 24, 1983, pp. 61–73.

[34]Quoted in Herman E. Drooss and Charles Gilbert, *American Business History* (Englewood Cliffs, N.J.: Prentice-Hall, 1982), p. 264.

[35]Schumpeter, *Capitalism, Socialism and Democracy*, pp. 389–90.

[36]A thorough discussion of the problem of double taxation of corporate profits, including objections to eliminating it, can be found in Charles McLure, Jr., *Must Corporate Income Be Taxed Twice?* (Washington: Brookings Institution, 1979). A recent argument for increasing corporate taxes can be found in Robert S. McIntyre, "The Corporate Tax: It's All But Disappeared," *The Washington Post*, November 16, 1983. For a rebuttal, see Bruce Bartlett, "But Business Pays More Than Its Share," *The New York Times*, January 29, 1984, p. 2F.

that is saved. At present, the tax law makes it twice as costly to save as to consume.[37]

3. Allow full deduction of capital losses. Presently, tax law allows individuals to deduct only $3,000 of capital losses per year. Losses above $3,000 may be carried forward into future tax years, but not backward into previous tax years. The effect of this provision is to seriously retard risk-taking.[38]

4. Develop a tax system that taxes consumption rather than income. The idea—again, to eliminate the tax on savings—is presently very popular among some economists and Washington policymakers.[39] However, they tend to talk about consumption taxes as being *in addition* to existing taxes, rather than a replacement for them.[40]

5. Drastically revise the estate and gift tax. Schumpeter thought Keynes's rationale for the tax—that it encourages consumption—was particularly wrongheaded.

There are, of course, any number of other tax reforms that could be enacted to encourage entrepreneurship, innovation, and risk-taking.[41]

In addition, there are obviously any number of non-tax reforms that could be made to improve the small business-entrepreneurship environment. For example, much more needs to be done in the area of deregulation.[42] As the Small Business Administration notes

[37]Irving Fisher, "Paradoxes in Taxing Savings," *Econometrica* 10 (April 1942): 147–58. See also Lawrence Summers, "The After-Tax Rate of Return Affects Private Savings," *American Economic Review* 74 (May 1984): 249–53.

[38]See Evsey Domar and Richard Musgrave, "Proportional Income Taxation and Risk-Taking," *Quarterly Journal of Economics* 58 (May 1944): 388–422.

[39]See, for example, "Why Washington Likes Consumption Taxes," *Business Week*, June 13, 1983, p. 80.

[40]Bruce Bartlett, "Revenue-Raising Redux: It's VAT Time Again," *The Wall Street Journal*, August 2, 1984, p. 24.

[41]See Michael J. Boskin, "Taxation, Innovation and Economic Growth," *Technology In Society* 3 (1981): 35–44; Joseph J. Cordes, "Tax Policies for Encouraging Innovation: A Survey," ibid., pp. 87–98; Eileen L. Collins, ed., *Tax Policy and Investment in Innovation* (Washington: National Science Foundation, 1982); Calvin A. Kent, ed., *The Environment for Entrepreneurship* (Lexington, Mass.: Lexington Books, 1984).

[42]See Israel M. Kirzner, "Competition, Regulation, and Market Process: An 'Austrian' Perspective" (Washington: Cato Institute, 1982); idem, *The Perils of Regulation: A Market Process Approach* (Coral Gables, Fl.: University of Miami Law School, Law and Economics Center, 1978).

in its latest report, the fastest growth in business starts during 1982 and 1983 was in deregulated industries.[43] Patent protection needs to be strengthened.[44] And there is also a critical need to stabilize macroeconomic policy in general, so that businessmen and entrepreneurs can have a more predictable economic environment in which to operate. Further efforts need to be made in reducing the overall burden of government in terms of both taxing and spending; trade barriers must be reduced; and efforts to help business through planning or industrial policies must be strongly resisted.

In short, entrepreneurship requires economic freedom. To the extent that high technology, industrial innovation, and more efficient markets are necessary to our nation's future, therefore, we are going to have to have more freedom, not less. Otherwise, our budding high-tech revolution will wither on the vine, for the record shows that an economy without entrepreneurship is like a plant without water—it simply can't grow.

[43]*Small Business Report*, March 1984, pp. 35–36.

[44]Milton Copulos, "Improving Patents to Spur Innovation" (Washington: The Heritage Foundation, 1983).

VI. Freeing Trade

Murray L. Weidenbaum

It is sad to report that our open international trading system is under assault at home and abroad. Here at home, every type of special interest is attempting to stem the tide of imports, especially those from developing nations. And overseas, international governmental organizations are seeking to thwart the efforts of private enterprise to participate in the development of poorer countries, meeting such efforts with a barrage of attacks followed by a burst of regulation aimed at the so-called neo-colonialist, greedy, profit-seeking multinational corporations.

Although one rarely thinks to group together the protectionists at home and the new breed of regulators abroad, these critics of open trade do share one common characteristic: their efforts will only exacerbate the current international debt problem and will eventually sour basic foreign policy relations among nations both poor and prosperous. A counterattack—aimed at freeing international trade—is long overdue.

The Importance of Free International Trade

The case for free trade is rooted in a basic economic law: the principle of comparative advantage. According to this principle, total economic welfare will be enhanced if each nation specializes in the production of items that it can make, in relative terms, most efficiently. This, of course, is an important case of Adam Smith's more general point concerning the advantages of the specialization of labor:

> It is the maxim of every prudent . . . family, never to make at home what it will cost . . . more to make than to buy. The taylor

Note: This paper draws on materials in Murray L. Weidenbaum, "The High Cost of Protectionism," *Cato Journal* 3, no.3 (Winter 1983/84): 777–91; and Murray L. Weidenbaum, et al. *Toward a More Open Trade Policy* (St. Louis: Washington University, Center for the Study of American Business, 1983). The author is indebted to Paul Tramontozzi for his substantial help in preparing this paper.

does not attempt to make his own shoes, but buys them of the shoemaker . . . What is prudence in the conduct of every private family, can scarcely be folly in that of a great kingdom.[1]

Smith's commonsense approach aside, arguments in favor of free trade are well supported by a good deal of historical evidence. Through most of the twentieth century the United States has played a strong leadership role in developing the system of world trade. We have already witnessed the severe effects on the world economy that the absence of such leadership produced in the 1930s. The "beggar-thy-neighbor" trade policies followed by the United States and many other countries at that time contributed substantially to worldwide depression.

Subsequent to the Second World War, our trade policy shifted to the negotiation of reciprocal trade agreements. Initially arranged bilaterally, they evolved into an effective multilateral trading system which broke down many of the historical barriers to world trade. An especially clear example occurred in the 1960s, when the acceleration of world trade and economic growth followed a sharp and mutual tariff reduction which contributed to lower prices for consumers. We continue to reap benefits from the policies initiated in those years.

The United States had similar positive experiences with open trade in the nineteenth century. This country began as a trading nation. If the concept of "Gross National Product" had existed in the eighteenth and nineteenth centuries, people would have pointed out the United States as one of the more open economies in the world as measured by the share of GNP involved in foreign trade.

Around the turn of the century the dynamics of the American economy shifted. Exports and imports became smaller shares of GNP, remaining relatively stable. U.S. investment abroad increased, gradually transforming the nation from an international debtor into a world creditor, and the American economy became increasingly self-sufficient. Only in the last 20 years has the international sector begun to grow in relative importance again.

Foreign business is now a crucial element in U.S. production and employment. Combined exports and imports of goods and services now represent almost 25 percent of our GNP, while 20 years

---

[1]Adam Smith, *An Inquiry into the Nature and Causes of the Wealth of Nations* (1776; reprint ed., New York: Random House, 1977), p. 424.

ago they were less than 12 percent of GNP. Much of this shift has occurred in the past decade.

In passing we should note that there is a close, though not generally appreciated, connection between imports and exports. A strong trade position requires a high volume both of imports and of exports. In fact, the only way to increase a country's exports in the long run is to increase its imports. U.S. exporters need to find foreign buyers who have the dollars necessary to buy their goods and services. In general, these dollars are obtained when Americans import and pay for foreign goods and services in turn.

Imports, therefore, put dollars into the hands of foreigners—dollars which can then be used to buy our exports. It follows that restrictions on imports will result in fewer dollars available to those in other countries who want to buy our wheat, aircraft, chemicals, or machinery—unless, of course, we make up the difference through loans or transfer payments.

In the short run, it is true that we can and do lend foreigners the dollars with which to buy our exports. When such loans are made at market rates of interest, trade is properly advanced. However, when government-subsidized credit is provided, such funds are denied other and often more productive uses in the domestic economy.

In some cases the connection between imports and exports is even more direct. Import restraints can reduce employment and profits in our more productive export industries. For example, in the non-rubber footwear industry U.S. exports of hides to foreign shoe producers suffered greatly as a result of restraints on the importation of foreign shoes.

To generalize from historical experience, the benefits of free trade are numerous:

1. Open trade contributes to lower prices by increasing the supply of goods and services competing for the consumer's dollar. Thus, the question of free trade is basically a consumer issue, and an extremely important one.
2. Open trade minimizes the role of government in influencing private-sector decisions. This allows individuals and firms to respond to the needs and pressures of the marketplace. Viewed in this light, free trade is crucial to promoting and maintaining economic freedom and the private enterprise system.
3. Open trade improves the efficiency with which our own

resources are allocated. Thus, we can see that free trade yields more growth, higher levels of employment, and an improved living standard here at home.

Aside from these direct and measurable benefits, free trade stimulates competition, stirs up creative activity, rewards individual initiative, and increases national productivity. Among nations, it speeds the exchange of new ideas and advanced technology. In the long run, open international trade means the creation of new jobs and the reduction of inflation. In sum, free trade contributes to a healthier economy—one with more job opportunities and a wider variety of goods and services for consumers.

Thus far we have focused on the obvious economic benefits of free international trade. The political benefits, however, are less clear, particularly to politicians. But it should go without saying that a healthy world economy offers real political stability. Such stability is not just a mere preservation of the status quo; rather economic well-being offers real opportunities for meaningful improvements in any political system.

Unfortunately politicians, unlike economists, are inclined more often than not to offer short-term solutions to problems that require long-term answers. Protectionism—a political response to rising unemployment and the decline in some industries—is just such a solution.

The Nature and Costs of American Trade Barriers

As with most issues of public policy, it is important to identify the costs of protectionism as well as the benefits. The short-sighted response or reaction of government officials is to ignore the long-term costs of protectionism—higher prices and lower living standards—and instead to focus on the immediate benefits. These benefits are viewed in terms both of the workers who keep their jobs as a result of trade restrictions (assuming that imports are their only threat) and of the political support that such workers can generate.

Many of the "benefits" of protectionist measures turn out to be very temporary, even to the group advocating them. For example, quotas on shoe imports led to an upgrading of the quality of such imports. As a result, American producers found themselves threatened in that part of the market which, prior to the protectionist action, they had firmly dominated.

The same process is taking place in the current case of "voluntary" restraints on Japanese auto imports. Auto import restrictions have essentially reduced competition among the Japanese producers themselves, guaranteeing domination of the American import market by the three largest producers—Toyota, Honda, and Nissan. Thus, restraints intended to improve the competitive standing of U.S. automakers have had the perverse effect of helping their most serious competitors, mainly by improving the profit margin on each Japanese car sold in the United States.

The process by which this has happened follows simple economic logic. Because of import barriers, the heavy U.S. demand for Japanese automobiles greatly exceeds the supply. But this has not led consumers to "buy American"; instead, many customers are waiting up to six months to buy a Japanese car at a premium price. Also, because the Japanese companies can send only a restricted number of cars, they have maximized profits by including a great deal of optional equipment and by upgrading their sales mix with higher-priced models.

In spite of its great drawbacks, however, protectionism has a great charm to it. In a society of 200 million individuals its beneficiaries are relatively few—perhaps ten thousand or a hundred thousand, depending on the specific industry involved. There can be very substantial benefits for each of the ten or hundred thousand. The costs, however, are usually far greater—typically, a hundred thousand dollars to maintain a job paying only a small fraction of that amount. But these costs are divided among 200 million consumers who never realize that in the aggregate they are bearing such an enormous financial burden. In public finance there is an old saying, "the best tax is a hidden tax." This is a statement based not on economics or equity, but on politics.

If consumers do not even know they are paying a tax, they are certainly not about to complain about it. Think of protectionism as that hidden tax.[2] A study at the Center for the Study of American Business at Washington University attempted to estimate that hidden tax for 1980. It came to more than $58 billion, or $255 for each American consumer.[3] Table 1 shows some vivid examples of the

[2]For an analysis of this phenomenon, see Morris E. Morkre and David G. Tarr, *Effects of Restrictions on United States Imports,* Staff Report of the Bureau of Economics to the Federal Trade Commission (Washington, D.C.: U.S. Government Printing Office, 1980).

[3]Murray L. Weidenbaum and Michael C. Munger, "Protection at Any Price?" *Regulation* (July/August 1983): 14–18.

Table 1

ESTIMATES OF THE COST OF PROTECTION TO U.S. CONSUMERS

Item Subject to Protection	Cost to Consumer
Automobiles (for each unit imported from Japan)	$1,900
Dairy Products (yearly)	$1.5–$4.9 billion
Meat (yearly)	$1.2 billion
Motorcycles (for each unit imported)	$400–$600
Peanuts (yearly)	$200 million
Radios and TVs (yearly until 1982)	$221 million
Shoes (1970–81 for each job protected)	$114,000
Steel (TPM, Quotas, and OMAs)	$7.2 billion
Sugar (yearly)	$3 billion
Textiles and Apparel (for 1980)	$18.4 billion

SOURCE: *How Much Do Consumers Pay for U.S. Trade Barriers?* (Washington, D.C.: Consumers for World Trade, 1984).

burdens on the American people that result from efforts to shield specific sectors of domestic production from foreign competition.

In addition, Figure 1 demonstrates the close relationship between import restrictions and domestic price increases. Prices of shoes imported from Taiwan and South Korea rose dramatically just as soon as import quotas went into effect in 1977. By contrast, the prices of these products to domestic consumers dropped sharply when these trade restrictions were eliminated in 1981.[4]

Many protectionist measures also act as a regressive tax whereby low-income consumers are more adversely affected than high-income consumers. If an item is a necessity, such as clothing or footwear, quotas are highly regressive for two reasons. First, the quotas raise the price of each imported shirt or sweater, resulting in larger percentage increases for the low-priced apparel generally purchased by low-income consumers. Second, the quotas induce a rise in the relative supply of higher-quality and higher-priced clothing,

[4]See Murray L. Weidenbaum, *Business, Government, and the Public* (Englewood Cliffs, N.J.: Prentice Hall, in press).

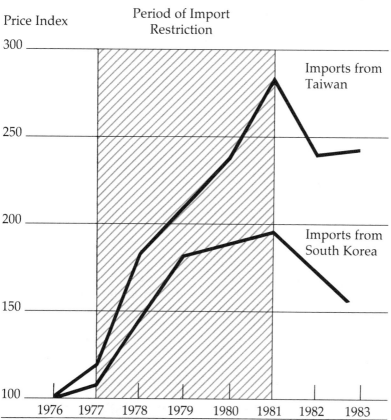

Figure 1
PRICES OF IMPORTED FOOTWEAR
(1976 = 100)

Price Index

Period of Import
Restriction

300

Imports from
Taiwan

250

200

Imports from
South Korea

150

100

1976   1977   1978   1979   1980   1981   1982   1983

SOURCE: Footwear Industry Association and International Trade Administration, U.S. Department of Commerce.

thereby resulting in lower price increases for items generally purchased by higher-income groups.[5]

Protection against import competition fails any reasonable

[5]Joon N. Suh, *"Voluntary" Export Restraints and Their Effects on Exporters and Consumers: The Case of the Footwear Quotas* (St. Louis: Washington University, Center for the Study of American Business, 1981).

benefit/cost analysis. The higher prices that consumers pay as a result of trade barriers far exceed the benefits for those who are being protected from the pain of adjusting to global realities. Given the recent tightening of restrictions on clothing imports, retailers have estimated, for example, that the costs associated with these restrictions could add as much as $4.4 billion to clothing costs for U.S. shoppers in 1984. See Table 2 for additional illustrations.

Trade restraint to shield a specific industry from imports is ultimately an internal transfer of income and wealth to that industry from U.S. consumers. Such a transfer takes the form of reduced employment and profits for American workers in and owners of our export industries, who bear the brunt of retaliatory trade restrictions. Workers in an industry that uses protected products (the auto industry with its purchases of steel, for example) find that they, too, lose their international competitiveness, and the pleas for protection rise again.

What emerges from any objective study of protectionism is the observation that the erecting of a single trade barrier sets off a chain of economic events that politically justify the enactment of even more protectionist measures. In other words, trade barriers spawn more trade barriers. This simple fact underscores the need to carefully and honestly evaluate our own obstacles to imports and exports alike. Before we complain about foreign governments and their role in "unfair" trading practices, we must be certain that the United States is not leading the charge in the current rush toward protectionism.

The problem can be explained with an elementary example. Country B has a large export surplus with Country A. Country A has great difficulty getting its exports into Country B. Sound familiar? Of course, Country B (large trade surplus) is Japan, and Country A (large trade deficit) is the United States.

But that is not the end of the story. If we take another look, we find that Country B (large trade surplus) is also the United States, and Country A (large trade deficit) is Western Europe. Though it has not received nearly as much urgent attention, the United States has enjoyed a trade surplus with the European Economic Community (EEC) over the last decade about as large as Japan's surplus with us. It would help to clear the air in international trade discussions if the United States would simply acknowledge that we too have been guilty of "unfair" competitive practices.

98

Table 2
Estimates of Annual Costs to Consumers Per Job Protected by Trade Barriers (1980$)

Product	Category of Restraint	Average Compensation	Subsidy from Consumer Per Job	Ratio of Subsidy to Actual Compensation
Apparel	Tariffs	$6,669	$45,549	6.8
Television Receivers	Tariffs, Quotas	12,923	74,155	5.7
Footwear	Tariffs, Quotas	8,340	77,714	9.3
Carbon Steel	Tariffs, Quotas	24,329	85,272	3.5
Steel	TPM	24,329	110,000	4.5
Autos	Domestic Content Bill (Proposed)	23,566	85,400	3.6
Citizens' Band Transceivers	Tariffs	8,500	85,539	10.1

SOURCE: Murray L. Weidenbaum and Michael C. Munger, "Protection at Any Price?" *Regulation* (July/August 1983): 17; Keith E. Maskus, "Rising Protectionism and U.S. International Trade Policy," *Federal Reserve Bank of Kansas City Economic Review* (July/August 1984): 3–17.

U.S. Barriers to Imports

The first step in any exorcism is naming the demons. Let us remind ourselves, however painful and embarrassing it may be to do so, of our many departures from free trade. An example is the "Buy American" statutes which give preference to domestic producers in government procurement. As a result of these statutes, a differential of as much as 50 percent is paid for military goods produced in the United States. In addition, the Surface Transportation Assistance Act, a mass transit subsidy program, requires most of the purchases over $500,000 that are made under its auspices to be limited to items utilizing American materials and products. Also, American flag vessels must be used to transport at least 50 percent of the tonnage of all commodities financed with U.S. foreign aid funds.

At the state level there are numerous "Buy American" laws of varying degrees as well. For example, New York requires its state agencies to buy American steel. New Jersey requires that all state cars be domestically produced. Numerous states and municipal authorities require the use of American-made materials in utilities, whether privately or publicly owned.

Moreover, there is the Jones Act. This piece of narrow, special-interest legislation prohibits foreign ships from engaging in commerce between American ports, effectively removing all competition in U.S. domestic marine transport. The perverse effects of such laws are greater than might be expected. For example, at times Canadian lumber—typically shipped by Japanese and not higher-cost U.S. flag vessels—has undersold domestic timber from Oregon in the lucrative southern California markets. In such a case, both the American merchant marine and any American industry that depends on it suffer obvious damage as a result of protection. With a friend like Jones, who needs an enemy?

Although our average tariff rates are low, high tariffs are levied on many items. Tariffs on textiles average some 20 percent, duties on fruit juices are over 27 percent, and the rate on ceramic products is over 14 percent. All these tariffs are additional to the numerous non-tariff barriers imposed at the federal, state, county, and municipal levels.

Despite this nation's overall free-trade posture, the wall of protection against imports now isolates some of our most basic industries—automobiles, steel, and textiles—from international competition. Pleas for further trade restrictions extend to such eso-teric sectors as mushrooms, clothespins, and even mechanics' shop towels. In light of these developments, it is no longer merely a question of accepting the existing array of protection. The real challenge is to deal with the rising pressures for further restriction of world trade.

Protectionist measures cut both ways. They may reduce imports from abroad, thereby aiding a declining domestic industry. But at what cost? The United States has been "successful" in getting the EEC, for example, to restrict its exports of steel to this country. But let us examine the results. First of all, the domestic automobile industry, a major purchaser of steel, bears the burden of higher costs, which in turn makes it less competitive. In addition, lower imports mean fewer dollars to buy American exports. All this gen-erates pressure for additional protection.

Furthermore, protection often generates retaliatory measures that hit unprotected sectors of the economy. For example, in January 1983 the U.S. government imposed import quotas on textiles and apparel from China. The Chinese government soon retaliated by cancelling new contracts for the importation of U.S. cotton, syn-thetic fibers, and soybeans. China's response to American restric-tions affected a very different sector of the U.S. economy and had a much broader effect than the supposed beneficiaries of the pro-tectionist action. The lesson is clear: protect one domestic producer from imports, and you are bound to hurt another domestic producer trying to export.

U.S. Barriers to Exports

Exports are even further limited by U.S. laws and regulations. In many ways—and often without considering the effects—we have enacted laws and promulgated regulations that prohibit U.S. exports or make it extremely difficult for American companies to export. For example, the Trans-Alaskan Pipeline Authorization Act prohib-its the export of oil from north slope fields. Also, a provision added to an appropriations act for the Department of the Interior bans the export of timber from federal lands west of the one hundredth meridian.

The Export Administration Act provides for controls on exports of certain goods and technology to protect national security. Now that is surely a worthy enough goal. In practice, however, the act mandates controls over a great variety of products, many of which are of dubious strategic value. These restricted products include domestically produced crude oil, refined petroleum products, unprocessed red cedar, and, of course, horses exported by sea. (We would not want the Soviet cavalry to get hold of those!)

Export controls do more than limit U.S. international trade for the period in which they are imposed. Indeed, such restrictions call into question the long-term reliability of the United States as a future supplier of products to other countries. As a result of such uncertainty, nations are likely to diversify their buying practices. For example, according to the most recent USDA estimates, American farmers will supply only a third of the Soviet Union's grain imports in 1984—down from the three-quarter level the United States had achieved prior to the 1980 grain embargo imposed by President Carter.

In the absence of other, well-established suppliers, nations are also likely to develop alternative sources. The main effect of the U.S. embargo of soybean products in 1974, for example, was to induce Japan to invest in other soybean-producing countries, particularly Brazil. Japan proceeded to spend huge amounts in that country to develop an alternative to U.S. soybean production, thus effectively and permanently reducing our share of the world market.

By no means is the United States the only nation with trade barriers; every nation has them. The EEC levies duties on wheat, barley, oats, sorghum, rye, and rice. Italy bans foreign-produced television commercials. Japan finds all sorts of reasons for keeping out baseball bats and oranges.

Still, even though the rest of the world's trade barriers are so plainly evident, our own trade barriers are ultimately far more important to the world economy. Despite all the short-term gloom left over from the 1981–82 recession, the United States is still the most important developed nation. American leadership in the world economy is undisputed. So, if we protect our most basic industries, there is every reason to suspect that every other developed nation will attempt to do likewise.

It is also important to remember that the United States is a world creditor. For this reason alone, free trade is a matter of enlightened self-interest. The developing nations need adequate access to the markets of the more-developed countries if they are going to be able to service the massive indebtedness they have incurred. However painful it may be to do so, the developed nations must adjust their economic structures to this reality. Default on foreign debt will do more to weaken the American economy than will any short-term trade deficit.

The Threat of International Regulation

One perennial bright spot in the international trade picture is the positive role of multinational corporations. Multinationals adapt to change more readily and are less likely to plead for protection than other companies.[6] They are also a private-sector alternative to foreign aid and other types of government intervention. This, of course, explains why so-called transnational enterprises are not terribly popular among the bureaucracies of international governmental organizations, and why the latter organizations are increasingly involving themselves in the regulation of private enterprise. The result is the threat of whole new sets of world trade obstacles.

To compound the problem, the advocates of this new level of regulation have ignored the shortcomings of existing regulation of business in the developed countries. Study after study has demonstrated that government regulators have often been oblivious to the burdens they impose on the private sector and—far more fundamentally—that such rules, regulations, and directives often do little to advance any intended social objectives. In reality, regulation is often counterproductive. One key finding permeates virtually all serious analyses of government regulation of business: it is the consumer who ultimately bears the costs that government, wittingly or unwittingly, imposes on business.

Leading the current assault on free international trade is the United Nations. Many of the UN's measures are in a state of evolution or negotiation in the form of "advisory resolutions" or "voluntary guidelines." Yet, in a growing number of instances, the new regulations are legally binding treaties. The form in which they currently exist is often an indication of the next step to be taken in the international regulatory process. Yesterday's studies lead to today's voluntary guidelines which, in turn, become the basis for tomorrow's treaties and directives. As shown in Figure 2, the regulatory activities of the UN cover every major aspect of business activity—operations, marketing, finance, technology, services, etc.[7]

[6]Ingo Walter and Kent A. Jones, "The Battle over Protectionism: How Industry Adjusts to Competitive Shocks," *Journal of Business Strategy* (1982): 37–46.

[7]Mary A. Fejfar, *Regulation of Business by International Agencies* (St. Louis: Washington University, Center for the Study of American Business, 1983).

Figure 2

REGULATORY ACTIVITIES OF THE UNITED NATIONS

	Operations	Marketing	Finance	Technology	Services	Information
General Assembly	■	■				■
Conf. on Trade & Development (UNCTAD)		■		■	■	
Environmental Program (UNEP)	■					
Development Program (UNDP)				■	■	■
Economic & Social Council (ECOSOC)	■	■	■		■	
Regional Commissions	■				■	
Comm. on Transnational Corps. (CTC)	■	■		■	■	■
Food & Agriculture Organization (FAO)					■	
International Maritime Org. (IMO)				■		
International Labor Org. (ILO)	■					
Int'l. Telecommunications Union (ITU)						■
Educ., Scientific, Cultural (UNESCO)		■				■
Industrial Devel. Org. (UNIDO)				■		
World Health Org. (WHO)	■	■				
World Intellectual Prop. Org. (WIPO)				■		

SOURCE: Center for the Study of American Business, Washington University.

Of all the actions of UN agencies designed to control the operations of private companies, the most ambitious (and perhaps the most troubling) is the draft code for the conduct of multinational corporations being developed by a commission of the Economic and Social Council. About two-thirds of the code's 71 provisions have been agreed upon.

The language contained in some sections of the code would make any sensible firm hesitate before investing overseas. One example is a provision that multinational corporations should "avoid practices, products, or services which cause detrimental effects on cultural patterns and sociocultural objectives as determined by the government." Where is the historical perspective of the authors of the code? Over the centuries civilization has been advanced by the transnational flow of science, art, music, culture—and commerce.

Moreover, should the UN be encouraging the governments of its member nations to set "sociocultural objectives" and to require private enterprise to follow the "cultural patterns" set and defined by government? This is not a traditional function of government regulation in a free society. It is, however, a mechanism used by totalitarian rulers to enforce their power.

Consumer Protection, UN-Style

The UN's Economic and Social Council is also considering a sweeping consumer protection code that would create new obstacles to international trade via controls on product advertising, safety, quality, and pricing. The proposed guidelines advocate replacing reliance on market competition—and consumer choice—with a system of government control.

One objective of the guidelines is "to facilitate production patterns geared to meeting the most important needs of consumers." In economies organized along private enterprise lines, the needs of consumers are always the strongest influence on production patterns; the pressures of the marketplace dictate that. But the guidelines suggest the need for a controlled, highly centralized economy in which consumer choices are in practice limited by the decisions of an all-wise government. This objective strongly implies that a central government must identify, and then control, the means of achieving the "most important needs" of consumers. We need only consult the dismal record of the world's centrally planned economies in feeding their citizens to know that promulgating this objective would severely hurt developing nations.

Such an objective overlooks the importance of world trade in meeting the needs of consumers. Most growing economies gear production for international markets as well as for the so-called more important needs of their own consumers. The case of Japan is instructive. If its postwar economy had been limited to meeting the needs of its own population, it surely would not enjoy its present strong position in world markets and its high standard of living.

Regardless of the motivation of their sponsors, many of the rules embodied in the proposed guidelines would increase costs to firms and ultimately to consumers. They would also create new barriers to the flow of trade and investment among nations. At a time when many of the developing nations are hardpressed to earn the foreign exchange needed to service their existing debts, such regulation would be counterproductive to their own development needs.

Rather than viewing the private corporation as the enemy of developing nations, proponents of international regulation should recognize that private enterprise has been the key to the successful development of Taiwan, South Korea, Singapore, Japan, and other developing societies that have prospered in our own time.

Unfortunately, the public at large knows little about the new trend in international regulation. There is little awareness of the extent to which the UN is becoming an economic body involved in radically changing the performance and character of private economies throughout the world. Its regulatory proposals are alien to consumers in Western nations that thrive on private markets and the principle of competition. Large private companies (the so-called multinational corporations) are given special attention—and penalized—in the UN's proposals only because they are the major alternative to direct government control and operation of the economic development process. More basically, these firms are singled out because they pose a viable threat to the establishment and maintenance of concentrated economic power in government— which is the hallmark of totalitarian societies. On the international regulatory front, we must stand our ground and encourage other nations that value economic freedom to do likewise.

A Program for Moving toward Free Trade: Four Positive Strategies

In view of the growing array of governmental obstacles to international commerce, what should be done? The United States should simultaneously pursue four positive and mutually supportive strategies for combating protectionism and promoting free trade.

First and most fundamental is carrying out domestic economic policies that expand production and incomes while holding down inflation. This, of course, is a plea for tax cuts, reduction in government spending, and regulatory relief. A healthy economy nips the protectionist bud at its source.

A second strategy for promoting free trade is to achieve greater stability and balance in macroeconomic policies. The shift in 1981 to tight monetary policy and expansive fiscal policy in the United States contributed substantially to high interest rates and a rise in the value of the dollar. Those trends, in turn, reduced the competitiveness of American producers in world markets. If government policymakers are not careful, they will now follow an easy-money policy that—coupled with outsized budget deficits—will lead to another inflationary spiral. Such a spiral would further reduce the competitiveness of U.S. products.

A third strategy for promoting free trade is to limit any governmental "trade adjustment assistance—apparently a politically necessary part of any comprehensive trade policy—to temporary aid in shifting labor and capital from industries hard hit by imports to more competitive activities. All too often, trade adjustment assistance merely maintains an inefficient and uncompetitive industrial structure. This in turn adversely affects our competitiveness in world markets and, predictably, generates further pressure for additional protectionist measures. The result is to lower domestic employment, which again generates additional pressures for government interference. All this exemplifies an important general principle: government intervention begets more government intervention.

In a healthy and dynamic economy we must expect that some industries and regions will grow more rapidly than others. We must also expect that some sectors will experience difficulty in maintaining their position and may even decline. We must rely primarily on market forces, not on government bailouts, to make the appropriate adjustments.

A fourth strategy for promoting free trade is to acknowledge once again the importance of multinational corporations in the world economy, particularly in the development process. With their ample supply of capital and technological ability, multinationals offer an effective alternative to foreign aid and other international transfers of wealth. Viewed in this light, the rise of international regulation can be seen as a stifling of multinational enterprise.

In addition—and as a possible fifth positive strategy—the United

States might consider responding to the various pleas for "reciprocity," but with a twist. In the past the notion of reciprocity had a very positive effect on world trade. It signified reducing trade barriers to countries that would lower theirs. Recently, however, the notion of reciprocity has been subverted. It is now used to cloak or justify erecting new or higher trade barriers supposedly against nations that inhibit our exports. This approach, however, ignores the trade barriers that we have already erected against those same countries.

Reciprocity, under the new definition, also fails to take account of the total flow of trade among nations. Thus, the advocates of reciprocity urge the United States to reduce imports from Western Europe even though, over the years, we have enjoyed a substantial trade surplus with the region.

Under the circumstances, the United States could initiate a process of freeing trade by reducing specific barriers to imports. Mindful of our large trade deficit, we could then "reciprocate" by reducing equivalent barriers we have erected to our own exports. This type of internal reciprocity would result in a lowering of trade barriers—just the opposite of the current style of reciprocity—without increasing the U.S. trade deficit. Reducing restrictions to the flow of commerce might begin, albeit slowly, to change the tone of foreign trade policy around the world. As other countries follow our new approach, we could accelerate the lowering of our barriers to imports and exports.

In any event, as the world's largest importer and exporter, the United States is extremely vulnerable to retaliation against the protectionist measures we initiate. Conversely, we stand to benefit greatly from a new round of lowered trade barriers.

Conclusion

Twin threats face the open world economy. First of all, the private sector of the United States itself is weakening the basic strength of the American economy by calling for protection from the effects of global competition. This is a case of labor and management in a given industry joining together at the consumer's expense. There may have been some justification for such protection in the case of "infant" industries in the eighteenth or possibly even the nineteenth centuries. But flabby, mature industries of the 1980s need to get themselves in shape to face competitive realities.

The United States is still, although by rapidly diminishing margins, the largest trading nation in the world. As this nation becomes more protectionist, it certainly is setting trends that are quickly followed around the world. Admittedly, should we become less protectionist we would likely find that our friends will be slower to follow our lead than they are when we restrict trade. Nevertheless, it is essential that this country take the lead.

Government action alone is not sufficient; American business must also assume a strong and meaningful free trade posture. The credibility of U.S. commitment to free trade has never been enhanced by companies sending their lawyers to Washington on Monday to seek the removal of import barriers overseas, only to send the same attorneys back on Wednesday to advocate import restrictions on the products of foreign competitors.

The second major threat to the open world economy is on the international regulatory front, where UN agencies are busy erecting what could turn out to be a colossal barrier to the expansion of world trade. The irony of an agency originally set up to promote world peace and prosperity now seeking to undermine the only realistic means of achieving such goals should not be lost on even the most optimistic among us. It is clearly time for the United States and its allies to put the UN back on the right track. A good start would be to derail the current regulatory juggernaut.

International trade is not a narrow matter of business or economics, but something basic to the relationships among nations. In this broader context, the resurgence of protectionism is troublesome because it raises tensions and irritates foreign policy relations among the nations of the world. The potential for strained political relations is greatly increased by heightened economic tensions. Conversely, open trade provides opportunities for improving relationships among nations and their peoples.

The serious question facing us is how best to encourage our trading partners to open their markets without using mechanisms that might harm the international trading system or setting off a spiral of retaliation. The current call for "reciprocity" raises such dangers.

The question is frequently asked, Other nations do not have a free trade policy, so why should we? But, instead of talking in absolutes, a more appropriate question is, Are the trade policies of other nations more open today than they would be without the continued pressure of agreed-upon international "rules of the game"—rules developed under the persistent and patient influence of the United States?

The answer to the latter question is a resounding yes. Trade policy, here and elsewhere, is far more open today as a result of our efforts and our example of an open domestic market. America's federal system, after all, was the original common market.

Is the United States better off with lower trade barriers? Again the response is affirmative. The goods we import are cheaper than domestic substitutes, America's 200 million consumers have greater product choice, and the markets for our exports are less restricted than they otherwise would be. Despite numerous real obstacles many American companies have experienced significant success in foreign markets, including that of Japan.

International trade policy will not remain static. The choice is between a creeping protectionism and a concerted multilateral effort to remove trade barriers. The longer the United States waits, the more firmly the obstacles will be in place and the more difficult it will be to deal with them.

VII. The Price and Perils of NATO

Earl C. Ravenal

Cost and Risk

In the past few years, the tides of discontent have been lapping at the base of the Atlantic alliance. Some observers have been struck by the unholy and unintended coalition of the European left (for example, the German Green Party and the radical wing of the German Social Democratic Party, or the left wing of the British Labour Party) and the American right (for example, the editorial board of the *Wall Street Journal* and such disaffected neo-conservatives as Irving Kristol).[1] The latter political manifestation feeds upon the former political phenomenon. Indeed, if NATO ever is washed away, it may well be attributable to erosion by these factions.

But there is another, more structural, reason for NATO's debility, which is at the causal root of the more obvious and superficial attitudes of the factions of left and right on both sides of the Atlantic: the unlikelihood of the American military guarantee of Europe, including our "nuclear umbrella." The incredibility of America's guarantee in turn proceeds from a tension inherent in the American assumption of this strategic commitment to Europe, 36 years ago. For the commitment to Europe presents the United States with a choice between unsupportable costs, associated with the confident defense of Europe with conventional forces, and unassumable risks, attributable to reliance on the earlier use of nuclear weapons. The direction in which this tension is resolved, by any particular American administration, is not rigidly determined; to some extent cost can be transmuted into additional risk, and risk can be transformed into mere cost. (That is what is meant by "raising" or "lowering" the nuclear threshold.) But, as long as the United States is committed to Europe, the choice, itself, is inescapable.

The Europeans have a somewhat parallel structure of choice:

---

[1]See his article, "What's Wrong With NATO?" *The New York Times Magazine*, September 25, 1983.

111

costly generation of sufficient conventional forces, or acquisition or expansion of their own national nuclear arsenals, with the accompanying more resolute and risky doctrines of employment. But there is an obvious difference: The European allies are situated more or less along the forward line of defense, down the center of Europe and in the eastern Mediterranean; the United States can "decide" (in that diffuse and objective way in which national decision-making systems, particularly plebiscitary democracies and polities of dispersed powers such as the United States, decide these matters) whether it wants to pitch its own security perimeter along that common line.

Those factors of cost and risk are shaped by the divergent options, with different costs and penalties, that arise from the relative situations of the United States and Western Europe. Thus, European allies alternately try to prolong their run of luck in attracting disproportionate American support (the response of nervous governments), and (the response of anxious peoples) try to avoid implication in the American style of defense, which periodically tilts to the substitution of nuclear strategies and the confinement of even a nuclear battle to the European continent. For its part, the United States continually attempts to mitigate the consequences of its commitment; and these attempts tend to diminish the deterrence of conventional war in Europe and to "decouple" the United States from Europe.

The factors of cost and risk are inevitable components of any assessment of America's role in the defense of Europe, and they are the most formidable reasons that could be presented for American withdrawal from Europe. It may be unpleasant to inquire about the problems of NATO from an American viewpoint; and it may seem crass to weigh those problems primarily on the grounds of cost to Americans. Yet cost (underlying the political pique voiced by conservative Americans at the Europeans, and traded off against the risk involved in holding our nuclear umbrella over our European allies) will decide the future of NATO. And that future will be disposed primarily within the American political, economic, and social process.

A History of Crises

The alliance of Atlantic nations, in its history, has been beset by many kinds of problems: There have been the periodic recrudescence of commercial and agricultural disputes; the irreconcilable antagonism of pairs of nations, such as Greece and Turkey; the threat of Euro-communism; the acrimony revolving around "burden-sharing"; the complaints about the "one-way street" of American military production for the alliance; the assaults of neutralists and anti-American political groups; the failures of "consultation" and recriminations over American "hegemony." But, whatever else is wrong with the Atlantic alliance, its essential problems are strategic: the United States and Europe have persistently failed to resolve their discordant strategic conceptions.

NATO's history, from its beginnings in 1949 to the present time, could be written in terms of a series of strategic crises:

- In the winter of 1950–51, there was the "great debate" in the U.S. Congress about dispatching troops to Europe.

- Between 1951 and 1954, Europeans devised, debated, and finally defeated the European Defense Community (EDC), inspiring John Foster Dulles's threat of an "agonizing reappraisal" of the American connection.

- The thwarting of the Suez adventure of Britain and France by the United States in October 1956 suggested the conditionality of American support for Europe and the divergence of American and European interests.

- In October 1956, the absence of U.S. opposition to Soviet suppression of the Hungarian uprising illustrated the limits of American interest in curing the division of Europe.

- The Cuban missile crisis of 1962 and the ensuing Limited Test Ban Treaty of 1963 marked the realization of a stalemate between the two superpowers at the strategic nuclear level.

- The unilateral American decision in 1962 to cancel the Skybolt air-to-ground missile, upon which the British relied for the perpetuation of their nuclear deterrent, indicated that the United States might put its own efficiency before its alliance responsibilities.

- The demise, in 1964, of the MLF—the multilateral nuclear force, the contradictory American scheme to endow Europe with its own nuclear deterrent, but with an American finger on the trigger—illustrated the insoluble dilemma of joint nuclear defense.

- De Gaulle's withdrawal of France from NATO in 1966 rendered uncertain the terms of participation of Western Europe's largest military force.

- The Soviet invasion of Czechoslovakia in 1968 proved both the persistence of Russian claims on deviant Communist countries and the meticulous abstention of the United States.

- Kissinger's "Year of Europe" in 1973 demonstrated that the United States might apply reverse linkage to its own allies, threatening to attenuate its military support in order to exact greater defense burden-sharing and more advantageous trade and monetary treatment.

- The Mideast war of October 1973 brought the denial by America's European allies of bases, overflight, and the use of ports. The ensuing oil embargo and the drastic raising of prices by the OPEC cartel evoked a discordant response from the West. It might even have illustrated that, in certain circumstances, Europe could be more of a liability than an asset to the United States.

- Soviet expansive probes, from Afghanistan in December 1979 to Central America in the early 1980s, have elicited divergent reactions from Americans and Europeans. The Europeans have been concerned to conserve "detente," at least in selected functional aspects; the Americans have stressed "linkage" in evaluating and attempting to restrain Soviet conduct.

- The recent crisis of theater nuclear weapons, or "intermediate nuclear forces" (INF), deserves more extensive discussion. In December 1979, NATO's foreign ministers allowed the deployment in Western Europe, to start in late 1983, of two new American theater nuclear weapons—108 Pershing II ballistic missiles and 464 Tomahawk ground-launched cruise missiles—with ranges, respectively, of 1,000 and 1,500 miles, long enough to strike almost all of the western Soviet Union. The Western European allies exacted a "two-track" compromise from the Americans: the deployment of the American longer-range missiles, but the seeking of a theater nuclear arms control agreement with the Soviet Union—the arms deployment to proceed only if the arms talks were to fail. Thus, although the proposed emplacement of American missiles was a response to German chancellor Helmut Schmidt's 1977 plea for some regional balance to the Soviet SS-20s, the compromise decision opened an abyss between the European and American allies, with the United States bent on a considerable deployment of intermediate nuclear forces, and the Europeans intent on the repair of detente with the Soviet Union and Eastern Europe.

The cohesion of NATO has weathered five years of Soviet bluster and the Soviets' excitement and orchestration of Western European peace groups; the American missile deployments began in November 1983. But the crisis illustrates a point of deeper, more abiding, significance. One might examine this by asking the question, why would the Europeans, or at least their governments—with some reluctance in Holland, Belgium, and Denmark—have wanted these longer-range nuclear weapons in the first place? Though measurements of the theater nuclear balance are so subjective that it is not clear what is being measured, the apparent edge goes to the Warsaw Pact. Europeans feel especially intimidated by the Soviet SS-20 missiles. By now somewhere in the neighborhood of 300 of these missiles have been deployed in the western part of the Soviet Union. But the additional protection afforded by the new American weapons is illusory; they will not even be subject to European control. The new missiles are not an additional implement of NATO's strength; rather, they represent another European attempt to secure America's commitment to the defense of Europe. They are a symbol of Europe's abiding distrust of America's "extended deterrence." They illustrate Europe's nervousness about the coupling of American strategic weapons to the defense of Europe and, in a larger sense, the coupling of the United States and Europe.

Coupling and Decoupling

What does all this history prove? First, the crises are not random. There is a common thread: they are all tests of confidence among the allies. Second, the crises are not accidental or superficial. They would not be crises if they did not have deep causal roots. In fact, they are crises because they derive from the divergent conceptions of alliance, the divergent security needs, and the divergent geopolitical situations of the United States and Europe. Third, the crises

115

are not novel. They stem from problems that have been implicit in the alliance from its inception.

Thirty-six years after the foundation of NATO, the defense of Western Europe still rests on the proposition that an American president will invite the destruction of our cities and the incineration of 100 million of our citizens to repel a Soviet incursion or resist a Soviet ultimatum in Western Europe. On its face, America's war plan—never denied by any president from Truman to Reagan, or by any secretary of state from George Marshall to George Shultz—is the first use of nuclear weapons, if necessary, to defend Europe. Thus America threatens to turn local defeat into global holocaust. But, under the surface, America's nuclear commitment to Europe is not so sure. The word that encapsulates this problem is "coupling." Not the title of an Updike novel or an anthropological treatise by Margaret Mead, coupling is a term of art used by strategic analysts to connote the integrity of the chain of escalation, from conventional war in Europe to theater nuclear weapons to the final use of America's ultimate strategic weapon.

In a larger sense coupling connotes the identity of the fates of the peoples, societies, and political systems on both sides of the Atlantic. The root of the problem is that America, the alliance guarantor, hoping to escape the destruction of nuclear war, will always seek to put time between the outbreak of war in Europe and the decision to escalate to nuclear weapons, and will take whatever advantage it can of its distance from Europe.

Not that an adversary is likely to test American will with an attack on Europe. Odds of, say, 65 percent of an American nuclear response will restrain a potential aggressor. (Even a whiff of American nuclear retaliation is probably enough to keep the Soviet Union from invading Western Europe.) But those odds will not convince allies of their protection. And the real efficacy of extended deterrence is in keeping allies, not just deterring adversaries. There is a nagging asymmetry about nuclear protection: it takes more credibility to keep an ally than to deter an adversary.

Whether America will fight for Europe, or whether it will in some way use the territorial depth of Europe as a buffer, is not a subject of polite conversation between Americans and Europeans. But decoupling from Europe is America's "secret" strategy. Not, of course, in the sense that our leaders are keeping it a secret, but rather because strategy (somewhat like "policy") consists of what a nation—a complex political-social system—will do at the time that

116

strategy must be invoked, not what its leaders profess or prefer, or even what they might have "planned" to do.

Europeans already suspect this. Virtually every American strategic move—up, down, or sideways—has evoked the specter of decoupling in one or another of its forms: either the avoidance of a nuclear response altogether or the attempt to confine even a nuclear conflict to the European theater. This is not something that began suddenly when President Reagan said: "I could see where you could have the exchange of tactical weapons against troops in the field without it bringing either one of the major powers to pushing the button."[2] The doubts had been sown long before that, in a series of American moves: the MLF; the emphasis on flexible response and conventional defense by the Kennedy-McNamara administration; the Schlesinger doctrine of 1974, which contemplated the selective use of the American strategic nuclear force; the interest in "mini-nukes," including such variants as the neutron bomb; and even the introduction of intermediate-range nuclear weapons, such as the Pershing II and the ground-launched cruise missiles. Though these may enhance coupling by perfecting the essential link of theater nuclear weapons, they may also allow the restriction of nuclear conflict to Europe.

More recently, President Reagan's "Star Wars," a design to protect American society from Soviet missiles, has stirred European concern that the United States could afford a "Fortress America" mentality and ignore forward defense in Europe. And, finally, America's current attempt to endow NATO with "emerging technology" has had the significance, to some Europeans, of further detaching the United States from its commitment to escalate to nuclear weapons, specifically by promising conventional coverage of some targets formerly requiring nuclear systems.

At issue here is not whether these American strategic moves are well planned or well meant, but whether they have the effect of attenuating the American connection with Europe; whether they provide reasons, or pretexts, for the United States to make its escalation to strategic nuclear weapons less than prompt and automatic; whether they give the United States additional buffers or "firebreaks." (A firebreak is any device, strategy, or doctrine that makes escalation to nuclear weapons less than prompt and

---

[2]Bernard Gwertzman, "President Says U.S. Should Not Waver in Backing Saudis," *The New York Times*, October 18, 1981.

automatic.) Coupling and firebreaks are inversely related. Coupling, across geography and between levels of warfare, is the essence of alliance protection in a nuclear age, but it contradicts the introduction of firebreaks. Firebreaks are an imperative of our security in an era of nuclear parity, but they impair alliance protection. This is more than a simple antithesis; it has the aspect of a paradox, since the enhancement of any level of military recourse can be regarded alternatively as a link to higher levels of escalation and as a self-contained effort. Improved conventional defense can postpone nuclear escalation and widen the firebreak between conventional war and nuclear war. On the other hand, earlier resort to discrete and controlled tactical nuclear weapons invokes the specter of limiting even a nuclear war to European territory, creating yet another firebreak, this one between theater and total nuclear war.

Henry Kissinger was clear and prescient about these matters when he addressed a private gathering of American and European strategists in Brussels in September 1979. In a remark that has since gained wide currency, he permitted himself some pessimistic reflections on the validity of the American nuclear guarantee:

> Perhaps even today, but surely in the 1980s, the United States will no longer be in a strategic position to reduce a Soviet counterblow against the United States to tolerable levels. . . . If my analysis is correct, we must face the fact that it is absurd to base the strategy of the West on the credibility of the threat of mutual suicide. . . . And therefore, I would say, which I might not say in office, that European allies should not keep asking us to multiply strategic assurances that we cannot possibly mean or if we do mean, we should not want to execute because if we execute, we risk the destruction of civilization.[3]

Kissinger's remarks should not have been surprising. Fourteen years earlier, he had pointed out that the disabilities of NATO are not peculiar; they afflict all alliances of sovereign nations. Kissinger discovered virtually a law of alliance: the contradiction of military effectiveness and political sovereignty.

> There is an increasing inconsistency between the technical requirements of strategy and political imperatives of the nation-states. . . . The dilemma arises because there is no scheme which

[3]Quoted in Kenneth A. Myers, ed., *NATO: The Next Thirty Years* (Boulder, Colo.: Westview Press, 1980).

118

can reconcile these objectives perfectly so long as the Atlantic Alliance remains composed of sovereign states.[4]

Nuclear weapons do not resolve this contradiction; they heighten it. Once they have spread beyond the monopoly of one nation, they corrode trust and dissolve the bonds of alliance.

Nuclear Risk

The American assumption of a guarantee to defend Western Europe carries with it a heightened risk of nuclear war. America's commitment to NATO can scarcely be understood, let alone evaluated, without plumbing at least two aspects of nuclear risk: (1) the progressive dominance of counterforce strategies, and (2) various attempts to mitigate the possible nuclear destruction of the United States.

America's drift to counterforce nuclear strategies is neither perverse nor accidental. Counterforce means the use of some fraction of our strategic nuclear force to attack a portion of the enemy's target system consisting of military installations, logistical complexes, command bunkers, and—to put the most important item last—missiles in their silos. In turn, it entails the acquisition of "hard-target kill capability." To grasp the rationale of counterforce, it is necessary to understand the logic of extended deterrence. Ultimately, it is adherence to alliance commitments that skews our strategy toward counterforce weapons and targeting and warps our doctrines of response toward the first use of nuclear weapons, prejudicing crisis stability and increasing the danger of escalation to nuclear war.[5]

The compelling motive for counterforce is damage limitation—that is, limiting the damage to the United States in a nuclear war. Part of that intent would be to strike Soviet missiles in silos (and, perhaps, also Soviet command bunkers and control and communication facilities). Such a damage-limiting attack, to have its intended effect, must be preemptive. Indeed, counterforce and first nuclear strike are mutually dependent. A first strike implies counterforce

[4]*The Troubled Partnership: A Re-Appraisal of the Atlantic Alliance* (New York: McGraw-Hill, 1965).

[5]An extended treatment of counterforce and alliance, their logic and their relation, is presented in Earl C. Ravenal, "Counterforce and Alliance: The Ultimate Connection," *International Security* (Spring 1982).

targeting, since the only initial attack that makes sense is a damage-limiting strike, the destruction of as much of the enemy's nuclear force as possible. In return, counterforce targeting implies a first strike, a preemptive attack, because a second strike against the enemy's missiles is useless to the extent that one's missiles would hit empty holes.

Any strategic policy will try to protect certain values that are at the core of our national identity and sovereignty. These values include our political integrity and autonomy and the safety and domestic property of our people. These are the proper—and largely feasible—objects of American defense or deterrence. It is when we attempt to protect more than these objects with our strategic nuclear force that we court the peculiar problems of *extended* deterrence. Then the calculus of credibility that we make with regard to strict central deterrence does not hold. The assumptions of deterrence apply to peripheral areas and less-than-vital interests with much less strength and validity.

As it happens, our protection of Western Europe requires *both* initial conventional defense and credible extended deterrence; one cannot be substituted entirely for the other. Extended deterrence, in turn, requires the practical invulnerability of our *society* to Soviet attack. (This is not to be confused with the invulnerability of our nuclear weapons.) I say "practical" invulnerability, since absolute invulnerability is beyond America's, or anyone's, reach. Rather, what is required is the ability to limit damage to "tolerable" levels of casualties and destruction. This is so an American president can persuade others that he would risk an attack on our homeland, or that he could face down a threat to attack that homeland, in the act of spreading America's protective mantle over Western Europe and other parts of the world.

To attain the requisite societal invulnerability, the United States would have to work through both its defensive and its offensive strategic systems. First, we would have to achieve a strategic defense. This might cost from half a trillion to a trillion dollars, over perhaps fifteen years, if we were to go about it seriously, not just symbolically. As a second condition of societal invulnerability, we must be able to hold in reserve, after any of the earlier stages of a protracted nuclear exchange, enough destructive power to threaten counter-city strikes. Finally, a significant requisite of societal invulnerability is the acquisition of a nuclear counterforce capability, specifically hard-target kill.

Counterforce "makes sense," then, as an attempt to fulfill some of the necessary conditions of extended deterrence—but, it is fair to say, *only* as such. Thus, our willingness to protect our allies rises and falls with the prospective viability of counterforce and, more generally, with our ability to protect our own society from nuclear attack. If there is any explicit doubt—technical, economic, political—that we will achieve that invulnerability, then there is implicit doubt that our extensive nuclear commitments, especially to Western Europe, can survive.

What emerges from this analysis is that the attempt to implement extended deterrence—to defend, say, Western Europe efficiently and thoroughly by substituting the threat of nuclear weapons for the conventional defense of the theater—requires conditions that, if they can be fulfilled at all, are expensive or dangerous or counterproductive.

First Use and Conventional Defense

In order to diminish the risk that stems from our extended deterrence in Europe, arguments have been made against the first use of nuclear weapons. The most notable statement in recent times has been the article by McGeorge Bundy, George F. Kennan, Robert S. McNamara, and Gerard Smith, "Nuclear Weapons and the Atlantic Alliance."[6] The article is classic, not only in its exposition but also in the problems it incurs in its premises and argument.

Its principal problem is that it insists on maintaining, somehow, the integrity of the American commitment to the defense of our Western European allies; and yet it seeks to obviate the risk to the United States of destruction in a nuclear war. If one is committed, as are Bundy and his fellow authors, both to defend Europe and to avoid the extension of conflict to our homeland, one must try to reconcile these awkward objectives. Thus, crucial in the Bundy-Kennan-McNamara-Smith proposal is that its apparent renunciation of the first use of nuclear weapons is *conditioned* on the acquisition of an adequate conventional defense.

But those who opt reflexively for conventional defense cannot mean just any conventional effort. They must mean the *high*

---

[6]*Foreign Affairs* (Spring 1982). I discuss the proposition of no-first-use in two places and contexts: first, here, as it affects the need for enhanced, and costly, conventional defense; later, below, in examining how various versions of no-first-use achieve or fail to achieve war-avoidance.

confidence defense of Europe with conventional arms. And they cannot just exhort or prescribe that the United States and its allies "must" do more to guarantee the integrity of Western Europe; they have the further burden of *predicting* that this is going to happen.

In order to determine the feasibility—and hence the predictive probability—of the conventional defense option, we must have a bill of costs. But seldom—and nowhere in the Bundy article—is that bill set forth. What would the conventional option in Europe cost the United States? One must look first at what we are already spending.

This requires that we attribute all U.S. forces either to the "strategic" or the "general purpose" side of the ledger and, in turn, attribute general purpose forces to some region of the world. For this calculation, combat forces are costed on a "full-slice" basis. For failing to state the full costs of forces prevents us from linking defense dollars and manpower with the defense of regions of the world. Both full-slice costing and the allocation of forces to regions of the world are necessary for making defense costs *intelligible*— that is, relating the primary inputs to the ultimate outputs.

In terms of forces, I judge (from an analysis of Secretary of Defense Caspar W. Weinberger's 1985 "Posture Statement," presented to Congress on February 1, 1984) that, for FY 1985, the Reagan administration intends the following regional attribution of our total of 20 active ground divisions: NATO/Europe, 11 divisions; East Asia, 4 divisions; Other Regions and the Strategic Reserve, 5 divisions. By applying these fractions to the total cost of our general purpose forces, $235 billion, we can calculate the rough cost of our three regional commitments. By my estimates, Europe accounts for $129 billion; Asia absorbs $47 billion; and the Strategic Reserve, including an expanded requirement for Rapid Deployment Forces, mostly for CENTCOM—that is, the Persian Gulf and Southwest Asia—takes $59 billion. One hastens to point out that the commander-in-chief of a given unified or allied command does not see all those costs. The American forces that he commands are just the tip of the iceberg; most of the costs involve support units and Pentagon overhead. The money is spent in the United States, but it is attributable to our commitment to defend each specified region.[7]

[7]A more ample explanatory section appears in Earl C. Ravenal, *Defining Defense: The 1985 Defense Budget* (Washington, D.C.: Cato Institute, 1984). My estimate of regional defense costs differs from several others, both official and unofficial, that have recently appeared. For example, a Department of Defense report is quoted as saying that "the total cost of European-deployed United States forces and all of the

Our present share of the conventional defense of Europe—and this is not even designed to be a self-contained conventional defense—is about $129 billion for FY 1985. This is over 42 percent of the $305 billion originally requested for defense by the Reagan administration. Given a reasonable projection of current cost growth, over the next ten years Europe will cost the United States $2 trillion. (It may be of some interest to compare this with the fact that, over the 36 years of its existence, the cost of NATO to the United States has been roughly $1.5 to 2 trillion. Each year, NATO-related costs have been between 40 and 50 percent of our defense budget.) The appropriate question is whether even those resources will be forthcoming, let alone the greater ones required for self-sufficient conventional defense.

Proposals for consolidating, enhancing, or improving NATO's conventional defense are called forth, of course, by the formidable Warsaw Pact forces, mostly against the central region of Europe. And the impressive Soviet buildup of conventional forces makes the requisite conventional force level for NATO a moving target. The current problem is expressed in a comparison of the forces in central, northern, and eastern Europe and the western USSR. The Warsaw Pact has 1,303,000 ground troops, including 825,000 Soviets; it fields 61 ready divisions (or equivalents), of which 38 are Soviet, including the 19 divisions of the Group Soviet Forces Germany (GSFG). Arrayed against them are NATO's 820,000 ground

United States-based forces that we have pledged to contribute as NATO reinforcements over the course of a conflict amounts to about $177 billion" for 1985, or about 58 percent of the Reagan administration's initial budget request of $305 billion. The General Accounting Office is reported to maintain that the United States actually spent $122 billion in FY 1982, or 56 percent of actual outlays (Richard Halloran, "Europe Called Main Arms Cost," *The New York Times*, July 20, 1984). Both estimates are undoubtedly too *high*. After several decades of underestimation, it is now almost becoming fashionable to over-allocate percentages of the defense budget to Europe. What seems to be happening is that the Department of Defense, when conducting its periodic estimate of the cost to the United States of defending NATO, as compared with the contributions of our European allies, has collected all forces that might plausibly be used in Europe and has attributed them to the Europe requirement, largely to impress audiences both internal and external that the United States is bearing more than its fair share of the burden of NATO defense. Some of those forces, however, are *primarily* attributable to other contingencies, notably the Persian Gulf/Southwest Asia. Thus, the Pentagon is probably double-counting those forces, for Europe and for the Gulf. The General Accounting Office may be selectively or disproportionately allocating certain items of support and overhead to NATO; it is also including a share of strategic nuclear forces.

troops and 27 division equivalents—much larger, on the average, than the Warsaw Pact's—including the 204,000 army troops and the 5 division equivalents of the United States (and including the French forces in Germany, 48,500 men and 3 divisions, which operate independently of NATO). The Warsaw Pact enjoys a preponderance of armor in these central and related European areas, having 32,100 main battle tanks against NATO's 13,716, and a substantial advantage in conventional artillery and multiple rocket launchers (10,500 pieces against 5,525). The Pact now has almost twice as many antitank weapons and has gained parity in tactical aircraft, with 1,742 fighter-attack planes against NATO's 1,706. NATO's position in this comparison has deteriorated markedly in the past five years.[8]

Hawkish and dovish experts argue about the numbers and the significance of the numbers. (They are not as conclusive as many allied and American observers take them to be.)[9] But the Russians have not made things more comfortable for the alliance. Certain aspects of their buildup—the number of troops, the types of weapons and combat support equipment, the configuration of forces, the qualitative improvements, the location of units, the publicized and observed tactical doctrine (which is clearly offensive, stressing surprise, shock, rapid advance, and deep penetration), the nature and intent of maneuvers—could be a cause of concern, or at least an occasion for wonder.

NATO's Responses

To all this, NATO and its critics have made responses that purport to provide sufficient conventional defense, or to adjust the American relationship to the alliance, or otherwise to meet the challenge

[8]*The Military Balance, 1984–1985* (London: International Institute for Strategic Studies, 1984).

[9]David T. Johnson, in a paper entitled "NATO's Military Situation: Back to Fundamentals," presented at the Amsterdam conference of the Transnational Institute, March 1–4, 1979, quotes the U.S. Defense Intelligence Agency to the effect that "Soviet posture opposite NATO has remained relatively stable numerically" for the past decade. "For about 10 years the Soviets have been in the process of correcting what they apparently viewed as serious deficiencies in their capabilities for theater warfare, deficiencies largely attributable to the policies of the Krushchev regime." He also cites the Brookings Institution to the effect that "since about 1970 the modernization of Warsaw Pact forces has been essentially matched by NATO improvements."

within acceptable parameters of NATO and American sacrifice and exposure to risk. Presented here, first, are two attempts to provide sufficient conventional defense.

NATO has proceeded, in a burst of planning in the Pentagon and in European defense ministries, with a long list of schemes to patch up its tactical deficiencies and repair its basic defensive stance. Energetic and often imaginative efforts have been made by the Office of the Secretary of Defense, beginning in the Carter administration. These moves fall mainly into the category of "quick fixes" in NATO's existing posture.

The moves suggested by analysts and planners have been in the following areas: increasing armament and firepower, including precision-guided anti-tank weapons, heavier American army divisions, and improved electronic warfare; bringing about greater military integration of NATO, in the areas of logistics, air defense, weapons procurement, communications and headquarters, and intelligence; refining doctrine, stressing maneuver; improving mobility and readiness; fostering greater use of reserves; and correcting the maldeployment of forces along the front.

Many of these moves have been accomplished between 1978 and late 1984. Some of them are sensible, as long as the alliance exists in roughly its present form, with more or less its present mission, in an international environment similar to the present one. But some of the "quick fixes" are not as quick or cheap as they might seem. And some moves would critically reduce the autonomy of our own national decision making, prejudicing American freedom and flexibility of action in the event of a crisis or the outbreak of hostilities. (Standardization is an example of this.)

NATO's second response is addressed to the more advanced offensive capabilities imputed to Soviet forces in central Europe. To this end, NATO has acquired an interest in "emerging technology" (ET) and associated tactical concepts. The emerging technology is almost literally a deus ex machina. It consists of revolutionary developments in long-range surveillance and target acquisition and in lethal specialized submunitions and accurate terminal guidance. The associated tactical concepts are bold attempts to target "second-echelon" armored units, logistical installations and choke points, and airfields, usually far behind the forward edge of battle. Sometimes generically labelled "Strike Deep," variations are the U.S. Army's AirLand Battle (the original scheme incorporated in the current Army Field Manual FM-105), the more advanced "AirLand

Battle 2000" (projecting requirements for the next 20 years), and Follow-On Forces Attack (FOFA), the planning concept of Supreme Headquarters Allied Expeditionary Forces (SHAEF) and General Bernard Rogers, the current Supreme Allied Commander Europe (SACEUR).

Many aspects of the new military technologies and tactical doctrines are constructive. Some should be adopted—provided they are cost-effective in relation to the promised gains in capabilities, and also absolutely economical. But serious questions have arisen. Some center on the technical feasibility of the new systems, particularly long-range identification and acquisition of moving targets, and "smart" submunitions. Other questions concern the high cost of these sophisticated weapons. Some estimates of overall acquisition costs over a ten-year period range from $10 billion to $30 billion. Such amounts might exceed the capabilities of the European allies' precarious political systems. Still other critiques challenge their relevance to the specific threat, the Soviet "Operational Maneuver Groups" (OMGs). These are mobile combined-arms units of less than divisional size that range laterally just behind the front edge of the battle to exploit opportunities that might open up. They would be hard to interdict with the new technologies and tactical concepts, since they operate close to the front and do not require significant massing.

Another objection is that the new weapons systems are provocative and destabilizing. Even though they are primarily designed to exist within the conventional range of the spectrum, the new munitions utilize the same delivery vehicles that are assigned to nuclear weapons. This might create a fatal ambiguity in a war. Though for the most part designed to push up the nuclear threshold, these weapons actually blur the concept of a recognizable threshold or a distinct firebreak. And the duality of delivery vehicles might subvert arms control by complicating verification. Indeed, from an arms control standpoint, emerging technology itself could touch off a *conventional* arms race in central Europe. After consideration of the technology and tactics of Strike Deep, it seems that NATO still lacks a proper doctrinal and organizational response.

The two foregoing responses—quick fixes and emerging technology—may not solve the conventional defensive problem, and probably aggravate the cost problem. Indeed, if the United States were to set for itself and its allies the task of providing a confident conventional defense against Soviet arms, principally on the central front of Europe, the costs of this in terms of American defense spending would be far higher than many proponents of conventional defense are willing to concede. One estimate of the entailed costs has been given by Leonard Sullivan, Jr.: "Expanding our conventional forces by 20% over the next 10 years to offset the numerically, qualitatively, and geographically expanding threat requires that defense outlays rise . . . to 9½% of the GNP."[10]

There are two reasons for citing, detailing, and documenting the present and projected costs of defending NATO. The first is to demonstrate the improbability of attaining self-sufficient conventional defense and thus obviating America's exposure to nuclear war and nuclear destruction, as long as the United States is attached to the defense of Europe. The second reason is to indicate that even the present level of defense (mostly conventional) of Europe is formidably high—not only the preponderant fraction of the defense budget, but the third highest "line-item" (more than one-seventh) of the entire federal budget, if it were to be identified as such; and that this expense is not likely to be reduced appreciably by the sorts of measures periodically proposed to mitigate the impacts of the American commitment to defend Europe. It is to these proposed measures that we now turn.

False Measures

The first of these approaches would adjust the roles and, to a much lesser extent, the burdens of the members of the alliance. In its most recent incarnation, this is the proposal of Henry Kissinger.[11] Kissinger identifies four problems that "are gnawing at the alliance," of which the most severe is the "lack of an agreed, credible strategy." He poses the classic dilemma: The present, and requisite, doctrines of flexible response—"a defense of Europe that begins with conventional weapons and then goes up the ladder of nuclear escalation"—are neither supported by adequate conventional ground forces nor buttressed by the credibility (or the objective sense) of an early recourse to nuclear war.

To this grave dilemma, Kissinger poses a remedy that is as irrelevant as it is trivial. The first part consists of an organizational rearrangement that would rotate hats: The Supreme Allied Com-

[10]"The FY 84 Defense Debate: Defeat by Default," *Armed Forces Journal International* (May 1983).

[11]"A Plan to Reshape NATO," *Time*, March 5, 1984.

127

mander Europe (SACEUR), traditionally American, would be a European; the Secretary-General of NATO, now European, would be an American. (It sounds a bit like a Gilbert and Sullivan denouement.) The second part of Kissinger's remedy has been widely and mistakenly advertised as the withdrawal of half of the American ground forces now stationed in Europe. But Kissinger posits this only conditionally, as a sort of punishment, "if Europe by its own decision condemns itself to permanent conventional inferiority" by failing "to build a full conventional defense and . . . express that commitment in unambiguous yearly obligations to increase its forces." As on other occasions, Kissinger leaves us with a problem gravely and implacably described, but only glancingly addressed and inadequately resolved, and thus abandoned as insoluble.

Other proposals demand more tangible "burden-sharing" by America's European allies. It is true that the Western European countries are spending on defense, in terms of percentages of their gross national products, only fractions of what the United States is spending, and that the gap is growing larger as European governments, in periods of economic stringency, slight their contributions to defense. Comparative contributions of key NATO allies, as percentages of gross national product, are as follows: United States, 7.3 percent; West Germany, 2.7 percent; Britain, 5.3 percent; France, 3.3 percent; the Netherlands, 3.2 percent.[12]

The reaction to these discrepancies, principally in the American Congress, is typified by an amendment proposed by Senator Sam Nunn (D-Ga.) in the spring of 1984. Nunn, normally a strong supporter of NATO, attempted to coerce our European allies into fulfilling their 1977 promise to increase their defense spending by 3 percent a year. (In 1983, non-U.S. alliance members, including Canada, increased defense spending by between 1.2 and 1.7 percent, while the United States had increased its NATO spending by 4.9 percent to 9 percent over the previous four years.)[13] Nunn

[12]Derived from *The Military Balance, 1984–1985* (London: International Institute for Strategic Studies, 1984). The figures are generally from 1983, a few from 1982. For some reason, they appear to overstate the United States slightly and to understate West Germany, and perhaps France, somewhat.

[13]Described in Helen Dewar, "Reagan Fights Nunn Bid to Cut Troops in Europe," *The Washington Post*, June 20, 1984. A more recent summary, on a slightly different basis, shows non-U.S. NATO averaging real year-to-year increases of 2.4 percent from 1979 to 1983, and a NATO *total*, including the United States, of 4.8 percent. ("Report on the Allied Contributions to the Common Defense," Department of Defense, 1984, cited in William Drozdiak, "Conventional Buildup Troubling NATO," *The Washington Post*, November 21, 1984.)

128

proposed that U.S. troop levels in Europe be cut by 90,000 (about one-third) by 1990, unless the Europeans either increase real defense spending growth to 3 percent or meet other logistical and force goals. The amendment was opposed by the Reagan administration and defeated, 55 to 41. Nunn's proposition is not a troop reduction, but a burden-sharing scheme. As he put it, "[Senator Mansfield's] goal was to get us out. Mine is to keep us in."[14]

Yet, in other terms, usually cited by those who support the present dispositions, our European allies appear to be paying the lion's share of the common costs of forces in Europe itself. A typical estimate has it that, "of the ready forces currently available in Europe, about 91 percent of the ground forces and 86 percent of the air forces come from European countries, as do 75 percent of NATO's tanks and more than 90 percent of its armored divisions."[15] Another reads: "If the Soviet Union were to launch an attack against Western Europe tomorrow, our NATO allies would provide 90 percent of the ground forces, 80 percent of the tanks and 75 percent of the naval and air units available to repulse the invasion."[16]

But comparing burdens is not the point, or the problem. The question has always been whether the United States is getting its own money's worth out of its forward strategy, and would be getting its money's worth even after some putative redistribution of burdens. Inevitably, we are thrown back on the economy of alliance. There are several ways of formulating this proposition. It may be that the actual costs of our preparations to support and implement the alliance, as such, exceed our gains, including as gains the benefits we derive from the contributions of allies. It may also be that in the ultimate calculus of war, the losses we would sustain through not defending forward are less than those we would incur through defending forward, even if successfully (and the value of both outcomes must be cut by their fractional probability, which is far less than certainty), plus the real costs we would have sustained in preparing to defend. And, in the encompassing calculus of deterrence, the future losses we might sustain by not even deterring attack or coercion against forward countries, reduced

[14]Quoted in Stephen S. Rosenfeld, "Putting a Test to Europe," *The Washington Post*, June 22, 1984.

[15]Stanley R. Sloan, *Defense Burden Sharing: U.S. Relations with NATO Allies and Japan* (Washington, D.C.: Congressional Research Service, July 8, 1983).

[16]Congressman Stephen J. Solarz, "To Buoy Europe's Defenses," *The New York Times*, January 10, 1983.

by the very low probability that such would occur because we failed to deter, might be less than the cumulative costs of deterrence. If we are assessing bargains, these more comprehensive and more complex calculations are the appropriate ones.

Yet another approach to mitigating America's burdens in NATO— a more far-reaching one—has been labeled "devolution." This scheme goes beyond mere shuffling of command slots and adjusting relative contributions. It comprises a deliberate, orderly, and militarily adequate effort by the United States to confer defensive capability and responsibility, including nuclear technology and the authority to use it, upon Western Europe. More than the other remedies, devolution is premised on European unity—political integration, beyond the French vision of a concert of independent national states (De Gaulle's "Europe des patries"). There would have to be a fit receptacle for the increased security capabilities and responsibilities. But even in the relatively unambitious sphere of finance and economy, the integration of the European states has not been impressive.

There is the more challenging question of combined military competence, particularly in nuclear arms. True, Britain and France have had national nuclear forces for several decades. But integrating and sharing nuclear deterrence is a problem that transcends the technicalities. There is not enough political trust between Paris and London, let alone between these capitals and Bonn, to create a truly effective (because truly common) nuclear force, not a mere bag of national nuclear forces. Simply adding up the damage potential of the several forces proves nothing. And just pooling peripheral technical, financial, and logistical items is not enough. True nuclear allies must share strategies, decision making, and targeting. The prospect of joint targeting particularly would produce mutual mistrust rather than mutual reliance, because of the lack of homogeneity of political will in the decision to strike targets or withhold fire. Even if it could be achieved, an independent European nuclear force, whether joint or a set of national nuclear forces, would be at best useless to the United States and at worst a considerable embarrassment.

Devolution combines aspects of commitment and decommitment, arraying them in a series of contradictions: The United States would have participation without authority, risk without control, involvement without the clear ability to defend, and exposure without adequate deterrence.

Another suggested approach to moderating the indefinite American

130

participation in Europe's defense involves a species of arms control: Mutual and Balanced Force Reductions (MBFR), a negotiated thinning-out of NATO and Warsaw Pact forces in Central Europe. Through five administrations, since the talks were endorsed by NATO in 1968 and initiated in Vienna in 1973, the prognosis for substantive agreement has remained dim. The approaches of the two sides have been incompatible. Essentially, NATO has insisted on unequal cuts, resulting in balanced opposing forces; the Warsaw Pact has insisted on equal cuts, resulting in unbalanced opposing forces. In June 1978, the Soviets apparently broke with their prior position and offered to set equal ceilings. But NATO immediately countered the Soviet offer by discovering or inventing the "data problem": the Soviets are unwilling to share intelligence about the starting figure for Warsaw Pact ground forces in the area, and Soviet admissions and NATO estimates differ by about 180,000. Moreover, it still appears that mutual force reductions will be defeated by the basic asymmetries of geography—the relative distances over which Soviet and American units would have to be reintroduced—and by the incommensurate types and functions of forces.

A further approach involves unilateral withdrawal of part of the American forces in Europe. The salient version of this approach was the Mansfield Amendment or Resolution, offered in Congress for eight years until 1975. This proposal, in its various forms, would have reduced American troops in Europe by as much as two-thirds, redeploying them to the United States but not (in all but one formulation) deleting them from the active force structure. But withdrawal of units saves nothing unless they are also deactivated. Nor would the Mansfield proposal have touched the forces kept in the United States *for* European contingencies. (Forces the United States keeps *in* Europe are only about one-third of the forces it maintains for the support of NATO.) Thus it would have made only a small dent in the amount, now $129 billion, that we are spending annually for the defense of Europe. Most significantly, our commitment to European defense would remain in full force. This is not a strength but a defect; the Mansfield type of initiative—centering on "troop reductions"—represents withdrawal without decommitment, a precarious stance.

Most versions of troop withdrawal are more trivial, some merely symbolic. An example was the amendment sponsored, in the fall of 1982, by Senator Ted Stevens (R-Ala.), chairman of the Senate Appropriations Subcommittee on Defense, that would have lowered the ceiling on our deployments in Europe in such a way as to return some 23,000 troops to the United States. But, as Morton H. Halperin said in rebuttal, it is cheaper to keep our troops in Europe.[17] But cheaper than what? Certainly it is cheaper than keeping our defensive commitment and just relocating our forces to the United States, providing even more prepositioned equipment in Europe and more airlift and sealift to return our forces there at the first sign of trouble. But it is not cheaper than absolving ourselves of the commitment, disbanding most of the forces we devote to it, and also saving the tactical air and surface naval units that go along with it. If we were to adopt such a non-protective attitude toward Europe, over a decade of progressive disengagement we could save half of the $2 trillion we are now committed to spend there, and at the end of that decade we would be spending three-quarters less than we will if we keep on our present course.

An Alternative Stance

Few realize how integral to our foreign policy stance has been the strategic paradigm of deterrence and alliance, or forward defense, that we have maintained for almost forty years—and therefore how much would have to change if we tried to achieve an alternative that would both allow lesser burdens and provide greater safety for Americans in an age of pervasive nuclear danger.

Implicit in a true alternative—a national strategy of disengagement—is the end of the American undertaking to defend Europe. But this is not to be equated with the current recriminations of America's isolationist—or, more accurately, unilateralist—hawks, who are simply disgusted with European neutralism, nuclear pacifism, anti-Americanism, commercial opportunism, and backsliding on defense spending promises.[18] These Americans threaten to dump Europe and shift our defense to the sea lanes and the Persian Gulf, but mostly to administer shock treatment to get the Europeans to come to their senses and make a larger and more docile contribution to an American defensive design. Such proposals proceed from motives that are not objectively strategic.

---

[17]"Keeping Our Troops in Europe," *The New York Times Magazine*, October 17, 1982.

[18]A cardinal example is Irving Kristol in such articles as "What's Wrong With NATO?" *The New York Times Magazine*, September 25, 1983, and in such a colloquy as "Should the U.S. Defend Europe?" *Harper's Magazine* (April 1984).

But the problem is a real one, not a kind of theater. There is a difference in geopolitical situation on the two sides of the Atlantic that leads inevitably to divergent strategic perspectives and preferences for different kinds of defense. Even understanding this problem from a European perspective will not change the policy orientations, let alone the underlying situations. The United States at least has the option of defending in the middle of the Atlantic. Europe, by definition, does not.

A thorough and consistent disengagement from Europe would shed the responsibilities as well as the burdens of alliance. The United States would devolve defensive tasks upon the European states, but not insist on the orderly and sufficient substitution of capabilities or harbor illusions of maintaining American political weight in European decision making. We would establish a measured and deliberate pace of disengagement and would maintain constructive consultation at all stages. Withdrawal from Europe would probably take a decade of preparation, diplomacy, and logistical rearrangement. But those are modalities, however important they may be. They would not alter the objective of scaling down our forces and setting temporal bounds on our commitment to European defense. We would progressively reduce Europe's strategic dependence on us and insulate ourselves from the consequences of conflict in Europe.

Most NATO loyalists mistake this criticism. One does not have to *urge* the dissolution of NATO, certainly not its instant and formal abrogation. NATO is an alliance that is less dependable year by year, as objective changes in circumstances erode the validity of the essential condition of the alliance: the American guarantee. Conversely, the loyalists should not take as compelling proof of the perpetual durability of the alliance the fact that something called "NATO" has not been formally repudiated. NATO can dissolve without a scrap of paper being torn up, without a journalist reporting it. NATO need not even perish in acrimony. It can expire in skepticism. The strategic content of the alliance can drain away, measured by the confidence allies repose in the ritual American commitment and by the hedges they erect against the guarantees the alliance still pretends to offer. NATO need not lose its form, at least until long after it has lost its substance.

Perhaps the situation can be summed up in a metaphor: NATO, after 36 years, is an old, unused medicine on the shelf. The bottle is still there and the label remains the same; but if you ever try to use it, you find that the contents have long since evaporated or spoiled.

War-Avoidance and Self-Reliance

It is important to reiterate that disengagement from the defense of Europe makes sense (or not) only as part of a broad alternative conception of a foreign policy and national strategy for the United States. Because the present and probable future states of the international system are more intractable than most critics consider them to be, and because our present capacity to meet the conditions of any of a number of interventionist strategies—even partial, "moderate," or "selective" ones—is much more inhibited than most critics understand, the resolution of our defense predicament and our fiscal dilemma suggests a more wholesale remedy.

An appropriate remedy would involve both strategic disengagement and a large-scale cut in defense spending. If we were to disengage, we could save on the order of $130 to $140 billion a year from current defense budgets. (Another $80 billion or more, to close the federal budgetary gap that looms each year for the rest of this decade at least, would have to come from stringent cuts in entitlements and other domestic programs.) But if we are to cut defense spending significantly, we must change our national strategies and our foreign policy. For the only way to save significant sums from the defense budget is to remove large, noticeable units from the force structure. And this would make it necessary, somewhere along the line, to reduce our defensive commitments in the world.

Specifically, both of the cardinal elements of the present American strategic paradigm would have to change. Instead of deterrence and alliance, we would pursue war-avoidance and self-reliance. Self-reliance is a response to (as well as a precipitant of) the dissolution of alliances, nuclear proliferation, and the practical demise of extended deterrence. Our military program would be designed to defend the most restricted perimeter required to protect our core values. Those core values are our political integrity and the safety of our citizens and their domestic property. However tangibly it is defined, that is a much smaller perimeter than the one we are now committed to defend. Precisely because America's stance in the world is essentially defensive, rather than aggressive and expansive, we would benefit from a compartmentalization of deadly quarrels between other nations. Compartmentalization must mean the delegation of defensive tasks to regional countries, and the

134

acceptance of the results of this, win or lose. We would, over time, accommodate the dissolution of defensive commitments, including NATO, that obligate us contingently to overseas intervention. The concomitant is that we would encourage other nations to hedge, to become self-reliant. In fact, other countries that are foresighted already discount American protection in a wide range of possible cases, despite our formal obligations to come to their assistance.

The other phase of our counter-paradigm, war-avoidance, is a response to the diffusion of power, the attainment of nuclear parity by the Soviet Union, and the risk of nuclear destruction to ourselves. It is based on the fact that we cannot any longer intricately and reliably manipulate or "manage" conflict. War-avoidance thus invokes primarily, though not exclusively, the strategic nuclear component of the counter-paradigm. We will always need a strategy that discourages direct nuclear attacks on our homeland, or intolerable coercion of our international political choices through nuclear threats. But today, given the parity between the nuclear arsenals of the two superpowers, our own safety depends on maintaining a condition that is called "crisis stability," where both sides have a strong incentive to avoid striking first with their nuclear weapons. A design for nuclear stability must include, among other elements, an *unconditional* doctrine of no-first-use of nuclear weapons. Thus, a *consistent* proposal of no-first-use of nuclear weapons—one that leads to war-avoidance—implies the dissolution of our defensive commitment to NATO.[19]

A Counter-Budget

The elements of the alternative policy and strategy that I propose—war-avoidance and self-reliance—are not mere rhetorical counters. They make real differences in forces and deployments,

[19]As we have discussed above, several of the most prominent recent proposals for no-first-use do not satisfy the requisites of a strategy of war-avoidance. The example we discussed at length was the proposal of McGeorge Bundy, George F. Kennan, Robert S. McNamara, and Gerard Smith. They raise, but do not dispose of, questions that go beyond tactical doctrine to the heart of extended deterrence. Correctly, they respond to their primary fear of the uncontrolled spread of nuclear war if we were to initiate it in Europe. But they complicate, and ultimately defeat, their own proposal by insisting on the integrity of the American defense of Western Europe against Soviet attack—that is, "coupling." For, unfortunately, it is the very fear of inevitable escalation of a local European conventional war to a global nuclear conflagration that constitutes the essential element in the coupling of our strategic nuclear arsenal to the local defense of our allies.

weapons and doctrines, defense budgets and manpower requirements. We could defend our essential security and our central values with a much smaller force structure than we now have. Such a force structure would provide the following general purpose forces: 8 land divisions (6 army and 2 marine), 20 tactical air wing equivalents (11 air force, 4 marine, and 5 navy), and 6 carrier battle groups. With the addition of a diad of nuclear forces, submarines and cruise-missile-armed bombers, this would mean manpower of 1,185,000 men (army 370,000, air force 315,000, navy 365,000, marine corps 135,000). The total defense budget at the end of a decade of adjustment would be about $154 billion in 1985 dollars. In contrast, the Reagan administration's requested authorization for 1985 is 20 land divisions and 44 tactical air wing equivalents, with 13 carrier battle groups; it requires 2,166,000 men and $305 billion.

One does not need a micrometer to measure those differences, and they will multiply enormously if we do not change our course. The way we are headed, the defense budget will be close to $700 billion by 1994, and cumulative defense spending during those ten years will be $4.8 trillion. Under a non-interventionist policy, the 1994 defense budget would be two-thirds less and the cumulative cost over ten years would be $2.6 trillion.

The savings from our present European spending, over a decade, would amount to an even larger fraction than the savings from the overall defense budget, since Atlantic-oriented forces constitute only 27 percent of my alternative defense program, compared with European-oriented forces of about 42 percent in the present defense program. Cumulatively, over ten years, instead of spending $2 trillion on NATO, we would have spent only $900 billion. At the end of a decade of adjustment, there would be no American forces in Europe; but in and around the United States, oriented toward the Atlantic, there would be 3⅓ divisions (3 army divisions and a marine brigade), 7⅔ tactical air wing equivalents (5 air force; ⅓ marine, which is equal to ⅔; and 2 navy), and 3 carrier battle groups.

Taking Threats Seriously

Because I propose a more restrained national strategy, with smaller forces and defense budgets, that does not mean that I take "the threat" as trivial or non-existent. Other kinds of critics may have to rely on creative negligence of the actions of the Soviet Union because the logic of their argument is that *if* the Russians were really up to something, we would need to rearm to the teeth. On the contrary, the essence of a true non-interventionist position, both historically and logically, is that it takes threats seriously. But it accepts some foreign damage, for fundamental reasons that have to do with preserving the integrity of our political, social, and economic system from the kinds of distorted effort and misguided control that proceed from unbalanced assessments of and responses to external challenge.

There are other kinds of answers, though they will not be absolutely and universally satisfying.

First, it is well to keep in mind that the alleged unfavorable consequences of disengagement that we should examine are not so much the immediate ones as the ultimate effects on basic American values—the integrity of our constitutional system, the safety of our lives and domestic property, the health of our economy, and the quality of our life. The possibility that we would have to confront a final threat to these basic values is very remote. Surely it is not the contingent certainty (1.0 probabililty) conjured up by those who fear any departure from the status quo. In short, the threat must be progressively *discounted*.

A second way of treating the threat is to consider our principal adversary, the Soviet Union. Of course, it is the action and potential action of the Soviet Union that drives almost all categories of our defense effort. So it is well to take seriously the facts of Soviet state and leadership. But such sobriety in itself neither disposes the factual determination nor dictates the policy conclusions. Odd as it may seem, there is no necessary connection between taking threats seriously and doing something about them. We could even grant most of the evidence of the hawks and still argue for non-intervention. The task is to assess the Soviet threat, not just factually, but logically, to see what connection might run, from Soviet politics and Russian character and Marxist ideology, to pressures on our regional allies and strategic points, to imputed danger to our own territory, people, property, and way of life, and finally, to some indicated American response. This approach does not deny the facts, but envelops them in a comprehensive *context* of logic and action.

For example, a recent tendency among critics is to denigrate the quality of the Soviet armed forces. An example of this is Andrew Cockburn.[20] Cockburn's research tells him that Soviet equipment is

[20]*The Threat: Inside the Soviet Military Machine* (New York: Random House, 1983).

crude, unsafe, and short on creature comforts, and that Soviet troops are sullen and unresponsive. Presumably, the size of Soviet forces, the multiplicity of equipment, and the magnitude of military spending are explained as compensations for deficient quality and dubious reliability. But such reportage can lead to some unwarranted predictive generalizations as well as to some tenuous policy conclusions. It is an unreliable and even dangerous basis for the obvious but superficial conclusion that the West could maintain the *same* level of military containment with fewer resources and less risk.

Another common interpretive point is that the positive aspects of Soviet military capabilities are considerably offset by the disabilities of the larger Soviet system: retarded economic growth, inefficiency and malinvestment, agricultural failures, and the rest of the familiar litany, including external factors as well.

What is the proper response of the United States to the opportunities these weaknesses might afford? Who is correct: the optimistic hawks, such as, during the Carter administration, Zbigniew Brzezinski and Samuel Huntington and, in the first Reagan administration, Richard Pipes and Richard Perle, who say that this is a time to press the Soviets hard, ideologically, politically, even militarily; or the optimistic doves, who say that we have nothing to worry about, since the Soviets are inhibited from projecting power abroad and have little stomach for external conquest?

The practical issue is linkage. As Nixon and Kissinger used to put it, linkage is "a fact of life." We have adversaries and competitors who have capabilities and ambitions as well as vulnerabilities and needs. Linkage supplies the intellectual connection and possibly also the program. But, although we can agree that linkages do exist in fact and in perception, we might do better to act if they did not. That is, we should compartmentalize areas of conflict and areas of bargaining in order to solve problems separately, on their own terms and on their own merits.

In any case, it is tenuous to speculate about alternative explanations for every element of Soviet strength, every troubling Soviet move. The general lesson that emerges is that detailed intelligence is not decisive. The problem is not one of knowledge as such— trying to achieve an authentic explanation of the motives of the Soviet leaders, and to make reliable predictions of their behavior. Rather, it is a problem of action—our action.

What ultimately matters is not putative threats but necessary responses. Beyond the simple fact of an adversary's pressure on another country is the connection our leaders forge between that disturbing fact and a "necessary" American military response. This connection is not itself a fact; it is a construct of our own discovery and devising. Thus it could be cut by the adoption of a different "major premise" of our action. Ultimately, the debate about the Soviet threat is not a question of facts, or even interpretation of facts, but a choice of responses and a choice of logics.

Europe without America

A third kind of answer to the doubts that follow upon American disengagement is a demonstration that Europe by itself has a strong basis for self-defense and therefore a good probability of deterrence.

The least likely, though most obvious, scenario is a calculated large-scale Soviet invasion of Western Europe. A more plausible challenge is that the withdrawal of the American presence might lay Western Europe open to Soviet influence and pressure—that because of its sense of impotence and exposure, Western Europe would lose its will and become malleable to Soviet manipulation. This is what is meant by "Finlandization." This possibility is a derivative of the ability of the Soviet Union to apply direct military pressure, and its analysis follows the same lines as the rejoinder to that other asserted threat.

True, Finlandization, and even more intensive satellization, have occurred in cases marked by special circumstances. (Finland itself is a sparsely populated nation, about 4.8 million people in all; it was a co-belligerent of Germany in World War II, and had been a duchy in the Russian empire for more than a century before 1917.) The real question is, does the model of Finlandization apply with all its force to a large, populous, rich, industrially capable, socially whole, politically resolute country, with a military force that would have far more than nuisance value—a country, in short, such as West Germany? It is hardly likely. Unlike direct attack, Finlandization takes two: a willing victim as well as a determined aggressor.

What would America's principal European allies do in the event of our disengagement? Their options range from (1) acquiring national nuclear forces, to (2) improving their conventional defenses, (3) forging a new European military community, (4) adopting unconventional defensive strategies (often suggested are forms of territorial defense or mobilization on the Swedish, Yugoslavian, Swiss, or Israeli models, or even less orthodox strategies of denial or attrition), (5) doing all or several of the above, or (6) none. Each nation, according to its external and internal situation, would adopt some combination of moves. It is far from certain that West Germany would independently go nuclear; that would worsen its position not only with the Soviet Union but also with its Western European partners. And since the aim of disengagement is not to shock or punish, the United States would not withdraw its forces, or even its commitment, precipitately. There would be time for European countries to deliberate, plan, and act.

Were Western Europe to coalesce, not only in a military compact but in a sort of federal union, it could become the second most powerful entity in the world—in theory more powerful than the Soviet Union (and in a few respects even more than the United States). Even now, Western Europe has greater population (372 million), more ample economic potential ($2.6 trillion in gross national product), about the same area of military manpower (over 3.1 million), a respectably competitive military technology, and the reckonable nuclear forces of Britain and France. Europe's aggregate defense spending, however, is markedly inferior ($83 billion).[21]

In any case, we do not need the premise of European unity and collective military superiority or equivalence to argue for American disengagement (as opposed to devolution, criticized above). The proposals of military analysts (including the quick fixes mentioned above, such as restructuring forces, adding equipment, and revising tactical doctrines, mobilization plans, and particularly reserve arrangements), though they are designed to improve NATO so it would be bearable for the United States to perpetuate its commitment, ironically hold possibilities for Western European conventional defense without the United States. First of all, a Soviet attack might encounter some problems that we do not clearly see now: Confronted by a thick NATO anti-tank defense, including the natural

[21]In this calculation I include the European NATO countries (including France) and Spain, but exclude Austria, Ireland, Sweden, and Switzerland. Figures are derived from *The Military Balance, 1984–1985* (London: International Institute for Strategic Studies, 1984). They are generally from 1983, a few from 1982. By comparison, the figures for the superpowers are: population, United States 237 million, Soviet Union 274 million; gross national product, United States $3.3 trillion, Soviet Union $1.6 trillion; military manpower, United States 2.1 million, Soviet Union 3.6 million (excluding 1.5 million command and general support troops); and defense spending, United States $239 billion, Soviet Union $308 billion (a figure that seems, for some reason, at the very high end of the range).

tank traps of wall-to-wall urbanization and parallel rivers, an attacking Soviet armored force could not push to the Rhine in three days, as the professional alarmists would have it. If the Germans chose to defend tenaciously, the Russians might have to halt and reduce each city by artillery and dismounted infantry assault, block by block. Also, the most convincing proposals for strengthening NATO *overshoot* the mark. If NATO forces have had weaknesses that are just beginning to be addressed (they are maldeployed, stretched thin, immobile, wrongly configured, badly integrated), and further, if the Warsaw Pact countries could have achieved their present military advantages from inferior production and manpower bases and from weaker economic and social systems, then it is not fanciful to imagine that the Western European countries—together or even powerful ones such as West Germany individually—if they were to make the most of their assets, could generate self-reliant military forces that would be adequate for defense and so also for deterrence.[22]

Values

Among NATO loyalists, when the question of American disengagement is broached, the automatic rejoinder is that we could not tolerate the loss of Western Europe, that shared values—cultural, political, social, economic—form both the basis of our attachment and the ultimate justification for our continued defensive support. Indeed, these loyalists argue (in an exercise of circular reasoning), our support itself is a value, something of transcendent moral worth beyond any calculus of net utility. Simply posing the question of values is supposed to imply its resolution in a particular way. Those who would challenge the existing relationship between the United States and Europe stand accused of gross negligence—even gratuitous destruction—of the rich network of ties that binds Americans to Europeans.

It is difficult—in a way, impossible—to answer such objections.

---

[22]Admittedly, in resorting selectively to the arguments of Steven Canby and others who have written compellingly, I am taking them in a direction that they would not follow. Certainly they do not argue for American disengagement. But their arguments could be enlisted to support such a strategy. See, for example, Canby's recent studies: "Military Reform and the Art of War," *Survival* (May–June 1983); a forthcoming work on emerging technology in the defense of NATO, skeptical of its promise; and, with Ingemar Dörfer, "More Troops, Fewer Missiles," *Foreign Policy* (Winter 1983–84).

For one thing, they are usually couched in generalities and frankly emotive terminology.[23] The purpose of replying, then, must be to say something about the structure of the issue and the logic of the non-interventionist position.

It should be recognized at the beginning that no argument about values is whole, or even clear, unless it is stated from the vantage point of some subject. Whether right or wrong, my argument is a view from the United States. If I were in the situation of a European, I might well "feel deeply disturbed" at American proposals either of no-first-use of nuclear weapons or of more extensive disengagement from the defense of Europe. But that is just the point: it is objective differences in their situations that dispose nations toward different ultimate decisions. Americans are faced with an increasingly demarcated choice between their own safety and the "salvation" of Europe. It is an option for Americans to pursue their own safety at the expense of European protection. That option is not available to Europeans. They must understand that these things are so by fact and definition, not by an author's device.

For the United States, there is, at best, a *tradeoff* of values; indeed, NATO loyalists do not realize what they are comparing, or even that there is something to compare. On one side, there is the minuscule risk of losing part of Western Europe to an opportunistic Soviet attack if we seemed unlikely to defend it. On the other side, there is the equally minuscule—but not fictitious—risk of the nuclear death of our own country, and possibly of civilization, if we joined in deterrence and deterrence were to fail. The only strategic sequence that could plausibly lead to such a dire result would be through the Atlantic alliance. Only absolute faith in the efficacy of deterrence (which, in theory, makes both eventualities—a Soviet attack on Europe and our own nuclear destruction—impossible) allows NATO loyalists to deny their implicit preference for nuclear annihilation. No one has a monopoly of values.

Almost invariably, when one critically or skeptically reviews America's strategic relationship to Europe and its commitment to defend Europe, people accuse him of "proposing" to dismantle

---

[23]An example is a letter to the editor of the *Bulletin of the Atomic Scientists* (September 1984) by Peter Schenkel, a citizen of West Germany, in response to my article, "No First Use: A View From the United States" in that journal in April 1984. Among other things, the correspondent would re-label my article "A View From the Soviet Union." I quote from Schenkel's letter in a few places below.

NATO, and consequently want to know why he would "want" to do such a thing. One might be tempted to reply that such proposals are no longer so rare as to imply a special animus or an aberrant train of thought. American isolationists of the right (one might dare to call them) have, in the last several years, made the attenuation of America's relationship to Europe, if not exactly respectable, at least not unspeakable or unimaginable. One has only to recall William Safire's pungent formulas: "The time is coming for an independent European defense. . . . 'Wayward sisters, depart in peace,' Horace Greeley told the seceding states. As Western Europeans turn inward, the U.S. should wish them well and look to its own vital interests." And this: "This scenario [of invoking American nuclear protection] is not hooked up to reality. . . . We would pull the biggest Dunkirk history ever saw. . . . The winds of change are growing, in Harold Macmillan's phrase, and will blow our forces homeward. The Europeans will have to choose: to come up with their own conventional defense, or to risk their birthright." (And Safire proceeds to outline a Franco-German axis of defense, a "new Gaullism.")[24]

Yet I would not want my remarks to be taken as a pure prescription for American withdrawal from the Atlantic alliance. Such a characterization would miss the point and misrepresent the tone of my argument. In short, I am not entirely "proposing." I could do so, but that would be incidental. Instead, a critic such as I is a messenger. Specifically, he is delivering a road map—a decision-tree, if you will (which, in a sense, is what a road map is). The critic insists only that the recipient see the structure of the problem. To kill the messenger is a response that is venerable, but not therefore less painful or more respectable.

[24]"NATO After Grenada," *The New York Times,* November 13, 1983; and "Winds of Change," *The New York Times,* April 2, 1984. The former German chancellor Helmut Schmidt has also sponsored such a "Franco-German security initiative," though not as a total substitute for American forces and the American nuclear guarantee; Schmidt's proposed joint defense, calling for a conventional force of 30 French and German divisions as well as the extension of French nuclear protection over Germany, is designed to raise the nuclear threshold and relieve some American troops (speech to the Bundestag, June 28, 1984). For other American remarks that are reserved or skeptical about NATO, see the references to Irving Kristol, above.

VIII. An Agenda for Regulatory Reform

Thomas Gale Moore

The challenge of the next four years in the area of regulatory reform is to move from administrative action and rhetoric to concrete congressional action. Without legislative changes in the statutes controlling the regulatory agencies, long-term improvements in the regulatory structure are impossible. Over the last four years, the Reagan administration has attempted a number of administrative reforms, but many have been struck down by court decisions. In some cases the law as enacted by Congress has also frustrated such administrative changes. Regulatory reform, therefore, should be given the highest priority by the new administration.

While a case can be made for changing virtually every regulatory statute, by either abolishing regulation or altering it to secure appropriate goals at minimum cost, several regulatory structures stand out as extremely costly to the economy and well-being of the United States. This chapter will focus on the most important regulatory issues facing the administration and Congress in the next four years.

Two regulatory reforms are especially needed. According to a study done for the Business Roundtable,[1] the single most costly regulatory statute is the Clean Air Act (CAA) and its amendments. Not only is that program costly, but it fails to achieve its goal of improving the quality of the air we breathe. A second vital reform should be the abolition of the regulation of natural gas. The current regulatory structure is making gas more scarce, inevitably driving up the price to consumers and making the United States less secure strategically. Other important areas of regulatory reform concern automobiles, transportation, communications, banking, and food and drugs. Each of these topics will be treated briefly below. However, the reader should realize that there are many other sectors in

---

[1]Arthur Andersen & Co., *Cost of Government Regulation,* Study for the Business Roundtable, Executive Summary (March 1979).

need of regulatory reform; only lack of space precludes their inclusion here.

The Clean Air Act

Federal legislation dealing with air pollution dates back to 1963, when the Clean Air Act gave the Department of Health, Education, and Welfare some authority to prosecute industrial polluters if the states failed to do so themselves. The act was strengthened somewhat in 1967, but it was not until amendments were added to it in 1970 that the federal government was authorized to set nationwide standards and to require the states to implement them. At that time the Environmental Protection Agency (EPA) was established and given five years to reduce air pollution to federal standards.

The CAA amendments (especially those of 1977) have converted legislation initially designed to improve the quality of the air into a regional and obsolete facilities protection act. At a monetary cost estimated by the Commerce Department to have been over $27 billion for 1982,[2] nearly half of total spending on environmental protection, the act and its amendments have also been very expensive.

Though very costly, the effectiveness of the air pollution controls, especially for non-automotive pollution sources, has been questioned. One knowledgeable observer concluded: "In its first twelve years the EPA *may* have reduced stationary-source emissions, but the extent of this reduction and its impact on air quality cannot be assessed from current data."[3] While there has been a decline in measured pollutants in major cities over this period, it is not necessarily attributable to EPA restrictions. The cities also experienced a decline in population and a sharp rise in fuel prices that decreased the use of fossil fuels—factors that should, by themselves, have led to a reduction in air pollutants. Moreover, most evidence actually suggests a faster rate of decline in air pollution in the decade prior to the enactment of the 1970 CAA amendments, as compared with the period since then.

The original act with its amendments requires the EPA to establish national ambient air standards for particulates, carbon monoxide, sulfur oxides, nitrogen dioxide, hydrocarbons, oxidants, and

[2]*Survey of Current Business* 64 (February 1984): 24–25.

[3]Robert W. Crandall, *Controlling Industrial Pollution: The Economics and Politics of Clean Air* (Washington, D.C.: The Brookings Institution, 1983), p. 31 (my italics).

lead. Primary standards are to be set, according to Congress, to protect the health of the most sensitive groups in the population. This requirement, taken literally, probably means that all emissions should be banned—shutting down American industry. There is no known safe level of pollutants; conversely, there is little evidence that existing levels of pollutants are harmful to the health of most individuals. To the extent that oppressive air pollution is a health hazard, it shortens the lives of those with severe respiratory problems, mainly the sick and elderly.

The country is divided into 247 air quality control regions, which are in turn designated "attainment" regions or, for those areas that do not meet CAA standards, "nonattainment" regions. For the attainment regions, which are rural areas and major portions of the Southwest, Congress established the policy of preventing any significant reduction in air quality, even if such reduction would leave the resultant air still within federal ambient standards. This policy results in much greater expense for firms moving major facilities out of the "frost belt" and into the usually cleaner air of the "sun belt." Such moves would reduce air pollution in congested areas and, as long as the national ambient standards were met, would mean lower costs and more efficient production.

Moreover, the CAA and its amendments stipulate that any new source of pollutants in attainment regions must use the "best available control technology" (BACT). They also require firms installing such technology to provide detailed environmental impact statements proving that the new facilities will not lead to a significant deterioration in air quality. Plants in nonattainment areas, for their part, must employ technology that achieves the "lowest achievable emission rate" (LAER). There is little difference in practice between this standard and BACT.

A great controversy has swirled over the meaning of the word "source." During the Carter administration, the EPA defined "source" for attainment regions as a *whole plant,* and "source" for nonattainment regions as *any point* of emission. In instances where a whole plant was defined as a source, firms could offset higher emissions of pollutants from one portion of the plant by lower emissions from another, reaping large savings in expenditures. This "bubble" concept, however, could not be applied in nonattainment regions.

The Reagan administration attempted to redefine "source" in nonattainment regions as the whole plant, thus producing a uniform definition and permitting the use of the bubble throughout the United States. After a legal battle that went as far as the Supreme Court the new definition finally prevailed, and the EPA is now implementing the bubble concept at the plant level. Extending that concept beyond the plant to whole air quality regions, an even more cost-effective procedure, is more difficult and cumbersome, however. The EPA does permit states (which actually do the regulating) to allow firms to trade off decreases in emissions from one facility for increases in another plant or for emissions from a new plant. However, the administrative cost is high and permission is not always granted.

One of the most costly aspects of the CAA amendments is their bias against new facilities. As mentioned above, such sources must meet very rigid technological standards. Moreover, in the case of new "fossil-fuel-fired stationary sources" the law requires in effect that flue-gas scrubbers be installed regardless of the sulfur content of the fuel. On the other hand, old facilities, even fossil-fuel-fired stationary sources, are required only to meet lower state standards or to comply with EPA-set "reasonable available control technology" (RACT) guidelines—both of which are much cheaper. For example, EPA estimates that the costs of meeting the new source standards for electric power are about 10 times more than the costs of meeting the standards set for existing plants. In the steel industry, the cost of meeting air pollution standards for a new source is 2 to 15 times as expensive as continuing to operate an old, higher-pollutant facility.

The requirement that all fossil-fuel-fired stationary sources use scrubbers is a blatant attempt to protect the jobs of miners of high-sulfer coal, who are located mainly in the Midwest and Appalachian regions. Low-sulfur coal from the West would be a cheaper alternative for power companies and consumers; it would also produce less air pollution! Such protection comes, therefore, at the expense of electricity users and of clean air.

Regulations should reduce emissions of pollutants, but at the lowest possible costs. The current clean-air law and its administration fail to satisfy this simple cost-effectiveness principle. For example, the cost to reduce particulates in the utility sector has been estimated at $36 to $680 per ton removed, while the cost to remove a ton from a coke oven may be as much as $30,880.[4] Consequently, if regulations permitted a coke oven to emit one additional ton of

[4]Crandall, p. 35.

particulates in exchange for a corresponding reduction from power plants, the resource savings would be over $30,000 for each ton so treated. (Actually, as additional trades were made, the gain would diminish. The cost of reducing particulates in power plants would rise while savings from allowing more particulates in coke ovens would fall.)

Correcting the biases described above is complex and politically difficult. Implementing a regional system of trading in emission rights is likewise complicated. Moreover, the unfortunate politicization of environmental issues that developed in the first term of the Reagan administration makes solutions more difficult to achieve and explain to the public.

Clearly, the elimination of the requirement that all stationary systems use scrubbers is desirable. Regulations should focus instead on the quantity of pollutants emitted. Thus a firm could choose to substitute low-sulfur coal or to organize its plant differently or to install a scrubber—whichever would achieve the objective of low emissions at the lowest possible cost. The law should, in addition, be rewritten to encourage the use of the bubble concept, not only for single plants but for entire air quality regions. A market for pollution rights could then be established in which, for example, a coke oven owner could purchase from a utility the right to emit a fixed amount of particulates. The utility and the coke oven would then adjust their emissions accordingly. The General Accounting Office (GAO) has concluded that such a market approach would reduce costs by some 40 to 90 percent.[5] This would permit either large savings in resources or more stringent standards and cleaner air at the same costs.

It is clear that the CAA should be amended to eliminate bias against new facilities. Such bias slows economic growth, makes American industry less efficient, and actually lowers air quality. To eliminate it the statute must be amended to put old and new plants on the same statutory footing. However, because of the difficulty inherent in reducing emissions from old plants and the political problem of closing such facilities if they fail to meet stricter guidelines, uniform standards should be phased in only gradually.

Finally, the treatment of attainment regions should be altered to

[5]U.S. General Accounting Office, *A Market Approach to Air Pollution Control Could Reduce Compliance Costs Without Jeopardizing Clean Air Goals* (Washington, D.C.: U.S. Government Printing Office, 1982), p. ii.

permit new plants to be built in such sections. While such sensitive zones as national parks and wilderness areas should be protected from undue degradation, there should be no prohibition against new plants in other attainment regions. Scientists recognize that the environment can safely dispose of a certain amount of pollutants; indeed, it already handles much natural pollution in this manner. Those areas of the country that more than meet ambient air standards hence could process more emissions without harm to society, leading to an increase in economic growth. New facilities, therefore, should not be required to meet stricter standards than elsewhere; in fact, requirements should be considerably lighter in places where new facilities would not degrade the air below federal standards.

Natural Gas Regulation

The federal government has had legal control over the price of natural gas since 1954, when the Supreme Court ruled that the Federal Power Commission must regulate prices at the wellhead. Strict bureaucratic control, however, was not imposed until the 1960s. From that period, prices for this clean, efficient fuel, which had been increasing rapidly with growing demand, have been kept below a free market level. As any student in an elementary economics course could have predicted, shortages resulted. Reserves that would have lasted 19 years at 1964 rates of production fell to 8.5 years of annual production by 1977. With the rapid escalation of world energy prices during the 1970s, U.S natural gas prices dropped so low compared with the prices of other energy sources that the shortfall became acute, resulting in short-term fuel cutoffs for some schools, factories, and communities.

The temporary gas shortages led an alarmed Congress to enact the National Gas Policy Act (NGPA) in 1978. This highly complex act provided for immediate deregulation of "deep gas" (gas found more than 15,000 feet below the surface). It also provided for a gradual increase in the prices of "new gas" and a large portion of older intrastate gas, and scheduled total decontrol of these categories for January 1, 1985. Other "old gas" would continue to be controlled until supplies were exhausted. At the time the act was written prices of new natural gas were programmed to escalate to meet an expected world oil price of $15 a barrel. With today's oil prices now at about $29 a barrel, there is growing apprehension that natural gas prices will jump significantly in 1985. Even if decontrol were permitted to take place as scheduled by NGPA, some 40 percent of production would still be subject to controls. At best, therefore, deregulation is only partial.

Regulation of natural gas prices has several serious economic effects. First, low prices reduce the amount of gas discovered, developed, and marketed. The result is that (a) we are more dependent on unstable Middle East suppliers and thus less secure strategically; and (b) our utilities and factories burn more coal as an alternative fuel, with a concomitant increase in air pollution and mine fatalities. Second, low prices also (a) encourage consumers to squander a scarce resource; (b) attenuate economic growth as a consequence of differential pricing and inefficient resource utilization; and (c) inevitably increase the fraud and waste associated with a controlled market system.

The objective of maintaining controls over old gas is to keep consumer prices down. Proponents argue that higher prices are necessary only to stimulate the search for new or expensive gas; existing gas fields will continue to produce whether higher prices are allowed or not. Decontrol, they contend, will simply enrich oil companies and owners of gas wells. The truth of the matter is quite different, however. While higher prices are indeed necessary to induce more exploration and drilling for new gas, they also provide an incentive to stimulate production from existing wells. The higher the price, the more that producers will invest to increase their current output. Consequently, continuing controls over old wells alone diminishes the amount of natural gas produced. Smaller supplies, in turn, prompt energy users to substitute dirtier and more dangerous fuels such as oil and coal.

Another undesirable feature of such price control is greater waste. The lower prices of the regulated market lead consumers to burn more gas than they would if prices were higher. Inexpensive fuel tempts consumers to overheat their homes, to let the hot water run wastefully, and to utilize gas in careless disregard for its relative scarcity. Conversely, high prices inspire conservation.

The problem of wasteful use is compounded by the creation of a variety of regulated gas prices. Until the end of 1984, only deep gas is uncontrolled. Some buyers have paid over $9 per thousand cubic feet (mcf) for deep gas, while the average price of that high-cost fuel has come down from nearly $7.50 at the end of 1981 to around $5.25 by mid-1984.[6] In comparison, the average price of all natural

[6]Energy Information Center, Department of Energy.

gas, less than $2.50 per mcf in 1982, is now (mid-1984) about $2.75. If deep gas can command, say, $7.00 per mcf, producers will invest up to $7.00 to obtain it. Thus consumers who pay under $3.00 at the wellhead are buying gas that took nearly $7.00 to produce. They are also utilizing it at the faster rate made possible by the unnaturally low price. In fact, in the absence of regulation, which permits gas pipelines to average high-cost gas with low-cost and to charge the consumer for the mixture, little if any of this deep gas would be produced at present. It would be stockpiled for future use, and more economical sources of energy would be exploited.

Moreover, as more deep gas is produced and less cheap old gas is available in the future, the average price of gas will go up—defeating the purpose of regulation, which is to keep consumer prices down. With partial decontrol these problems are only compounded. Because gas from old wells is still subject to price control, some relatively low-cost gas is not profitable and hence is not produced. At the same time, to meet the needs of the public, pipelines buy somewhat higher-cost new natural gas. The result is that the average price of gas could, under continued controls, become as high as or even higher than its price under no controls.

Therefore, in 1985 the administration should move toward total deregulation of natural gas. Partial decontrol would produce inefficiencies and might even fail to hold prices below a free market level. Removing all controls would produce the most gas in the shortest period of time, swiftly reducing our dependence on foreign suppliers.

If gas were decontrolled now, its price would rise to roughly equal that of substitute energy sources. Nearly half of the natural gas produced in this country is used in the industrial sector, and about one-third of U.S. gas is burned in industrial boilers that can employ either gas or fuel oil. With residual fuel oil selling for the equivalent of approximately $4.60 per mcf and with the cost of transporting gas from the wellhead to the utilities roughly $1.00, the price of gas would probably settle somewhere between $3.00 and $4.00 per mcf. If controls were lifted, the price increase at the wellhead might be as much as 30 percent, but the boost to consumers would only be about 16 percent, since transportation, distribution, and marketing costs would not be affected. However, the American Gas Association, which advocates continued controls, estimates that decontrol would increase wellhead prices by only 13 percent, and the price to consumers by 11 percent.[7] At all events, any price increase would probably be temporary. Without controls, more gas would be produced and the increased supply would eventually bring the price down.

Even if prices did increase for a longer period, however, several important benefits would result. Conservation would be spurred. Sales of fuel oil would diminish, decreasing oil imports and thus threatening the tenability of the OPEC cartel. Even the taxpayer would benefit, for producers would pay a portion of their added earnings to the government in taxes. Because our resources would be employed more efficiently, and because energy supplies ultimately would become more plentiful and cheaper, economic growth would be fostered. Decontrol would thus be highly beneficial to our economy.

Finally, because the wealthy consume more energy and gas than the poor, decontrol would affect the rich more than anyone else. Indeed, the poor would benefit from the economic growth spurred by decontrol. The appropriate policy to take toward those who cannot purchase such necessities of life as fuel, housing, and food is to provide more income, not to hold down for the sake a small minority the price of a product that everyone buys.

That being the case, the new administration should assign a high priority to removing the vestiges of natural gas regulation. We have suffered from these controls long enough. It is important for our national security to minimize our dependence on foreign energy sources. Decontrolling natural gas would spur domestic production, reduce imports, and foster conservation.

Automobile Regulation

Starting in the mid-1960s with the introduction of federal regulation of exhaust pollutants, federal controls of the automobile industry have been extended to encompass safety, fuel efficiency, and sales practices. The motor vehicle industry is one of the most regulated in the country.

There is good economic justification for controlling automobile emissions. No manufacturer would voluntarily attach pollution control devices to its cars, for such devices add cost and make a vehicle perform less well. Moreover, no consumer would

[7]"Historical and Projected Natural Gas Prices: 1983 Update" (Washington, D.C.: American Gas Association, November 1983).

153

voluntarily purchase a vehicle that produces less pollutants, for the effect of one car's emissions on the air—and hence on the health of the individual consumer—is negligible. As a result, although emission controls would, in fact, be beneficial to everyone, the market cannot provide for such controls. Consequently, regulation does make sense.

However, there is good reason to believe that the standards for exhaust control devices are too strict. The 1965 standards, which came into effect for the 1968 model year, reduced hydrocarbon emissions by 28 percent and carbon monoxide by 44 percent. These standards added little to the cost of a new car. In 1975–76 the federal standard was tightened to reduce the allowable emission by 6.7 grams per mile of hydrocarbons (45 percent), 75 grams per mile for carbon monoxide (83 percent), and 0.3 grams per mile for nitrogen oxides (9 percent) from uncontrolled levels. It has been estimated that this reduction cost $728 per car (1984 dollars). In 1981, standards were tightened again, requiring a further reduction of 1.09 grams per mile of hydrocarbons (7 percent), 11.6 grams of carbon monoxide (13 percent); and 2.1 grams of nitrogen oxides (62 percent). The additional cost of these much smaller reductions is estimated at about $864.[8]

Whether the benefits of the 1981 standards over those of 1975–76 are worth the extra cost is an open question. There is little evidence that typical levels of these pollutants even in the most polluted urban centers of the United States have significantly detrimental effects on health. Hydrocarbons, together with nitrogen oxides, do form photochemical smog and ozone that can cause discomfort and reduce visibility. Health dangers from pollutants are more generally attributable to particulates and sulfates. Auto exhaust is only a minor source of the latter. Particulates, mainly in the form of lead components, were not controlled in automobile emissions until 1981, and the first actual reduction in particulate emissions is not scheduled to take place until 1985. However, lead particulates have already been reduced with the use of unleaded gas in new cars. The benefits of the 1981 program may be summarized as follows:

> Some mild adverse effects on health have surely been prevented for some sensitive individuals. The degradation of visibility in

[8]Lawrence J. White, *The Regulation of Air Pollutant Emissions from Motor Vehicles* (Washington, D.C.: American Enterprise Institute, 1982), pp. 4, 15, 61.

154

areas with photochemical smog has been moderated, and some damage to agricultural crops and other vegetation may have been avoided.[9]

It would thus appear that the tight 1981 standards are probably unwarranted from the standpoint of health, providing benefits only in a few places such as Los Angeles where smog is a major problem. Since much of the country is largely free of smog problems, and since little permanent harm results from smog even where it is a problem, there is good reason to relax auto emissions standards.

In addition to regulating emissions, the federal government now prescribes vehicle safety standards. While there is an argument for requiring good brakes, adequate headlights, turn signals, and so on to protect innocent second parties, the case for protecting driver and passenger is less evident. Moreover, there is no justification for regulations whose purpose is to guard against property damage, such as standards for bumpers. Clearly, auto purchasers should make their own decisions concerning the importance of stronger bumpers.

The best justification for requiring safer cars is that society today bears the cost, to some extent, of medical care for people injured in auto accidents. On the other hand, there is evidence that drivers who feel safer drive with less care, causing more accidents and hurting more pedestrians. As a consequence, part of the reduction in mortality that results from safer vehicles is offset by additional mortality among pedestrians and other drivers.

A major dispute in recent years has focused on the desirability of imposing mandatory automatic restraints in automobiles. The insurance lobby has been advocating airbags for all vehicles, while auto manufacturers have bitterly opposed such requirements. Early in the past administration, the government rescinded a rule imposed by the Carter administration requiring mandatory restraints. After the Supreme Court held that the Reagan administration had acted arbitrarily, the Department of Transportation (DOT) undertook a careful review of all evidence. In July 1984 DOT ruled that unless states containing two-thirds of the total U.S. population enact mandatory seat-belt use laws, all vehicles manufactured for sale after September 1, 1989 (the beginning of the 1990 model year) would have to contain automatic restraints to protect the driver and

[9]Ibid., p. 58.

frontseat passenger. Ten percent of each manufacturer's cars for the 1987 model year must meet this standard; for 1988, 25 percent; and for 1989, 40 percent.

According to DOT data, lap and shoulder belts used together are more effective in preventing injury than airbags used alone. Airbags used with both belts, however, are slightly more effective than both belts used alone. But the combined use of airbags and belts is unlikely. If airbags were mandated without a corresponding requirement to use seat belts, people would feel protected by the airbags and probably would use seat belts even less than they do now. Accordingly, from the standpoint of safety, it would be at least as effective for a state to require and enforce the use of seat belts as it would be for the federal government to mandate the use of airbags. Automatic seat belts, unless disabled by drivers, would provide more safety than airbags. Airbags, however, are less likely to be removed by drivers than are automatic seat belts, especially by the group most prone to accidents, young males, who are also likely to ignore seat-belt use laws.

DOT contends that mandatory seat-belt use laws are best from a cost-effectiveness point of view. While such laws would not require additional expenditure by consumers, they do involve such extra "costs" as the requirement to "buckle up" and the possibility of being arrested and fined for noncompliance. There is also the additional cost to the states of enforcing such legislation. Automatic belts are estimated to add $51 to the lifetime cost of a new car; airbags, $364.

If the government had to do something, the decision to follow DOT's recommendations was probably correct, although the plan for the transition to mandatory passive restraints presents some problems. How will the auto companies sell the 10, 25, or 40 percent of their cars that will have passive restraints if a purchaser is free to buy a car that lacks such equipment and hence is produced at lower cost? The car companies will have to sell restraint-equipped vehicles at below cost and add a premium to the price of nonequipped cars.

From the point of view of a free society, this whole affair has been a sorry exercise. The consumer-driver should have the option of purchasing or not purchasing additional safety for vehicle occupants. Neither mandatory seat-belt use nor mandatory airbags make sense in a free society. However, those auto owners whose cars are not equipped with automatic seat belts should pay higher auto taxes to reflect the higher medical costs to society expected to result from voluntary seat belt use. In addition, those wishing to drive without wearing seat belts should purchase the right to do so by paying an additional sum for their driver's licenses, which would then indicate that they have secured that right. Drivers stopped by the police and found not wearing seat belts should be fined heavily if they have not purchased the right to go without. These steps would internalize the externality of additional medical costs originating in the decision by some not to wear seat belts.

A simpler regulatory problem facing the auto companies concerns the "corporate average fuel economy" (CAFE) standards. Now written into law, these rules require that the average car produced by manufacturers meet or exceed a certain miles-per-gallon ratio. For 1985, the standard is 27.5 miles per gallon. These rules were written at the time of the gasoline shortage—itself a result of government regulation. For a considerable period, the relatively high price of gasoline had induced consumers to purchase small, gas-efficient vehicles; thus, automakers had no trouble meeting CAFE standards. With the decline in oil and gasoline prices since decontrol in 1981, however, consumers have been purchasing a greater number of large vehicles with lower gas mileage. By 1985, the auto companies may have to pay large fines if these standards—which have no real justification—remain in effect. The new administration should give priority to abolishing such rules. Consumers should be able to purchase any car they wish at any gas mileage, as long as they are willing to pay the full cost of their fuel.

Transportation Regulation

The surface transportation industry has been only partially decontrolled. The Interstate Commerce Commission (ICC) continues to maintain some controls over entry into the motor carrier industry; requires the filing of rates; and regulates railroad abandonments, pricing, and merger activity. Controls still exist on freight forwarders, barge lines, and pipelines. With the exception of pipelines, these are all highly competitive businesses. (Ironically, the only industry that is relatively monopolistic is the one the commission fails to regulate adequately—pipelines.) Hence, all surface transportation regulation could and should be abolished. The ICC itself should be quickly abolished before its hundredth birthday in 1987.

Admittedly, regulation has been relaxed greatly in recent years, and many of its inefficiencies have been eliminated. Certainly for trucking, entry has become almost completely free. Nevertheless, some controls of the surface transportation industry remain. There is potential for significant regulation even in the motor carrier industry, should the ICC fall into the hands of those wanting to extend regulation. As I write, there is before Congress a bill to reduce the authorized number of commissioners from seven to five. If this bill passes and becomes law, the composition of the commission is likely to shift from the current three-to-one pro-degregulation majority to a three-to-two pro-regulation majority. Thus, the only way to completely foreclose the possibility that entry barriers might be raised again is to abolish all regulation of the motor carrier industry.

An unregulated railroad industry also would have significant advantages. Even in today's relatively free economic environment, railroads are not able to price freely or to abandon unwanted trackage easily. Although shippers fear that an unregulated railroad industry would be able to price monopolistically, there is in fact considerable competition between railroads and other modes of transportation. So-called captive coal mines may have to ship by a single railroad, but a railroad cannot price so high that coal mines are unable to make money. If it does, the railroad will carry no coal. Because coal is sold in a competitive market, the most that a railroad can do is to capture whatever added profit a coal mine might earn due to low costs or privileged location. From the standpoint of the economy, who keeps such extra profits is totally irrelevant. Naturally, coal mine owners wish to keep their profits; just as naturally, the railroads would like to get them.

The airline industry has been totally deregulated for about six years. This deregulation has been a great success, working to the benefit of airplane passengers and airline stockholders. In addition, more workers are now employed in the industry than before deregulation. There are, however, latent tendencies to reregulate the industry. As a result of the air traffic controllers' strike, the Federal Aviation Authority (FAA) allocates landing slots at a few of the most congested major airports. Recently, traffic has increased sharply and congestion has risen, bringing considerable pressure for such controls at other major airports. Control over landing slots, however, is control over entry into the airline market—no government agency should have such power.

There is a simple market solution to the problem of scarce landing slots: the airports and/or the FAA could auction them. In fact, the

158

FAA is already considering allowing the trading and selling of such slots. That market should be encouraged and extended, as it would eliminate the pressure to regulate and control entry.

Communications Regulation

The Reagan administration has made some progress in reducing federal control over broadcasting and, through the settlement of the AT&T antitrust case, has changed the whole nature of telecommunications. At the same time, the Federal Communications Commission (FCC) has made some questionable decisions that might have, but did not, permit more broadcasters.

In the future, it is important that the FCC be as permissive to new technologies as possible. Competition among various media should be welcomed. For example, direct satellite-to-home broadcasting should be encouraged to compete with multi-point distribution systems (MDS) and with cable systems, which in turn compete with standard over-the-air television broadcasting.

The FCC should also eliminate remaining controls on broadcasting content. For example, its access rule prohibiting networks from broadcasting between 7:30 and 8:00 p.m., while never making much sense, now makes no sense at all in view of the highly competitive television market. Moreover, FCC restriction on network participation in financing and originating programing simply reduces competition and is a barrier to entry in the field. It is now time for the commission to eliminate these restrictions, even though it faces considerable opposition in doing so.

The breakup of the AT&T monopoly of long-distance telephone service is an excellent opportunity to establish a competitive structure in that market. However, the FCC has been unwilling to permit AT&T to compete actively with its rivals. This has been due in part to congressional pressure to block the necessary shift in costs from long-distance users to local-rate payers. The FCC should move, as soon as possible, to put AT&T on a basis comparable to that of its rivals. Moreover, the FCC should seize the opportunity for total deregulation of rates and service in long-distance communications provided by the courts when they ruled that the unregulated sector be separated from the regulated.

Banking Regulation

In recent years, a considerable loosening of controls on banking has been forced on the industry and its regulators. These changes have been due, in part, to innovations in technology that significantly lower the cost both of data and fund transfers and of handling. Lower costs meant that larger banks with widely distributed branches were not only possible but desirable. Relaxation of bank controls has also resulted from the ballooning of interest rates in the late 1970s and early 1980s that made ceilings on interest charges impossible to enforce. As other financial organizations moved into banking, banks have pressed for the right to expand into other financial fields.

These changes have been complicated by the recent financial difficulties experienced by some banks, such as the failure of Continental Illinois. The fact that Continental's demise had little to do with banking "deregulation" is being ignored by those who want to stop the trend toward deregulation. Actually, had banks been given greater freedom to move into other lines of business, and had interstate banking been permitted, Continental would probably not have become so deeply involved in the oil industry and in questionable overseas loans. Had Continental not been subject to the unitary banking laws of Illinois, it would have been able to build up a more stable depositor base. If the Continental experience teaches us anything, it is that more deregulation is needed, not less.

Barriers to regional and nationwide expansion should, in particular, be abolished. This requires legislation. To compete in the world market, U.S. banks must be able to expand nationwide, making possible better service for depositors and borrowers. In addition, restrictions on banks moving into related financial services should be removed. If Merrill Lynch can offer banking services, banks should be able to sell and underwrite securities and offer insurance.

The Continental Illinois collapse demonstrates a major problem facing banking regulators: the incentive to excessive risktaking provided by deposit insurance. Under current law and practice, the funds of depositors are guaranteed by an agency of the federal government. Thus, banks can make risky loans at no risk to the depositor. Moreover, if a bank runs into trouble and its stockholder equity erodes, bankers have every incentive to engage in risky loans in an attempt to recover. The taxpayer becomes the person at risk, not the depositor or the stockholder.

The purpose of deposit insurance is to eliminate panic runs on banks and the risk that such runs pose to the monetary system.

160

The problem is that the scheme has worked too well; too much risk has been eliminated. We need a system that protects the payments system and the small depositors, but forces large, sophisticated depositors to monitor the lending behavior of financial institutions. One possible solution would be for the government to restrict insurance coverage to deposits earning less than 5.5 percent interest. Small depositors, usually those with ordinary savings and checking accounts, would thus be covered by federal insurance; but large depositors, those with money market accounts or certificates of deposit, would have to look to the safety of the bank.

Food and Drug Regulation

Everyone wants safe, sanitary, and nutritious food. Further, we all want safe and effective drugs. However, the attempt to provide these benefits through food and drug regulation has had a number of undesirable side effects that may have caused more harm than good. Unfortunately, politicians have been unwilling to face the political heat that an attempt to amend these statutes would inevitably generate.

Two pieces of legislation, in particular, stand in need of change: the Delaney amendment (1958), and the Kefauver-Harris amendments (1962). The Delaney clause prohibits the use of any food additive that has been found to cause cancer in humans or in test animals. The Kefauver-Harris provisions require the manufacturer of a new drug to prove its efficacy and safety. The effect of these two provisions is to deprive people of needed new drugs and to slow the introduction of drugs into the marketplace.

The Delaney amendment has been interpreted as rigidly banning the use of any substance, no matter how beneficial, if tests show it to be related to cancer in laboratory animals. The idea, of course, is that people should be protected from any exposure to cancer-producing substances. Since 1958, scientists have learned that many normal foodstuffs are mildly carcinogenic; in fact, it is virtually impossible to follow a normal diet without eating foods shown to have carcinogenic effects.

The rigidity of the Delaney amendment has caused so many problems that in several cases, most notably those of saccharin and DES (diethylstibestrol, an additive to cattle feed), Congress has passed legislation that permits the continued use of certain carcinogenic substances. Legislated exceptions are, however, an inefficient way to build flexibility into the act. The saccharin case is

161

most illustrative. Invoking the Delaney amendment, the FDA had earlier banned the artificial sweetener, cyclamate. Now we know that the evidence for doing so was inadequate and misleading and that there is no firm evidence that cyclamates are carcinogenic. On the other hand, saccharin, the additive that the FDA had allowed as a substitute for cyclamate, has now been shown to be mildly carcinogenic in laboratory animals. The FDA is considering whether to lift its ban on cyclamates.

What is needed is legislation permitting more flexibility in FDA regulation to allow the benefits of a substance to be weighed against its potential harm. Even more desirable would be to allow consumers to decide for themselves whether or not to use certain substances, with the FDA's role consisting simply of publishing studies evaluating the potential effects of those substances. For example, the FDA could weigh the potential of sugar for causing diabetes, heart disease, tooth decay, and obesity against the possible carcinogenic harm of an artificial sweetener. Individuals would then consider the relative risks for themselves.

The Kefauver-Harris amendments also need modification. To prove the effectiveness of a given substance is very expensive. The high cost of doing so has impeded the development of new drugs, causing some individuals to suffer who otherwise would not. Moreover, effectiveness is subjective. To one consumer a product may be effective while to another it may not. What right or obligation does the government have to tell consumers whether they can use a substance?

Other Regulatory Reforms

There are other areas, obviously, that stand in need of regulatory reform. A national product liability law should be enacted that would limit liability to cases in which firms acted in a negligent or careless manner. Farm regulations should be abolished so that farming can operate in a free market environment. The minimum wage should be abolished or at least lowered for teenagers. Certification-of-need controls for hospitals should be abolished. The federal 55-mile-per-hour speed limit law should be returned to state jurisdiction. Because the Consumer Product Safety Commission provides no visible benefit, it should be eliminated. Occupational Safety and Health Administration (OSHA) regulation should be severely curtailed or eliminated; its major impact to date has been to raise costs for small firms without producing any measurable increase in safety.

Finally, in 1985 the administration should consider overhauling the most significant, and among the oldest, regulatory statutes—antitrust. It has long been recognized that many of the antitrust laws are anticompetitive, and recent evidence suggests that very few of them are beneficial to the market economy. A major reform could stimulate economic growth significantly.

There is no expectation that a political administration will, in January 1985, adopt these recommendations outright. The purpose here has been to lay out some of the major goals of regulatory reform and allow the politicians to compromise, moving from the ideal to what they consider possible. However, many of the reforms are of great importance to the economy and should be addressed seriously over the next year or so.

IX. Antitrust

Catherine England

What do the U.S. antitrust laws actually accomplish? Popular wisdom argues, of course, that antitrust laws protect consumers from the evils of predatory corporate behavior and monopolies. But do they? A closer look reveals that the antitrust laws have had some unexpected consequences: They are often used to protect inefficient firms at the expense of more successful competitors. They frequently slow the pace of innovation and damage the competitive standing of American businesses in world markets. And, in some cases antitrust laws may actually serve to raise prices and reduce output. Indeed, a careful consideration of the historical results of antitrust enforcement finds few consumer benefits.

As a result, the list of antitrust critics is growing. University of Hartford professor of economics D. T. Armentano and Court of Appeals Judge Robert Bork have written two of the most widely read attacks on antitrust enforcement.[1] But Armentano and Bork have been joined by economists Yale Brozen, Harold Demsetz, Robert Tollison, and Lester Thurow, among many others, in critically reexamining the statutes.

Those advocating significant reform—if not eventual repeal—of the antitrust laws seem to arrive at their position through one of two lines of reasoning.

The libertarian view holds that the right to fix prices is part of an individual's right to enter freely into contracts and dispose of his property as he sees fit. As Fred Smith explained in an article for *Regulation*, "The activities prohibited under antitrust laws are invariably *peaceable* activities—whatever their merit under an efficiency standard—and thus should be allowed in a free society."[2]

---

[1]See Dominick T. Armentano, *Antitrust and Monopoly: Anatomy of a Policy Failure* (New York: John Wiley and Sons, 1982); and Robert H. Bork, *The Antitrust Paradox: A Policy at War with Itself* (New York: Basic Books, 1978).

[2]Fred L. Smith, Jr., "Why Not Abolish Antitrust?" *Regulation* (January/February 1983): 25.

Others conclude through a more complicated series of observations that the antitrust laws have done more harm than good. They note that the economic rationale on which antitrust laws are believed to have been based is flawed, particularly with regard to its emphasis on the "perfect competition" model. A more dynamic view of the competitive process leads these individuals to the conclusion that efforts to fix prices or monopolize an industry are generally futile in the absence of government protections. In addition, these critics of antitrust are troubled by the anticompetitive potential of antitrust statutes. Like every other form of government regulation, such laws have been used to shift competition from the market, where it belongs, to the courts and political system.

The case for personal freedom argued in the libertarian view is important and the rights to which property owners should be entitled will be alluded to later in this chapter. But the focus of the following discussion will be on the series of arguments concerning the obsolescence, futility, and counterproductive nature of the antitrust statutes. The first part of this chapter will review the case against current antitrust statutes, and the second will consider where policy should be headed.

The Case Against Antitrust

This section will discuss four points in the case against the antitrust laws: (1) the misplaced emphasis on perfect competition, (2) the court interpretations resulting from this emphasis, (3) the role of private antitrust cases in producing counterproductive results, and (4) the incentives created by the historical enforcement of the antitrust laws.

The Antitrust Ideal: Perfect Competition

In building models and studying market behavior, economists often use the tool of the "perfectly competitive market." In the theoretical perfectly competitive industry consumers are well served. They receive goods at the lowest price possible given the cost and availability of the resources necessary for production. Society is able to choose among competing goods with maximum efficiency, and firms that do not produce what consumers want at a fair price are quickly eliminated. Thus, the perfect competition model frequently serves as a benchmark in economic analyses of market conditions.

Unfortunately, in the past the Federal Trade Commission, the Antitrust Division of the Justice Department, and the antitrust courts have attempted to use this theoretical tool as an ideal toward which real world markets could be moved through proper application of the antitrust laws. But the perfectly competitive market is a highly restrictive model applying stringent standards.

To be considered perfectly competitive, an industry must contain a large number of buyers and sellers who have complete information about market conditions, especially prices. The products sold by the firms within the industry must be identical, so that customers will develop no brand loyalties or company preferences. Each firm must be small relative to the industry as a whole so that the entry or exit of one firm will have no effect on market price.

Obviously, no industries meet these strict criteria. For example, the mere fact that one gasoline station has a more convenient location than its competitors bestows some market power (control over price) on that station and thus invalidates the conditions of perfect competition. The extensive resources spent every year on advertising by manufacturers attempting to build brand loyalty and the perception of real product differences among such essentially similar products as toothpaste constitute another violation of perfect competition standards. In fact, none of the behavior generally associated with competition appears in this model. When both consumers and producers are assumed to have complete information about product quality, market conditions, and price, there is no need to attempt to find new price/quality combinations or other improvements that will serve the public. Indeed, any firm able to discover and implement a product or process improvement would immediately violate the model criteria by gaining an advantage over its competitors.

This apparent inconsistency arises because the perfect competition model is essentially static. Like a photograph, it describes an industry at a point in time but reveals nothing about how the industry got there or where it is going. By contrast, real world markets are extremely dynamic. Because they lack complete information and perfect foresight, businessmen and consumers continually revise past decisions and attempt to correct earlier errors. Firms enter and leave the industry; new production and market processes are discovered; and consumer demand adjusts to changing fashions, fads, economic conditions, and products.

Thus while perhaps useful as a theoretical tool, the perfect competition model is unsuitable as a benchmark in antitrust enforcement. To their credit, the federal antitrust enforcement agencies are moving away from the perfect competition ideal. But despite improvements discussed more fully later, the historical use of the perfect competition model has set unfortunate precedents, leading to many of the perverse consequences identified earlier.

Competitors over Competition

In the competitive process, when a firm (or firms) finds a better way of delivering a product or service, it will frequently cause other competitors to fail, particularly those unable or unwilling to adjust. This is especially true if the more efficient production process involves economies of scale, thus biasing the industry toward fewer and larger firms. But increasing concentration traditionally makes those enforcing the antitrust laws nervous.

The courts, obviously, have no control over many of the facets of the perfectly competitive model. Judges cannot ensure that all consumers will have complete information or will act wisely when using the information they do have. The government cannot force manufacturers within an industry to produce identical products. Indeed, consumers appear to want some diversity and often impart subjective differences to products that are essentially the same. In fact, the only aspect of the perfectly competitive model over which the judicial system has any control is the number of firms within an industry. Competitive markets, the theory says, require a large number of relatively small firms. So in their pursuit of the illusory perfectly competitive market, antitrust courts have often favored *competitors* over *competition*.

Consider the *Alcoa* case, for example. In the late 1930s, Alcoa was charged under the Sherman Act with illegally monopolizing the aluminum industry. Yet Alcoa's monopoly was not protected by patents, nor was there any evidence of predatory tactics being used to eliminate competitors. Alcoa's practice of adding new capacity in anticipation of increased demand drew criticism from the court, but that was only normal, efficient business behavior.[3]

There are two possible explanations for Alcoa's admittedly dominant market position: superior management or economies of scale. On the face of it, neither of these would seem to be acts for which Alcoa should have been punished, and indeed, Alcoa was found innocent of all monopoly and conspiracy charges by the first court

[3]Richard A. Posner, *Economic Analysis of Law*, 2d ed. (Boston: Little, Brown and Company, 1977), p. 233.

168

to hear the case. But the government appealed. The special Appeals Court that heard the case in place of the U.S. Supreme Court reversed the lower court's decision and found Alcoa guilty of monopolizing virgin ingot aluminum.[4]

The reasoning behind the majority opinion, written by Judge Learned Hand, is instructive. Apparently the court concluded that Alcoa's dominant position resulted from a combination of the two factors mentioned above. Alcoa's size enabled the firm to operate more efficiently than smaller businesses; therefore, economies of scale existed. In addition, Alcoa had been able to achieve its efficient size through "superior skill, foresight, and industry." Although nothing more evil or predatory was uncovered, Alcoa was still convicted of monopolization. Its superior management techniques were branded "exclusionary" and therefore illegal.[5] Furthermore, Judge Hand interpreted the Sherman Act as having been motivated by a congressional desire to preserve a system of small competitive units, *even if that meant higher costs*.[6]

A larger number of other court decisions have since reflected that attitude. Individual firms have been protected despite the potential—often realized—inefficiency of doing so. In 1966, for example, the Supreme Court struck down a merger between two grocery chains in Los Angeles that would have produced a firm with 1.4 percent of the stores and 7.5 percent of the sales in the Los Angeles market.[7] The decision to stop the *Von's Grocery* merger was based on the observation that the number of single-store owners had declined substantially as grocery chains became increasingly important.[8] To derail this trend toward concentration "in its incipiency," the merger was denied—even though it could have produced efficiencies that allowed the new firm to compete more effectively against growing national chains.

More recently, in 1980 the Federal Trade Commission charged DuPont with "attempting to monopolize" because its research staff had discovered and patented a less expensive means of recovering a particular chemical, and DuPont had attempted to pass the savings along to its customers. "Unfair competition," charged the FTC

[4]Armentano, p. 101.
[5]Ibid., p. 111.
[6]Posner, p. 223.
[7]Bork, p. 217.
[8]Ibid., p. 219.

legal staff. By forcing its competitors to match its price cuts, DuPont was charged with preventing them from generating funds for pursuing corresponding research.[9] Although eventually exonerated, DuPont was forced to spend time and money defending itself for finding a more efficient means of providing consumers something they wanted.

The important point is that an overemphasis on so-called perfect competition has led antitrust courts to attempt to force many industries into a mold for which they are not suited. Even in cases where firms gained their large market shares by offering lower prices and/ or improved products, or where economies of scale dictated a more concentrated industry, the courts have often admittedly sacrificed consumers' welfare to the perfect competition construct.

Private Antitrust Actions

As a result of widespread economic and legal criticism, important changes are occurring in the interpretation of the antitrust laws, particularly at the federal enforcement agencies. President Reagan's appointees at both the FTC and the Justice Department have encouraged their staffs to look beyond "concentration ratios" and "market shares" to ask about the actual impact of proposed mergers or internal growth on consumers and the existence of efficiencies before bringing suits. But serious problems remain. The courts, as creatures of precedent, often continue to interpret the statutes as they have been interpreted in the past. So while the federal government may no longer press the more frivolous antitrust cases, that does not imply that the number of private antitrust suits will decrease.

Since the 1950s, the number of private antitrust suits has steadily increased, accounting for at least 94 percent of the antitrust cases brought every year during the 1970s.[10] Frequently, these cases are brought by less successful businessmen against their more prosperous competitors. Because court decisions have often protected competitors at the expense of the competitive process, there is always a chance that firms with larger market shares will be told to discontinue whatever practice is drawing customers to them.

[9]Betty Bock, *The Innovator as an Antitrust Target*, Information Bulletin No. 174, The Conference Board, 1980.

[10]Betty Bock, et. al., *Antitrust in the Competitive World of the 1980s*, Research Bulletin No. 112, The Conference Board, 1982, pp. 18–19.

Antitrust targets may even be ordered to share the special knowledge or distribution networks responsible for their success.

Betty Bock, director of antitrust research at The Conference Board, notes, for example, that it has been argued in antitrust cases attacking patent holders that innovative leaders should be required to grant production licenses to competitors harmed by a significant technological development, or that they should be required to "pre-disclose" to competitors new products or processes before they appear on the market. It has also been argued, Bock says, that leading innovators should not be allowed to pass along cost savings to customers when price reductions would make it more difficult for competitors to match R&D investments.[11]

In addition to these efforts to stop industry leaders from competing, treble damages are automatically available to successful litigants. Less successful innovators may also find advantages to delaying the introduction of new products and processes through antitrust suits, even when the targets are eventually absolved of guilt.

The Antitrust Message: Compete, But Not Too Hard

The message implicit in U.S. antitrust policies is: Compete, but not too hard; succeed, but not too much. Serving consumers so well they beat a path to your door to the obvious detriment of your competitors can lead to expensive antitrust challenges.

The threat of divestiture or dissolution, often recommended as an antitrust remedy, creates further perverse incentives. As Court of Appeals Judge Richard Posner notes in his analysis of the antitrust laws, the threat of divestiture may actually lead to higher prices and lower output—the very results against which the antitrust laws are supposed to protect consumers. As Posner explains:

> As a firm's market share approached the level that would subject it to a dissolution order, it would have an incentive to limit further growth by increasing its price. If the other leading firms in the market followed the same policy, the result would be a price level higher than the previous monopoly level, and with worse output effects, especially since inefficient entrants would be attracted to the market by the price umbrella held over their heads by the existing firms.[12]

[11]Bock, *The Innovator.*
[12]Posner, p. 232.

The U.S. auto market is a typical example. Before the entry of the Japanese during the 1970s, there appeared to be little robust competition in the industry. Prices, models, and services were very similar among the Big Three—General Motors, Ford, and Chrysler. Antitrust advocates bemoaned the apparent lack of competition and pointed to the evils arising from concentrated industries. But it is equally likely that the situation was a direct result of the antitrust laws. With politicians and scholars periodically contemplating the dissolution of General Motors, for example, GM executives certainly realized that any strengthening of their market position would mean the death of the corporation as it existed. No one had a stronger interest in seeing that American Motors and Chrysler survived than GM and Ford. The result was most likely a carefully calculated *lack* of competition to avoid entanglement with the antitrust statutes.

Furthermore, as MIT economist Lester Thurow has noted, breaking up a company like IBM into three or four smaller companies would benefit no one—except possibly, foreign computer manufacturers.[13] Where economies of scale exist, unnecessary inefficiency will be the result of forced divestiture. In other cases, dissolution would punish the superior management and/or innovative leadership most people believe it is designed to protect.

Antitrust laws, then, have some quite perverse results. They undoubtedly discourage innovation. Not only does research and development have a lower pay-off if successful innovations must be defended against possible antitrust challenges, but proposed cooperative industry-wide research efforts directed at solving widely recognized problems are also stymied. In addition, U.S. law has made it unnecessarily difficult for domestic firms to compete overseas. Joint ventures, designed so that two or more firms may combine resources and more easily enter international markets, are made more risky by their vulnerability under the antitrust statutes. Further, many of the declining U.S. industries face the stiffest competition internationally. If the steel industry, for example, is to have any hope of regaining its competitive status, mergers will undoubtedly be necessary to allow for the consolidation of the more efficient plants. This process is made significantly more difficult by current antitrust laws.

---

[13]Lester C. Thurow, *The Zero-Sum Society* (New York: Penguin Books, 1980), p. 148.

Antitrust Reform

This section will consider (1) recent changes in federal antitrust activities so that the picture of current enforcement practices can be brought up to date, (2) the problems (if any) that antitrust should be directed at solving, (3) the costs and benefits of continued antitrust enforcement, and (4) short-run steps toward reform.

Changing Antitrust Enforcement

A new outlook on the role of federal antitrust policy, debated during the 1970s, came to the forefront with the election of Ronald Reagan. James C. Miller III at the Federal Trade Commission and William Baxter at the Justice Department brought with them a new attitude toward the definition of "acceptable business practices."

Soon after the Reagan administration appointees took office, three of the government's largest antitrust suits were settled. After nine years, the FTC decided not to appeal the administrative law judge's negative findings in the "shared monopoly" case against Kellogg's, Post, and General Mills. The Justice Department also settled with both IBM and American Telephone and Telegraph. While many disagree with particular aspects of these settlements, at least the costly enforcement processes were brought to an end.

A more important indication of future federal enforcement policies is the Justice Department's revision of its merger guidelines and the FTC's "statement" outlining its policies on horizontal mergers. The new guidelines of the FTC and the Justice Department gave economic arguments precedence over political and social consequences. Under these guidelines vertical and conglomerate mergers will be challenged only when they are believed to have substantial anticompetitive horizontal effects.[14]

Despite these changes both the FTC and the Justice Department continue to view horizontal mergers as a threat to consumer welfare and, as such, justifiable targets for continued antitrust enforcement. But attitudes at both agencies have become much less restrictive. In unconcentrated markets, for example, few mergers will receive even a second glance from enforcement authorities. By contrast, the 1968 merger guidelines prohibited mergers between companies controlling as little as five percent of the market each. For moderately to highly concentrated industries the guidelines have been

[14]Joe Sims and William Blumenthal, "The New Era in Antitrust," *Regulation* (July/August 1982): 25–26.

relaxed only slightly from the 1968 standards, but the new guidelines do take into consideration a long list of other factors which may influence federal decision makers. These include product homogeneity, transaction size and frequency, and pricing structure.[15]

On the issue of efficiencies, the Justice Department and the Federal Trade Commission are somewhat at odds. The Justice Department believes it has set market-share enforcement thresholds high enough to allow the realization of all economies in the vast majority of cases. Therefore, officials at Justice are not likely to accept an "efficiency defense" in a merger they would otherwise find illegal. On the other hand, the FTC's Miller believes scale economies should be part of the legal analysis. Because other commissioners are not yet ready to accept his position in its entirety, however, the Commission's official position is that efficiencies should be considered when the FTC is making a decision about exercising its prosecutorial discretion, but that efficiency arguments are too vague to be considered a legal defense.

Federal authorities are also trying to make it easier for failing firms or firms within declining industries to combine. Consider, for example, efforts made during early 1984 by the LTV Corporation and Republic Steel to merge. If there is a textbook example of a declining U.S. industry that should be allowed to consolidate its resources in order to modernize and survive, it is the U.S. steel industry.[17] After some initial objections, the Justice Department and the affected firms were able to reach an agreement allowing the merger to go forward. However, continued federal activity in this area unnecessarily raised the costs for those companies in time, legal fees, and foregone opportunities—an unnecessary additional burden for an already troubled industry.

In short, while concentration ratios and market shares have been deemphasized, they have not been dismissed. Similarly, the view of economies of scale taken by enforcement authorities, while more tolerant than in the past, remains ambiguous. And while moves toward instituting a "declining industries" defense are laudable, continued antitrust activity still produces a chilling effect on

[15]Ibid., p. 27.

[16]Ibid., p. 28.

[17]Naturally, a streamlined steel industry should also be forced to forego current protections against foreign competitors.

174

potentially beneficial mergers simply by forcing troubled firms to defend themselves.

The Trust Problem

Before moving on to recommend reforms of current antitrust laws and guidelines, it is necessary to ask: What should the goal of antitrust policy be, if anything?

When the Sherman Act was passed in 1890, political rhetoric supporting enactment was addressed to the "trust" problem. Farmers' organizations, unions, small business organizations, academics, and "progressive" journalists formed a coalition promoting early antitrust legislation. The congressmen who spoke for these groups told of small businesses subjected to unfair competition by growing trusts. It was argued that " 'giant monopolies' were creating a 'dangerous concentration of wealth' among the capitalists of the day."[18]

Once monopolies were outlawed, some firms attempted to coordinate their economic activity without actually merging. That is, they attempted to devise agreements dividing territories, setting market-wide prices, and/or specifying quality. These so-called cartels were viewed by many as presenting the same pitfalls for consumers as outright monopolies, and hence the antitrust statutes were expanded to outlaw collusions as well.

Regardless of the actual or perceived problems addressed by the antitrust statutes when they were written, it is certainly valid to question the existence of an antitrust problem today. In considering the need for antitrust laws, the dynamic nature of competition must be more fully understood. Driven by the profit motive, businessmen are constantly searching for better ways to serve their customers or more efficient ways of organizing their businesses. Success in these areas is, after all, the way profits are increased. But the story does not end there. Once a successful innovation attracts above-normal profits, it also attracts attention from the market. Investors are constantly searching for a greater return on their funds. Thus, in the absence of government-imposed barriers to entry, any firm that begins to earn an unusually high rate of profit will naturally attract competitors. Funds from individuals seeking to start new

[18]Thomas J. DiLorenzo, "The Origins of Antitrust: An Interest Group Perspective," working paper at the Center for Study of Market Processes, George Mason University, p. 16.

175

businesses and from existing firms wanting to expand their markets will flow into the industry in an attempt to capture some of the extra-normal profits. If government trade barriers are absent, new competitors may appear from overseas as well.

For similar reasons, it is as difficult to form a successful cartel in the free market as it is to establish a lasting monopoly. In the first place, the many facets of the competitive process—price, research and development, service after the sale, and location, to name a few—make successful anticompetitive cooperation all but impossible. No cartel can possibly define all the terms of competition. Making the task even more formidable, cartel members have strong incentives to cheat on their agreements. There are large profits to be made by the cartel member who manages to cut prices just a little or offers a slightly better product at the agreed-upon price. This temptation to cheat becomes even stronger during periods of declining sales. A firm's excess capacity can drive up average costs and lead to lower profits. Additional sales may be needed just to help cover fixed costs. The result is usually an extremely unstable system which often collapses from internal pressures. Even if it manages to contain the competitive impulses of its members, however, a cartel's success is far from assured. As with a monopoly, any successful collusion will, by definition, earn higher profits than the norm for similar industries. Barring government intervention, additional firms will be attracted to the cartelized industry. Unless each new entrant can be included in the cartel successfully, which is highly unlikely, competition soon returns to the industry.

In the absence of government-imposed trade barriers, it is unlikely that even a single-firm industry within the United States could constitute an effective monopoly as far as American consumers were concerned. Consider, for example, the tremendous competitive pressure exerted by foreign automakers in this country. Even with "voluntary" import quotas, American car manufacturers are forced by their overseas competitors to keep a close watch on prices and quality.

In addition, the presence of large conglomerate firms within the economy makes it difficult to imagine an industry where entry would not occur in the face of monopoly profits. Any number of American firms have the marketing expertise, capital resources, and distribution networks to enter almost any industry they want. Thus, the likelihood of a monopoly developing in an economy unprotected by government regulation is very slim.

176

Furthermore, it is often difficult to determine who is competing with whom. Just defining a "market" that may be monopolized is extremely difficult. The suit brought by the FTC against the ready-to-eat cereal manufacturers is a case in point. Besides the fact that there were four firms, not one, named in the original indictment, there was also a serious market definition problem. With what other goods does Cheerios compete? With Kellogg's Corn Flakes or Post Raisin Bran alone? Of course not. There are a large number of other breakfast options—bacon and eggs, frozen waffles, oatmeal, cream of wheat, and liquid instant breakfasts, to name a few. Certainly, some options are even as easy to prepare as cold cereal. Given this range of choices, even a single cereal manufacturer would find it difficult to exercise any significant market power.

Fundamental to understanding the foregoing discussion is an appreciation of the role profits play in a capitalist system. Profits, especially abnormally high profits, are a key element in the smooth operation of a market economy. They should be applauded rather than denigrated, for extra-normal profits are the consumers' means of signaling their approval of a new product, better quality, or improved service. Profits are the ultimate source of consumers' power in revealing to businessmen what they want and in offering the incentives to ensure their demands are met.

The Costs and Benefits of Antitrust

Notwithstanding the strength of the case outlining the anticom-petitive effects of the antitrust statutes and the difficulties inherent in forming monopolies or effective cartels, most critics continue to argue for antiturst *reform* rather than *repeal*. While recognizing the flawed nature of historical antitrust enforcement, they continue to support the basic notion behind antitrust. Most frequently they assert that regardless of how short-lived a monopoly or cartel might be, consumers are harmed during the period it is in existence. Therefore some antitrust laws should remain: those outlawing price-fixing and predatory behavior are mentioned most often.

In fact, in a July 18, 1984, presentation at a Cato Institute Policy Forum, Timothy J. Muris, director of the Bureau of Competition at the Federal Trade Commission, likened price-fixing to theft. Muris remarked that he failed to see any difference between someone stealing a television from his home and two television manufactur-ers agreeing to take more money than necessary when selling him a television. This analogy has strong emotional appeal. It is useful, however, to review several factors that deserve consideration before defending the concept of antitrust too strongly.

Can the government act more quickly than the market? In many cases the answer is no. By the time federal authorities identify a problem and satisfy the necessary legal requirements, judicial proceedings, and appeals, the market has long since responded with new competition forcing down prices. Where the market does not respond more quickly, there is almost always some government regulation inhibiting entry. Private antitrust suits are often equally time consuming.

Furthermore, consumers almost always have a choice. There are substitutes for almost any good that may be subject to price-fixing or monopoly. In Muris's example, no one can force him to buy a television from manufacturers who are colluding. Muris could buy a used television instead, or have an old set repaired. He could rent a television or invest in a radio or stereo. Ultimately, he could do without. In most cases, therefore, if consumers feel a good is not worth the price charged for it, they can refuse to deal with those fixing prices, thus hastening the return of competition.

In addition, in a republic based on the principles of individual freedom and private property, one ought to be able to sell his property for whatever price he and a buyer agree to. Does the government really have more right to interfere in a private contractual arrangement than in the contents of a private conversation?

Ultimately, even granting the potential of the antitrust laws to stop collusions or discourage monopolies in a few cases, a strong case can be made that the costs of antitrust protection outweigh its benefits. It is true that many firms challenged under the antitrust laws are ultimately exonerated, but only after having devoted substantial resources in terms of funds, executives' time, and legal staff efforts to their defense. These resources are, as a result, unavailable for more productive pursuits—increased research and development or capital investment, for example.

Steps toward Reform

Regardless of exactly what steps are taken first or how far they proceed during the next four years, it is important to reexamine the antitrust statutes. Despite positive changes at the FTC and the Justice Department, the bulk of the antitrust problem remains in the private sector, untouched. Only statutory change can have a lasting impact in discouraging private "nuisance" cases, and only statutory change can ensure that later revisions of the government's merger guidelines do not retreat to a counterproductive emphasis on the number of competitors within a narrowly defined industry.

Writers such as D. T. Armentano advocate eliminating all anti-trust restrictions. Others, like Robert Bork and Lester Thurow, would retain restrictions against price-fixing and predatory pricing (pricing below costs for the express purpose of eliminating com-petitors). And while the eventual abolition of the statutes should certainly be given serious consideration, political realities probably dictate a more cautious approach in the short term.

The following suggestions are meant to identify possible reforms about which there is at least some agreement. Once these initial steps are taken, we may hope that reform can build on their suc-cess.[19]

1) Modify Section 2 of the Sherman Act to ensure that competitive success is not considered a violation of the antitrust laws. Active competition cannot exist without hurting some com-petitors. Indeed, the very essence of competition is to benefit consumers by eliminating the less-efficient producers. Firms rewarded by consumers for providing better quality, a lower price, or enhanced service certainly should not be punished by the Justice Department, the Federal Trade Commission, or disgruntled competitors.

2) Repeal the "unfair methods of competition" provision of Sec-tion 5 of the Federal Trade Commission Act. The vague nature of the current law unnecessarily increases the risk faced by businessmen because they are subjected to ex post facto deter-minations of what constitutes a legitimate or illegitimate way of doing business. The only clearly unfair methods of com-petition are those that involve practices that are already illegal without Section 5, such as enforcing a patent fraudulently obtained or threatening physical violence to deter competitors.

3) Modify Section 7 of the Clayton Act to ensure neither large firm size nor concentration of the industry are presumed to be anticompetitive. Under Section 7, mergers have been denied on the basis of "concentration ratios" that often have little or nothing to do with monopoly power. This has made it

[19]See Catherine England, "Bringing Antitrust Laws into the Twentieth Century," Heritage Foundation *Backgrounder* No. 344, April 18, 1984, pp. 13–14.

unnecessarily difficult to consolidate declining industries or to achieve the economies of scale necessary to compete effectively in world markets. Attention should, therefore, be directed more toward government-imposed barriers to entry rather than to market-determined firm size.

4) Abolish the automatic trebling of damages for antitrust violations and adopt a rule of reason in establishing assessable damages. With more than 90 percent of the antitrust cases being brought by private litigants, a changed attitude at the FTC or Justice has little effective impact on reducing the chances that a particular firm will face a court battle. To reduce the number of cases brought by private litigants merely to harass successful competitors, treble damages should not be guaranteed even where legal violations are discovered.

5) Remove current disincentives to innovation and research by making it clear that no use of a patent or copyright lawful under the "intellectual property" laws should be considered a cause for action under the antitrust laws.

Conclusions

The case against the antitrust laws continues to grow. Antitrust enforcement has often proven counterproductive and has done little, if anything, to promote consumers' interest. Indeed, a greater understanding of the dynamic nature of the competitive process reveals that in most cases antitrust laws have been ineffective precisely because there is not much of an antitrust problem to solve. Just as vertical and conglomerate mergers have been shown to have more benefits and fewer costs than was believed to be the case a decade ago, research is beginning to indicate that cooperative behavior among competing firms—now viewed as collusive and damaging to consumers—may have many more benefits than was first suspected.

Ultimately, the only sources of permanent monopoly power are governments. California almond growers can determine the supply of almonds reaching U.S. markets because their agreements are backed by the U.S. Department of Agriculture. New York City taxicabs are able to earn extra-normal profits while often providing consumers with poor service because the city government controls the number of cabs that may operate there. Such examples abound. As Milton Friedman has observed, "the problem of monopoly, as a matter of policy, is largely a problem not of getting government to enact legislation against monopoly but of keeping government from enacting and enforcing legislation strengthening and preserving monopoly."[20] Thus, if there is a role for federal antitrust authorities, it may be in highlighting the anticompetitive activities of municipalities and state governments. But, then, who will protect consumers from the equally damaging activities of the federal government?

[20]Milton Friedman, *An Economist's Protest*, 2d ed. (Glen Ridge, N.J.: Thomas Horton and Daughters, 1975), p. 285.

X. The Information Revolution

Milton Mueller

The implementation of the AT&T divestiture at the beginning of 1984 finally made the "information revolution" something more than an academic cliché. The American public, and indeed the entire world, began to take notice of telecommunications policy. By divesting the world's largest corporation of its telephone operating companies, the United States made an irrevocable break with over fifty years of that policy.

But the divestiture was only the most visible element in a radical transformation of the nation's communications laws and regulations. Although the seeds of this legal revolution were sown decades ago, the past four years have been critical. During this time AT&T has been freed to enter the computer business, long distance telecommunication has emerged as a highly competitive field involving hundreds of players, and full price deregulation has become a near-term possibility. Thousands have entered telecommunication markets using newly authorized technologies: low power television (over 12,000 applicants), multipoint distribution service (over 16,000 applicants), cellular radiotelephone, direct broadcast satellites, and so on. In addition, most state governments are following the initiative of the Federal Communications Commission (FCC) by permitting competition for the toll calls within their respective borders.

Local telephone service, however, is still a monopoly, and many of the divested Bell operating companies are fighting hard at the state level to keep it that way. Moreover, the FCC's attempt to overhaul the way local telephone companies determine their rates by imposing a system of "access charges" was stymied by Congress, local telephone companies, and state regulators. These bodies contended that such a change would lead to higher local rates; in reality, the access charge stalemate is a threat to both local and long distance competition.

FCC chairman Mark Fowler, a former broadcaster ideologically committed to deregulation, has spearheaded a drive to release existing broadcasters from the constraints of the 1934 Communications Act. The results of his efforts have been mixed. Such regulations as the prime time access rule and the financial interest and syndicated exclusivity rules, which limit the networks' control of prime time programming and of reruns, respectively, have withstood his challenge, at least for now. Other regulatory reform has been set aside.

The most salient feature of the information revolution is not new technology per se, but reorganization. In cybernetic theory, "information" is synonymous with order and control; it is the opposite of randomness. So intimate is the relation between communication and control that Norbert Wiener, one of the mathematical geniuses who contributed to the creation of computers in the 1940s, classed the two together. "When I control the actions of another person," Wiener wrote, "I communicate a message to him. . . . Furthermore, if my control is to be effective I must take cognizance of any messages from him which may indicate that the order is understood and has been obeyed." Wiener noted that "the commands through which we exercise control over our environment are a kind of information we impart to it."[1] Thus, the "information economy," usually taken to include communications, education, law, government, and banking, could just as well be called the "control economy" or perhaps even the "political economy." It pertains to the way humans organize their affairs through the production and exchange of symbols.

A revolution in information technology—the means by which we transmit, process, store, and retrieve knowledge—can therefore be expected to produce profound changes in the social order. It does not simply mean that our mail will be delivered by computers instead of by mailmen, or that we will have access to 150 channels of television programming instead of 3 or 4. The restructuring of the telephone system, easily one of the largest-scale and most rapid industrial reorganizations in history, is only the first of many other organizational changes in store for us as the new information technology works its way into the social fabric.

This chapter conducts a broad survey of the domestic and international policy issues posed by the information revolution. The emphasis throughout is on how information technology is transforming the economic, legal, and political relations governing this

[1]Norbert Wiener, *The Human Use of Human Beings* (Boston: Houghton Mifflin Co., 1950), pp. 24–25.

country and its relations with other nations. The information revolution, I will contend, can be described most accurately as an extension of the capitalist mode of organization—that is, social coordination based on private property and exchange relationships—into the information economy, which was formerly largely exempt from it.

This thesis is discussed only in relation to three critical sectors of the information economy: the telephone system, banking, and international telecommunications. The complexity and ubiquity of the information revolution requires concentration on these areas to the exclusion of other important concerns such as copyright, broadcast regulation, and the First Amendment.

The Transformation of the Information Economy

Today we take it for granted that workers can be hired and fired and can move from one employer to another in search of the best opportunity. Likewise, we think of land as a commodity capable of being bought and sold on the market. However, these conditions did not always exist. They were the outcome of a profound upheaval in social organization that took place between the fifteenth and eighteenth centuries in Europe: the emergence of capitalism. It is my contention that the most striking feature of the "information revolution," and the aspect that makes it truly revolutionary, is its virtual reenactment of the capitalist revolution within the context of the information economy.

The transition from feudalism to capitalism was a complex process spanning centuries, and there is plenty of room for disagreement and debate concerning how this transformation took place.[2] Nevertheless, its eventual results are relatively clear. The local manor economy of feudalism was supplanted by a wider, national economy with a correspondingly greater division of labor. Land and labor, which under feudalism had been bound together in an intricate chain of obligations based on the requirements of military defense, became alienable, freely transferable commodities. The

[2]On the transition from feudalism to capitalism, see Douglass C. North and Robert Paul Thomas, *The Rise of the Western World: A New Economic History* (Cambridge: Cambridge University Press, 1973); William Parker and Eric Jones, eds., *European Peasants and their Markets* (Princeton: Princeton University Press, 1975); Paul Sweezy et al., *The Transition from Feudalism to Capitalism: A Symposium* (New York: Science and Society, 1954); R. H. Tawney, *The Agrarian Problem in the 16th Century* (London: Longman, Green & Co., 1912).

185

establishment of a market in land and labor was both cause and consequence of a process known as "enclosures," whereby communally regulated agricultural land was appropriated to individually owned plots.

The capitalist revolution replaced feudal obligations with property and exchange relationships. However, what we today would call the "information economy" was largely exempt from this revolution. Indeed, in this area the breakup of feudalism took a different direction altogether.

With the rise of modern Europe, the traditional role of the church in the preservation and dissemination of knowledge was gradually taken over by the new European nation-states. Rather than allowing markets to evolve, the nation-states invariably established monopolies over the networks of transportation and communication tying their territories together. Both the monarchs and the parliaments of the period, for example, felt compelled to establish postal monopolies in order to maintain their hegemony. The early governments made no bones about the purpose of postal monopoly: it was to monitor potentially treasonous or seditious communications. Rationalizations about "natural monopoly" had to await the invention of economics centuries later.

In the eighteenth century, the dependency of political hegemony on the control of information became explicit as Enlightenment democrats such as Condorcet and Rousseau argued for free, universal, compulsory education as a means of fortifying the nation-state's hold on the minds of its people. To Thomas Jefferson, the subsidization of knowledge via common schooling and state-supported universities was as much a part of his approach to the information economy as was a belief in the First Amendment and an uncensored political press.

Industrialism brought with it the invention of the railroad and of telegraph, telephone, and radio communication. For a brief period these technologies evolved privately and competitively. Eventually, however, they either fell under the direct control of the state, as in most of Europe, or became enmeshed in a system of public utility regulation as in the United States. While utility regulation preserved private ownership, it made the social organization of these technologies a virtual mirror of the state. Like governments, utilities were organized as territorial monopolies. Just as the authority of the state is supposed to assure each individual of justice and equality before the law, so utility regulation was supposed to guarantee

186

the public just, non-discriminatory rates. In effect, the new industrial transport and communications technologies, like the post office, were absorbed into the preexisting pattern of control dictated by the nation-state.

The fact that telecommunications were kept out of the nexus of marketplace relations governing the bulk of the Western economy set the stage for today's information revolution. The regulatory scheme imposed on the industrial transport and communications infrastructure was a throwback to precapitalist times; the concepts of "just price" and "common carrier" on which utility regulation is based are feudal in origin. The landmark case in which the U.S. Supreme Court validated early utility regulation, *Munn v. Illinois* (1873), took its precedent from medieval common law. The utility historian Martin Glaeser notes that the tendency for competitive enterprise to replace royal monopolies during the emergence of capitalism stopped short in certain areas designated as "public callings." "In the case of these public callings, the essential elements of the medieval framework of regulation survived its general collapse." Modern utility dealings, Glaeser concludes, are the "direct lineal descendants" of feudal economic organization.[3]

The information revolution is nothing less than the systematic transformation of this neofeudal order. The invention of computers and the accelerated development of electronics technology during World War II was of course its catalyst. However, it was the attempt of business users to appropriate the economic value of these technological developments that proved to be truly revolutionary, for in order to do so they had to transform the organization of the telecommunications industry. Although this process is usually described as "deregulation" or as the introduction of "competition," what is really going on is the emergence of specialization and the creation of property and exchange relationships where none existed before. We are not deregulating an existing industry so much as *creating* the legal underpinnings of an exchange economy in telecommunications. The information revolution of the late twentieth century is making information distribution channels into alienable, freely transferable commodities, just as the capitalist revolution did for land and labor.

A brief survey of the evolution of U.S. telecommunications policy

[3]Martin Glaeser, *Public Utilities in American Capitalism* (New York: MacMillan, 1957), p. 199.

over the last 25 years bears this analysis out. The origin of "competition" in telecommunications is usually dated to the FCC's *Above 890 Mhz* decision of 1959, which opened up the microwave spectrum—heretofore reserved for the monopoly common carrier—to private companies. As Dan Schiller demonstrates in his study *Telematics and Government*, the impetus for this change came not from the commission's devotion to abstract economic principles regarding competition, but from businesses interested in constructing their own specialized communications networks. "The Above 890 Docket . . . can best be viewed in terms of a far broader process of private network development, itself crucial to the more general expansion of business throughout the postwar period."[4]

The next crack in the old regulatory order emerged around terminal equipment—the telephone device at the end of the line. Under the old principle of "end-to-end service," the provision of a telephone was inseparable from the provision of dial tone and switching. Moreover, the phone companies prohibited what they called "foreign attachments" to their networks. But as communications technology advanced beyond the simple voice telephone invented by Bell in 1876, business users developed specialized needs and began to demand the right to attach non-telephone-company equipment to their lines. The proliferation of private networks contributed to this movement, as businesses wanted to be able to connect their separate networks into the public switched network to achieve universal intercommunication when necessary.

The alienability of terminal equipment forced the FCC to redefine the property relation between the user and the telephone company. In its *Carterfone* decision of 1968, which concerned the attachment of a device that fed mobile radio calls into AT&T's network, the commission began to establish the principle that no device suiting a subscriber's convenience and causing no technical harm to the network can be prohibited by the telephone companies. Closely related to the *Carterfone* docket were the FCC's two "Computer Inquiries" initiated in 1966, in which businesses fought for the right to attach their own computers and message-switching facilities to the public network. As an outgrowth of these inquiries, the commission adopted in 1975 and 1976 new technical standards establishing the now-familiar modular plug permitting any licensed terminal equipment to be readily attached to the telephone system.

[4]Dan Schiller, *Telematics and Government* (Norwood, N.J.: Ablex, 1982), p.14.

The public network became further divided into separate realms as specialized, competitive long distance carriers arose and began to attract heavy users of long distance away from AT&T. In 1971, the *Specialized Common Carrier* decision authorized new entry into the private line market. In 1975, MCI introduced its "Execunet" service, a discounted, switched long distance service that competed directly with AT&T's toll service. From 1975 to 1978, the litigation surrounding *Execunet* established the right of "Other Common Carriers" (OCCs) to connect to the Bell system's local exchange to originate and terminate calls. The need to interconnect the Bell system with its competitors made the whole legal/economic relation between local exchange and long distance service a critical regulatory issue.

The AT&T divestiture sought to resolve this problem by legally severing local exchange and long distance service. The divested local telephone companies are barred from the long distance market. By 1987 they must provide "equal access," or the same interconnection services at the same price, to all long distance companies. In a closely related development, the FCC's "access charge" decision of 1983 sought to replace the old administrative formulas for transferring revenues from long distance to local exchange service with a new system based on fees levied on local subscribers and interconnecting long distance companies.

The strand unifying this long process of change is the eruption of specialization and the coordination of diverse needs through market relations. An integrated telephone network has been broken up into separate components: terminal equipment, inside wiring, local exchange service, and long distance service. These components are coordinated by means of market exchanges between consumers on the one hand and separate and competing business entities on the other. The system as a whole is no longer under the control of a single entity: an *organization* has become a *market*. For this to be accomplished a new set of property relations between users and carriers, and between the carriers themselves, had to be formulated.

A similar course of development is changing the way radio frequencies are allocated. Out of the old system of government licensing and allocation, a market system founded on private property rights is emerging. This development is all the more remarkable because radio engineers and regulators have insisted for decades that such a market would be "impossible" or "impractical" to create.

The invisibility and variability of radio emissions and the need to control interference were thought to justify centralized government control. Its "impossibility" notwithstanding, however, over the past five years the FCC has been quietly laying the foundation for property rights and a market in radio frequencies. As in the case of telephone regulation, this has not been a conscious policy but a spontaneous, incremental adjustment to the economic and technological realities of the information age.

The proliferation of telecommunications technologies has caused an explosion of demand for radio frequencies. Often these demands are mutually exclusive. To authorize multipoint distribution services (MDSs), for example, the commission had to take away frequencies from educational broadcasters in the instructional television fixed service (ITFS). Once it authorizes services, the commission is often confronted with hundreds of mutually exclusive applications for the same channel. Thus it received 12,000 applications for low power television (LPT) licenses, 16,500 for MDS (about 70 per channel group), and nearly 200 for the two cellular radio licenses in the top 30 markets. The commission's administrative channel allocation and assignment procedures are simply inadequate for making rational choices among competing uses and users under such circumstances. Therefore, it has inched its way toward instituting a market for radio frequencies.

In some cases, the commission has authorized subleasing or resale of radio channel capacity, as in the MDS-ITFS conflict. Subleasing allows frequencies to be shifted from one use to another without the FCC having to take away the licenses of existing users. Resale allows current licensees to sell excess channel capacity to other users who otherwise would have to go to the commission in search of a channel.

In other instances, the commission has given licensees the technical flexibility to "mine" their channel more intensively, thereby permitting new radio services to be introduced without the need for a new allocation. Most noteworthy in this respect are the FM subcarrier and TV teletext decisions of 1983. The teletext decision authorized TV broadcasters to use their vertical blanking interval to transmit textual information to homes with specially equipped receivers. The FM subcarrier decision authorized FM broadcasters to multiplex their baseband to create additional channels for non-broadcast-related, profitmaking services such as data communication, radio paging, telemetry, and so on. Thus the holders of

190

broadcast licenses have been given the right to carve completely new, potentially profitable services out of their existing channels. In both cases, the broadcaster need not provide the service himself, but can sublease his subcarrier or teletext capacity to someone else.

These directions make the broadcast license approximate a property right, for the broadcaster is able to appropriate the profit created by more efficient technical exploitation of his channel. The broadcast license is no longer merely an authorization to provide a certain type of mass entertainment service. It is a grant of control over a valuable commodity that can be exploited in a number of different ways. The decision undermines the traditional scheme of centralized frequency allocation as well, allowing frequencies to be transferred from one use to another without government approval.

Recently, the commission's drift toward creating a radio market has become conscious and explicit. In September 1983 the FCC's Office of Plans and Policy issued a proposal to create a "decentralized radio service" in the UHF band.[5] The decentralized radio service would be neither devoted to any specific service (like broadcasting, mobile radio, or data communications) nor bound to any technical standards save those pertaining to interference. Licensees would be able to configure their transmission systems in any way and offer any service they wished as long as they did not surpass the interference limits. The detailed proposal lays to rest the old questions about the technical feasibility of radio property rights. It draws on the commission's newly developed computerized procedure for assigning low-power television channels to demonstrate that interference can be controlled without prior specification of service or system configuration. Although the proposal is too controversial and too radical a break with the past to be implemented soon, the mere fact that it came from the FCC itself is an indication of how far the commission has come in supporting a regime of property and exchange in radio.

Issues in Communications Policy

Although the information revolution as defined above has progressed considerably and has gathered a great deal of momentum, it is far from complete. Outside the United States, the old order of

[5]Alex D. Felker and Kenneth Gordon, "A Framework for a Decentralized Radio Service" (Washington, D.C.: Office of Plans and Policy, Federal Communications Commission, September 1983).

monopoly/utility regulation is still the norm. Even within the United States, most of the changes have taken place only at the federal level. The focus of telephone regulation is now shifting to the states, whose utility commissions must confront all the issues pertaining to competition and telephone pricing anew. Moreover, the future direction of policy is far from predetermined. The confusion and delay engendered by the AT&T reorganization and the FCC's access charge order have generated a strong political backlash that could slow or divert the evolution of capitalist relations in the information economy. The following section surveys the most critical policy arenas.

Access Charges

Local telephone exchange access pricing is by far the most important unresolved policy problem in telecommunications regulation today. The transition to a competitive regime in telecommunications will be incomplete, imperfect, and unstable until and unless a market for local exchange access is instituted. Such a change would not only consolidate the reorganization of the telephone system into a set of discrete markets, but would also force telephone companies and their regulators to thoroughly reorder the economic relationships underlying telephone rates.

Under the "end-to-end" service principle of telephone industry organization, there was no such commodity as "local exchange access." Subscribers purchased access to the local and long distance network on a bundled, undifferentiated basis. Only one long distance network, that of AT&T, connected the 23 Bell operating companies and the approximately 3,000 independent telephone companies. These local telephone companies were reimbursed for terminating long distance traffic by an arrangement that pooled all long distance revenues and distributed them according to cost allocation formulas established by a joint board of federal and state regulators.

Once new long distance companies entered the market in the 1970s, an economic boundary between *exchange* and *interexchange* carriers began to evolve. When the courts established the right of the new interexchange carriers to originate and terminate calls over the local exchanges of the Bell system, the local telephone companies were for the first time in their history faced with multiple interexchange carriers seeking interconnection. Thus what had once been the purely administrative problem of planning and engineering the local and long distance components of an integrated network became the locus of a market.

But the creation of a market for local exchange interconnection was beset by three severe complications. First, the court decisions ordering AT&T to connect necessarily left the price of interconnection unresolved. The Bell companies, as wholly owned subsidiaries of the dominant long distance firm, were in no position to hold an unbiased auction for interconnection rights. Second, there was a huge difference between the quality of interconnection available to AT&T and that available to its fledgling competitors. Not only were the connections available to "Other Common Carriers" inferior in technical quality to those of AT&T, but the nature of these connections made it impossible for OCCs to serve subscribers with rotary telephones and forced OCC customers to enter 12 extra digits to complete a call.

The most fateful obstacle to the creation of a market for local access, however, was the fact that such a market could not be instituted without disturbing the vast cost- and rate-averaging scheme lodged at the heart of the telephone system. Fully one-half of the costs of the telephone system were fixed or "non-traffic sensitive" (NTS) in nature, which meant that they did not vary with the number of calls placed. Under our system of utility regulation, regulators were able to arbitrarily allocate these costs between the local and long distance services. Regulators used this latitude to subsidize local service. As improved technology lowered the costs of long distance, more and more of the local loop's NTS costs were shunted over to the interstate rate base, to be recovered through long distance charges. From 1943 to 1982, the proportion of NTS costs allocated to long distance recovery rose from 3 percent to a system-wide average of 26 percent.

Costs were spread out among different regions of the country as well as among different service offerings. Small independent telephone companies and rural areas were permitted to allocate an ever larger portion of their NTS costs to the interstate jurisdiction, sometimes as much as 50 or 60 percent. Regions with denser populations and lower costs, on the other hand, contributed more than their share of costs to the nationwide pool.

Thus, rate increases were avoided in basic subscriptions, the most visible and politically sensitive rates administered by state commissioners, and long distance rates were kept artificially high. Of course, this arrangement was viable only as long as there was no competitive alternative to AT&T's switched long distance service. In December 1982, on the eve of the AT&T settlement, the FCC adopted its access charge order. The FCC's plan would have gradually ended the recovery of the local exchange's NTS costs from interexchange carriers by phasing in a flat fee on all local subscribers over a five-year period. The transition was scheduled to begin in 1984 with a $2 additional charge to residential subscribers and a $4 additional charge to multiline business subscribers. By 1989, local rates would increase by an average of $10 a month to recover all of the local exchange's fixed costs. Relieved of their NTS contribution, long distance rates would be expected to fall by 40 percent.

Despite the commission's determination in the same proceedings that competition was in the "public interest," and despite repeated invocations of "cost-based pricing" and "competition" in the text, these were not the reasons the decision to end the subsidy was made. Rather, the FCC feared that continued reliance on artificially high long distance charges would make it economical for large business users of long distance to construct their own telecommunications facilities to originate and terminate calls. This "bypass" by high volume users, the commission feared, would eventually cause an even greater revenue shortfall than the loss of the long distance subsidy. Their concern was backed by data showing high concentrations of demand: close to 40 percent of AT&T's business interstate long distance revenues came from only 1 percent of its customers.

Nevertheless, the prospect of higher local rates raised a storm of controversy. With "universal service" as their battle cry, Congress and state regulators rose up in opposition to the access charge order. Rep. Edward Markey of Massachusetts spoke darkly of the possible "loss . . . of millions of users to the telephone network in the years ahead."[6] Rep. Timothy Wirth, chairman of the House telecommunications subcommittee, opined that "without a rededication to the principles of universal service, we could witness the creation of information haves and have-nots. We certainly cannot tolerate that kind of division. We must assure that economic status does not become a barrier to access to telecommunications services."[7] In a

[6]House Committee on Energy and Commerce, *Hearings before the Subcommittee on Telecommunications, Consumer Protection, and Finance*, 98th Cong., 1st sess., March 22, 1983, p.1.
[7]Ibid.

rare moment of unity on telecommunications legislation, the Republican-controlled Senate and Democrat-controlled House cooperated to draft legislation aimed at preventing the FCC from implementing its access charge order. The commission was forced to back down. In February 1984, in a move designed to preempt congressional intervention, it deferred the implementation of access charges for residential and single-line business users until June 1985—well after the 1984 elections. The situation is now suspended somewhere between the old system and the new, in an unstable and untenable position.

There is no factual basis for the hysteria fostered by Congress and the telephone monopolies. Indeed, the greatest threat to affordable telephone service comes from the remnants of regulation, not from access charges or competition. A detailed study by Congress's own Congressional Budget Office debunked the argument that universal service is threatened by access charges.[8] It showed that increases in basic subscription rates would be partially (and in some cases wholly) offset by decreases in terminal equipment and long distance costs. Local rate increases are also being accompanied by the institution of "lifeline" rates, allowing low-income subscribers to opt for less expensive access alternatives than before.

However, the impasse over access charges has deeper roots. As long as local telephone companies are governed as rate-base regulated monopolies, local rates will continue to rise. The "rate base" from which the local telephone companies derive their charges is simply a static accounting of all the expenses the utility incurs in providing service. It gives us no assurance that those costs were actually necessary to provide service, nor does it guarantee that other, less expensive ways of doing so could not be found. As long as the utilities are legally entitled to recover all of these "costs," deregulating any portion of the market necessarily puts rate pressure on the shrinking monopoly base of customers. Thus for those, mainly residential, subscribers as yet unreached by competition, utility regulation makes competition a zero sum game.[9]

The only antidote to the rate increases is to allow cable companies

[8]Congressional Budget Office, "The Changing Telephone Industry: Access Charges, Universal Service and Local Rates" (Washington, D.C.: U.S. Government Printing Office, June 1984).

[9]Nina Cornell, Michael Pelcovits, and Dan Brenner, "A Legacy of Regulatory Failure," *Regulation Magazine* (July/August 1983): 38.

and others to compete with the local exchange, and to deregulate local ratemaking. Unfortunately, many congressmen, state regulators, and consumer advocates have interpreted local rate hikes in the opposite way and have responded by restricting competition. Their conservative tendencies are reinforced by telephone companies seeking protection from the rigors of the marketplace. The California Public Utilities Commission, for example, reacted to the divestiture and access charge decisions by flatly prohibiting all intra-LATA competition with Pacific Bell.[10] It also announced that it intended to find ways to ban carrier bypass of the Bell monopoly. The purpose of these draconian measures was allegedly to prevent local rate increases by allowing Pacific to charge higher than competitive prices for intra-LATA toll calls. In other words, the CPUC is trying to re-create the old long-distance-to-local exchange subsidy within the narrowed confines left to it by the AT&T divestiture.

But regulators who try to protect consumers by obstructing competition will in the end simply lock them into dependency on an inefficient monopoly whose rates will continually ratchet upward anyway. This pattern is already becoming apparent. Local rates began their upward climb in 1980—four years before the divestiture and the access charge order were implemented. State commissions granted $6.8 billion in intrastate rate increases from 1980 to 1983, making the price of local subscriptions rise faster than the rate of inflation. The same telephone companies that cry to state commissions for shelter from competition in order to keep rates down think nothing of asking for hefty rate increases in the next breath. Pacific Bell—undoubtedly the exemplar of this kind of hypocrisy—was granted a $131 million rate hike in June 1984 the same day the ruling prohibiting intra-LATA competition was made and only six months after another, $434 million, increase. In the fall of 1984, Pacific announced that it would seek yet another rate hike, this time of $1.5 billion. Local subscribers can expect more of the same as long as rate-base regulation continues and exchange carriers are sheltered from competition.

Telephone companies are also requesting—and usually getting—restrictions on the right of cable television companies to carry business data communications. Recently the state of New Mexico, on a

[10]"LATA" is the acronym for "Local Access and Transport Area." LATAs form the territorial boundaries of the local exchange companies as defined by the Modified Final Judgment of the AT&T settlement.

motion filed by Mountain Bell, ruled that any company providing two-way communications qualifies as a "telephone company" and is subject to the same certification requirements as established telcos. Since cable companies do not want to be subjected to the systematic control that comes with common-carrier status, this ruling effectively bars them from the data communications market. In a related development, the House telecommunications subcommittee amended its "cable deregulation" bill in such a way as to erect a veritable legal wall between one-way delivery of television signals and two-way transmission of data and voice. The intent, once again, was to keep cable off the telephone companies' turf.

The problem of revising local exchange access pricing is inseparable from that of opening up exchange telecommunications to competition. Efficient, pro-competitive access pricing cannot be achieved through traditional tariff regulation. The byzantine complexity and arbitrariness of the FCC's modified access charge order should serve as a reminder that rate regulation is capable only of giving us political compromises among competing interest groups, not efficient prices. Even the positive features of the plan, such as the decision to shift all NTS costs to local subscribers, were forced on the FCC by the threat of "bypass" (in this context just another word for competition). Prices will gravitate toward costs if and only if competition for local traffic spreads and the telephone companies learn that any attempt to price their services above economic cost will drive customers away.

Unfortunately, regulatory authority over local exchange telecommunications and over its actual and potential competitors is highly fragmented among the three levels of government. It will probably be necessary, therefore, for the FCC to preempt state and local authority and institute a nationwide, uniform set of rules governing entry into exchange telecommunications. There is ample precedent for such an action. In order to carry out its program of terminal equipment deregulation, the FCC preempted state pricing regulation of telephone equipment and equipment interconnection standards. By preempting state and local regulation of exchange carriers, the FCC could pave the way for open competition in exchange telecommunications, just as it did in the terminal equipment market.

Although the reorganization of the telephone system is abolishing the rate-averaging and territorial monopoly that once constituted the public element in telecommunications, it has not abolished public intervention altogether. The public component of telecommunications now centers on the rights and conditions of interconnection. It stipulates that all users, regardless of the competition they might provide, have a right to exchange traffic with the public network. For example, telephone companies are prohibited from discriminating against resellers of their services. To make access lines available to one, they must make access lines available to all on equal terms. This is a modification, not an elimination, of traditional common-carrier principles. There is still an important distinction between the public network and the myriad private networks that have grown up to supplement it. Indeed, the utility of these private networks is enhanced by the indiscriminate availability of a public network, just as the viability of the public network is enhanced, not diminished, by the attempt to realign rates and costs to make each of its components self-sustaining.

Banking Reorganization

The banking system, another pillar of the information economy, is also undergoing an organizational transformation. Information technology has contributed to the dissolution of the economic boundaries separating banking from other financial services such as securities and insurance. It is also eroding the geographic restrictions that kept banking localized. As a result, the nation's banking system is in the throes of its most systematic restructuring since the Great Depression.

It was the depression that spurred banking legislation promoting security and stability at the expense of competition. The profitability of established banks was assured by controlling market entry and by setting limits on the amount of interest that could be paid on deposits. The scope of competition was further narrowed by legislation restricting or prohibiting branch and interstate banking. With these restrictions, the United States has sustained 14,600 separate banks—roughly the same number that existed in the 1930s—while Canada, for example, supports only 11.

This system began to unravel in the late 1970s, when the rate of inflation spurted above the regulation-imposed ceilings on the interest banks could pay. Vast sums of money were removed from banks and transferred to higher-interest-bearing money market accounts. From 1978 to the end of 1981, the amount invested in these alternative instruments rose from $4 billion to $185 billion. Traditional

198

depository institutions found it increasingly difficult to attract and hold funds.

The companies best positioned to fill the gap created by regulatory constraints on depository institutions were those with nationwide retail distribution outlets and sophisticated data processing networks: Sears, American Express, Merrill Lynch, and so on. These competitors were also free of the geographic restrictions applied to banks and so were able to experiment with nationally advertised electronic funds transfer, home banking and home security trading services. As new businesses were drawn into competition with banks the economic boundaries between banking, securities, and insurance began to crumble.

Eventually, bank regulators were forced to phase out pricing regulations and to ease geographic restrictions, with the result that interstate banking is rapidly becoming a reality. Six New England states have already passed regional banking laws permitting interstate banking. As of March 1984, 35 states were involved in or were proposing regional interstate banking arrangements. Many state regulators view these laws as a preparation for national banking, which is widely considered to be only a few years away.

The emergence of a nationally integrated financial services industry will probably result in a major shakeout. Financial service firms have already become a popular target of corporate acquisitions: *Business Week* listed $8.5 billion in acquisitions from 1980 to 1984 involving companies such as Sears, Xerox, American Can, and Gulf and Western.[11] Regional and national banking is also expected to produce some consolidation of banks. A Booz, Allen, Hamilton report estimates that only one-third of the nearly 15,000 banks now in existence will survive the decade.[12] Despite a net reduction in the number of banking entities, however, an increase in competition can be expected as protected pockets of monopoly or oligopoly are exposed to national competitors capable of entering any market in the United States.

The "decentralized" banking system of the past in fact depended on centralized regulation and a central banking network, the Federal Reserve System. This dual structure—thousands of local outlets linked by a nationwide monopoly clearinghouse—follows the

[11]"The Peril in Financial Services," *Business Week*, August 20, 1984, p. 54.

[12]"On the Edge: Banking World Seems Less Safe," *Philadelphia Inquirer*, June 3, 1984.

pattern of the nation's broadcasting system, in which thousands of local broadcasters are (or were) linked by a network oligopoly. The similarity is significant because it shows that the United States has structured its information economy according to certain consistent, albeit tacit, principles. In order to demonstrate this consistency, a brief digression concerning broadcasting is necessary.

Rather than conceiving of broadcast channels as distribution outlets for nationwide programming entities, the FCC deliberately assigned channels to local communities and set stringent limits on the number of broadcast outlets a single company could own. However, the economies of scale inherent in the production of programming made the emergence of nationwide program producers—the networks—inevitable. The networks were able to use their control of the best programming to secure the affiliation of local outlets and gained control of the bulk of the broadcast day. Moreover, FCC-imposed limits on the number of channels available to each community shut out any new networks, for few of the top cities had more than three VHF channels. So while the FCC's policies ensured that there would be thousands of independent radio and television stations, it severely restricted competition at both the local and national level, just as banking regulation did. As might be expected, the production of new conduits into the home via cable and Pay TV has led to the growth of many new television programming entities, all national in scope.

The geographic realignment that is occurring in banking is only the first phase of a deeper reorganization of the nation's banking system. The partial deregulation of banks raises questions about when and if banks should be allowed to fail, and more generally whether the Federal Reserve System should be completely over-hauled.[13]

International Communications

I have argued that "control economy" is a better label than "information economy" because information is exchanged among individuals and institutions in order to regulate or alter their environment. A corollary of this position is that we can expect a revolution

---

[13]For a discussion of alternatives to the Federal Reserve System, see Lawrence H. White, "Competitive Money, Inside and Out," *Cato Journal* 3, no. 1 (Spring 1983): 281–99; and Leland B. Yeager, "Stable Money and Free-Market Currencies," *Cato Journal* 3, no. 1 (Spring 1983): 305–26.

in information technology to be conjoined with a rearrangement of society's relations of economic and political control.

Perhaps the most challenging policy choices raised by the information revolution are those pertaining to the international flow of information and the production and regulation of transnational telecommunications conduits. Domestically, information technology is abolishing territorial monopolies in telephony and eroding localism in banking and broadcasting. This border-eroding effect is visible at the geopolitical level as well, and has sparked a momentous debate over the conflict between national sovereignty and the free flow of information.

The importance of international communications is a reflection of an increasingly integrated world economy. The amount of direct U.S. investment in foreign countries rose from only $7.2 billion in 1946 to $192.6 billion in 1979. World trade in goods and services during roughly the same period grew at an average annual rate of 5.1 percent, significantly faster than world output. Moreover, imports now comprise an increasing proportion of the industrialized nations' GNP, rising from 6.2 percent in 1970 to 9.6 percent in 1980.

The effects of the eruption of market relations in the gigantic U.S. telecommunications infrastructure cannot help but ripple across the globe. Domestic deregulation gives hundreds of U.S. computer and telecommunications producers an incentive to expand their markets by vending to foreign post, telegraph, and telephone authorities (PTTs). Computer and communications technologies are now the fastest-growing sectors of the U.S. economy, and Commerce secretary Malcolm Baldridge has asserted that by 1990 they will surpass agriculture to become our number-one export opportunity. Thus much of the international communications policy dialogue in this country revolves around opening up foreign markets and revising our regulatory scheme to increase the global competitiveness of U.S. corporations. Concern about the international scene is also forcing the United States to consolidate its international communications policymaking apparatus, which is now divided among five federal agencies: the State Department, the National Telecommunications and Information Administration (NTIA) of the Commerce Department, the U.S. Trade Representative, the FCC, and the Department of Defense.

Global economic interdependence introduces the need for an integrated, transnational communications system. But most of the world's telecommunications systems are organized as territorial monopolies closely aligned with, if not an appendage of, the state. In certain respects this raises the familiar problems of free trade versus protectionism. But the imperatives of technological change and the pressures exerted by transnational telecommunications users bring other factors into play. Transnational users who are aware of and benefit from the freedom and flexibility of the U.S. system are eager to extend policies similar to those in the United States to other national systems. In Europe, telecommunications users associations with a pro-competitive orientation similar to that of the user groups who successfully pushed for deregulation in the United States are emerging.[14] European telecommunications authorities are beginning to concede that the survival of their domestic industries will require products and services that are competitive with the Americans and the Japanese. They are also beginning to realize that a competitive position cannot be attained as long as their domestic industries exist within small, sheltered markets. As a result, European nations are gradually liberalizing their telecommunications systems.

Britain began in 1981 by authorizing competition with its telephone monopoly, British Telecom. West Germany's economics ministry forced the German Bundespost to permit up to 80 percent of the telecommunications equipment used by businesses to come from alternative suppliers. Holland is expected to open its terminal equipment market to private competition next year and to authorize some competition in data communications and value-added services. The need for larger markets is pushing European PTTs as a group toward a transnational, Europe-wide telecommunications and computer marketplace. Such a market would be achieved through technical standardization and through reciprocal agreements to strike down market barriers.

Japan, too, is opening up its telecommunications monopoly. A 1981 agreement with the United States permitted American companies to sell telecommunications equipment to Nippon Telephone and Telegraph (NTT). In April 1985, NTT becomes a privately held corporation subject to competition. Twenty-five Japanese firms, primarily banks and electronics companies, have already formed a joint venture to compete with NTT in the provision of transmission services. Liberalization along these lines is intended to cultivate private investment and a more competitive telematics production capacity.

The gradual movement of the world's telecommunications systems toward a market will eventually lead to an integrated and more or less uniform set of rules regarding technical standards, pricing, and market entry. In the meantime, a substantial amount of friction still exists between the competitive regime of the United States and its monopoly counterparts overseas. Two instances of such friction come to mind.

The first example concerns Intelsat, a consortium of telecommunications authorities in 108 nations formed by treaty in 1965 that provides international satellite communications on a monopoly basis. A comparison of the Intelsat monopoly with AT&T's erstwhile long distance monopoly in the United States is irresistible. Intelsat's relations with national telecommunications authorities, like AT&T's arrangements with its former local operating companies, are administrative in that operating agreements between two monopolies are negotiated and a division of revenues is agreed upon free of market pressures. Like the old AT&T, Intelsat averages its rates (globally) and complains that new competitors will force it to lower rates for dense routes and raise them for thin (usually Third World) routes.

The FCC now has applications from five U.S. corporations to provide international satellite communications in competition with Intelsat. Intelsat and its U.S. member, Comsat, have strongly urged the FCC to deny the competitors permission to operate, and Intelsat's board passed a resolution urging member countries to refuse to do business with the monopoly's competitors. But even if the U.S. companies are denied permission to operate, Britain and France are expected to launch competing satellite services soon. It seems likely that PTTs in developed countries, like the American local exchanges, sooner or later will have to deal with a multiplicity of interconnecting competitors, with all the attendant pressures toward reorganization and repricing.

A second case underscoring the friction between the old and new regimes was the FCC decision to authorize the resale and sharing of international leased lines. In 1976 and 1981 the FCC permitted domestic entrepreneurs to lease AT&T and OCC private lines for a flat monthly fee and to resell them to customers who would normally have to use more expensive direct dialing. These moves were highly successful in bringing new competitors into U.S. telecommunications and in allowing smaller users to benefit from volume discounts. Foreign PTTs, however, view resale as a revenue-loser because it diverts traffic from expensive direct dial lines. Their reaction to the FCC decision was so negative that U.S. users who would benefit from resale and sharing now oppose it for fear that the PTTs would, in retaliation, eliminate flat-rate private line tariffs altogether. It is becoming increasingly difficult to authorize competition domestically without exporting it to other countries.

The integration of the world's communication system has given rise to a political reaction against the "free flow of information." As might be expected, the reaction comes from the representatives of national governments, in both the developed and the developing worlds. Developing countries in particular tend to see the free flow of information as inimical to their efforts to cultivate autonomous political and economic institutions. The position outlined below by Zimbabwean journalist Chen Chimuntengwende is typical:

> We must have planned development, and the role of the media has to be planned too. Its role must be strictly defined for maximum contribution to development. A nation in a hurry to develop is like a nation in a state of emergency: freedom to criticize must be restricted by government according to its priorities.[15]

The reaction against free flow found a forum in international bodies such as the United Nations and its agencies UNESCO and the International Telecommunications Union (ITU). It is not surprising that "international" institutions should emerge as the primary means of defending the prerogatives of nationalism, for their constituents are not the world's *people* but the *national governments* represented in their delegations and supporting them financially. Ironically, then, the world's only international institutions are beholden to the interests of nation-states and hence are incapable of adopting a truly transnational perspective.

In the mid-to-late 1970s, the reaction against free flow was consolidated into a demand for a "New World Information Order," a demand that national governments be allowed greater control over the flow of information into and out of their countries. Thus in September 1979 a UNESCO seminar pronounced that "free flow of information is a grossly commercial concept serving the interests of transnational corporations, especially with the development of new communication technologies such as satellite telecommunications

---

[15]Cited in Rosemary Righter, "Battle of the Bias," *Foreign Policy* (1978): 125.

and computer systems."[16] Three years later, the UN passed a resolution upholding the right of governments to control the TV signals
their citizens can receive from foreign satellites. The endorsement
of the "prior consent" doctrine, a throwback to the days of royal
publishing monopolies, passed by a vote of 88 to 11.

The intellectual leader of the attack on the free flow doctrine was
communications scholar Herbert Schiller of the University of California at San Diego. Ironically Schiller, a leftist, based his attack on
an explicit defense of "national sovereignty." Schiller's abandon-
ment of the internationalism of the classical left illustrates the profound ideological dilemma the information revolution poses for the
left. Modern leftists claim to support free expression, but they are
first and foremost opposed to capitalism. The extension of capitalist
economic relations into the information economy therefore forces
them into a sterile defense of the preexisting state monopoly system. Thus, would-be "radicals" are transmuted into reactionaries—
apologists for the regulatory status quo ante despite all its obvious
defects, defenders of "national sovereignty" and traditional culture
despite the oppression that prevails in so many nations. Perceiving
this pattern, the late Ithiel de Sola Pool issued this eloquent
warning:

> Nationalism is the doctrine of the right wing that most easily
> coopts the left. Historically, liberals and radicals have been inter-
> nationalists. . . . [It is astonishing] how widely people of the sin-
> cere left have been absorbed in classical doctrines of conservatism
> as a consequence of nationalism. Increasingly they find them-
> selves pushed by the logic of their position to see themselves as
> more opposed to liberalism than to traditional culture, to assert
> that the free flow of information is a goal that must be reconsid-
> ered, to conclude that preservation of traditional ways is more
> important than a rapid rise in GNP, and to justify the use of state
> power to control the communications that reach the people. Their
> ideological predecessors sought to liberate the print media from
> state control, but increasingly people who call themselves men of
> the left find themselves advocating state monopoly control of the
> newer media. Thus a strange alliance puts conservative military

[16]Cited in Peter Hirschberg, "The War over Information," *Washington Journalism Review* (March 1980): 24.

regimes or theocratic oligarchies at one with nominal progressives in defense of censorship.[17]

A New Approach for a New Era

The information revolution must be understood as a revolution in the relations of social control, a transformation of the political and economic organizations that make decisions and regulate production. The emergence of market relations in the information economy, first in the United States and eventually in the rest of the West, portends far-reaching changes in social organization. It is unlikely that these changes will follow any pattern that can be extrapolated from developments in the past. A social transformation of this scale calls for a policy response that transcends old ideological categories, requiring innovative ideas about social organization in general and political economy in particular. Above all, it requires a willingness to clear the ground of the controls and rigidified rules of an earlier epoch so that the seeds of a new, hopefully better social order can germinate and grow.

---

[17]Ithiel de Sola Pool, "Direct Broadcast Satellites and the Integrity of National Cultures," in *National Sovereignty and International Communication,* ed. Kaarle Nordenstreng and Herbert I. Schiller (Norwood, N.J.: Ablex, 1979), pp.139–40.

XI. Solving the Education Crisis: Market Alternatives and Parental Choice

Clint Bolick

Public education in America is in a widely recognized shambles.

For more than a century, Americans have cherished the concept of universal education and have embraced monopoly public schooling as the mechanism to achieve that goal. But somehow, the means and the ends have become confused to the point that we are now sacrificing the goal of universal education in order to preserve the public school mechanism as an end in itself. In the process, educational quality has declined alarmingly and public schools have ceased to provide opportunities for social advancement to minorities and the poor.

Nobly inspired reform proposals abound, but all are addressed to the symptoms rather than the disease. Indeed, some of the proposals are akin to the medieval practice of using leeches to remove poison from the bloodstream: the "cure" may be worse than the malady. Unfortunately, even worthwhile peripheral changes in our educational system will leave intact those fatal flaws that are at the core of monopoly public schooling. What is clearly needed instead is a movement away from governmental control toward a free market in education.

Two landmark events relating to American education occurred during the past administration. The first helped to identify the magnitude of the problem, while the second opened the door to the solution.

The principal event that dramatically revealed the extent of the educational crisis was the report of a blue-ribbon presidential commission, which assessed the state of public education and pronounced it abysmal. The commission regretfully observed that "for the first time in the history of our country, the educational skills of one generation will not surpass, will not equal, will not even approach, those of their parents."[1]

---

[1]National Commission on Excellence in Education, *A Nation at Risk* (Washington, D.C.: U.S. Government Printing Office, 1983), p. 11.

The event that signaled hope for change was a landmark decision of the Supreme Court that upheld a statute reducing the tax burdens of parents choosing private-sector educational alternatives. Speaking for the Court in *Mueller* v. *Allen*, Justice Rehnquist declared that a tax deduction designed "to defray the cost of educational expenses incurred by parents—regardless of the type of schools their children attend . . . plainly serves [the] purpose of ensuring that the state's citizenry is well-educated."[2]

Viewed in tandem, these events underscore both the necessity and the timeliness of realigning our priorities toward a more rational educational strategy. But any strategy that leaves essentially undisturbed the present failed system cannot possibly solve the educational crisis. If our goals are individual opportunity and universal education, we must attack the very root of the problem and remove the governmental impediments that for generations have stymied parental attempts to secure the best education for their children. As Clarence Pendleton, chairman of the U.S. Commission on Civil Rights has emphatically declared, "we must turn to the moral superiority of the marketplace to ensure a quality education for all of America's children."[3]

Origin of the Crisis: The Public School Monopoly

The failures of the monopoly public school system are legion. The presidential commission identified the following as among the most alarming symptoms:

- Twenty-three million Americans, including 13 percent of all 17-year-olds, are functionally illiterate by the simplest tests of everyday reading, writing, and comprehension.
- SAT scores show a virtually unbroken decline between 1963 and 1980, with average verbal scores falling more than 50 points and mathematics scores declining by 40 points.
- International comparisons of student achievement reveal that on 19 academic tests, Americans did not score first or second a single time and were last among industrial nations seven times.
- Half of the nation's gifted students do not perform on a level commensurate with their abilities.

[2]*Mueller* v. *Allen*, 77 L. Ed.2d 721, 728 (1983).

[3]Clarence Pendleton, Jr., "Education and Minorities," *Journal of Social, Political and Economic Studies* 9 (Spring 1984): 78.

- Science achievement has declined precipitously since 1963, and remedial mathematics courses in colleges have grown by 72 percent since 1975.

Such dismal results, the commission concluded, demonstrate that "the educational foundations of our society are presently being eroded by a rising tide of educational mediocrity that threatens our very future as a Nation and a people."[4]

The commission assigned the blame for these results to several deleterious developments in education. Curricula, for instance, have been "homogenized, diluted, and diffused to the point that they no longer have a central purpose," resulting in "a cafeteria-style curriculum in which the appetizers and desserts can easily be mistaken for the main courses."[5] Indeed, in many schools classes in cooking and driving count as much toward graduation as mathematics, English, or biology. Moreover, the typical school provides an average of only four hours of academic instruction per day and requires less than one hour of homework per night. Students are increasingly being taught by teachers who themselves ranked in the bottom quarter of their college graduating classes. Discipline problems are often so disruptive that whatever learning environment is possible given other impediments is soon destroyed.

It is noteworthy that all of this has occurred amid massive increases in educational subsidies and burgeoning federal involvement. Yet the commission report calls for more of the same. Implementation of the commission's recommendations is priced at $23.1 billion, and would further inflate an already bloated public educational bureaucracy. Some of the proposed solutions—more stringent graduation standards, tougher discipline, and courses relevant to the real world—certainly work in the private sector and could marginally improve public education. But others, such as substantial pay raises for teachers, tend to compound the problem by rewarding mediocrity and boosting financial incentives to maintain the status quo.

Were public education a private corporation, wasting vast resources entrusted to it for such questionable results, the shareholders would surely cash in their certificates and place their investments elsewhere. But it is precisely the public and monopolistic nature of government schools that prevents individuals from diverting their financial

[4]*A Nation at Risk,* p. 5.
[5]Ibid., p. 18.

209

investments to more responsive, effective, and efficient producers. And it is for this reason that the mounting failures of public schools are not merely temporary problems which may be eliminated with moderate doses of reform, but are instead fatal flaws inherent in the public monopoly process. Consequently, an enduring solution requires nothing less than a systemic overhaul in the way children are educated in America.

The *public* nature of education inevitably leads to problems associated with the public provision of any service. Economist Walter Williams argues that "while there might be some social argument for taxing people to finance education, there is no social argument for the state to produce it."[6] As a matter of course, public education is a political process, which lends itself to special interest pressures. Indeed, many of the present problems of public sector education—tenure laws, skyrocketing costs, declining standards, inefficiency—can be traced in large measure to the "capture" of public schools by teachers' unions, which utilize their carefully crafted skills to benefit members through sophisticated manipulations of the political process, at enormous costs to educational quality.

Moreover, the very nature of public control requires homogenization in virtually every aspect of the educational process, at tremendous cost to individuality and diversity. Public enterprises are run as bureaucracies under established sets of rules, and bureaucrats choosing to make exceptions for individuals can properly be charged with not treating all citizens equally. This avoidance of "rocking the boat" manifests itself in such ways as the frenzy for equalization of expenditures and the imposition of uniform textbooks and curricula, thereby sacrificing individual needs and desires.

Perhaps most tragically, the public nature of schools makes them susceptible to government experimentation through which students' academic needs are subordinated to nebulous social goals. As attorney Maxwell Miller has declared, "the undergirding problem with American education is its failure to view schools as primarily institutions of learning rather than laboratories for achieving social ends."[7] The tragic legacy of such programs as forced busing,

---

[6]Walter E. Williams, "Inner City Parents and Freedom of Choice," *Black Education and the Inner City* (Washington, D.C.: Lincoln Institute for Research and Education, 1981), p. 10.

[7]Maxwell A. Miller, "Can Education Survive the 'New Equality'?" *Journal of Social, Political and Economic Studies* 9 (Spring 1984): 8.

racial quotas, and avant-garde teaching fads is one of mis-education and missed opportunities.

As if these flaws in the public provision of education were not enough, they are exacerbated by its *monopoly* status. The massive burdens of tax financing render it difficult, if not impossible, for most parents to opt out of public education. With both a steady source of funds to which private sector schools are not privy and a student body held captive by compulsory education laws—in essence, artificial supply and demand—public schools are subject to virtually no competitive pressure to produce a quality product. There is consequently little wonder that public school administrators and teachers are consistently at the forefront of efforts to thwart any meaningful choice in education.

The real crux of the problem is indeed the monopolistic privilege enjoyed by public education. Only in the absence of competition from the private sector can public schools indulge themselves in such luxuries as administrative top-heaviness, inflated salaries, political lobbying efforts, and a smug attitude toward parental demands. It is therefore clear that the typical reform proposals—none of which address the monopoly issue—are insufficient to fully cure the crisis confronting American education. No matter how much additional money is spent to "improve" public schools, the present maladies will recur time and again until meaningful competition and choice are infused into the system.

Parental Response: Turning to the Marketplace

Growing numbers of parents are facing the sobering realization that they must pursue alternatives in order to secure quality education for their children. Many are removing their children from schools altogether and are teaching them at home. But others are turning to the private sector. That fully 11 percent of all parents are willing to devote enormous financial resources to invest in private alternatives—simultaneously paying taxes for public schools and tuition for a private school—is a testament to the intense desire of many Americans to provide the best possible opportunities for their children.

The parents who are pursuing the private alternative include not only those possessed of substantial resources with whom private schools are most commonly associated, but increasingly those whose children need quality education the most—ethnic minorities and the poor. Indeed, fully *half* of urban private school families have incomes of $10,000 or less, twice the percentage of the U.S. population as a whole. Such families often make extraordinary sacrifices to patronize private schools: they raise tuition from welfare checks, from members of extended families, or by working multiple jobs. A recent study confirmed that urban private schools consist largely of

> the minorities of the 1980's—blacks, Puerto Ricans, and Mexican Americans. Like this country's earlier minorities—the Irish, Germans, Italians, etc.,—who built these schools and used them as a means by which their children could more fully enter the stream of American life, today's inner-city private school clients have similar expectations.[8]

The market has responded to these desires in a most impressive fashion. Another study recently found more than 300 independent schools operated by and for minorities.[9] Indeed, over half the students in urban private schools are black, and another third are Hispanic. Parochial schools, in particular, provide minorities enormous opportunities. All other factors being equal, blacks are more likely than any other group to enroll in such schools.

Because private schools have to be fiercely competitive in order to survive, they must be responsive to consumer demands and produce superior results. These results are achieved in three principal ways: greater educational expectations manifested by stress on basic skills, rigorous academic courses, and more hours of homework; an orderly learning environment buttressed by stringent disciplinary standards; and operational efficiency, eschewing the bureaucratic malaise that permeates the public sector. Those public schools that are successful are typically those exhibiting these characteristics; but while in public schools such efforts represent policy options which are always subject to change, they are the very key to survival in the competitively disadvantaged private sector.

As a consequence, parental investments in private schools usually earn substantial returns. The impact of private schools on academic success is often substantial, particularly for minority youngsters. Private school students score well above the national average

---

[8]J. Cibulka, T. O'Brien, and D. Zewe, *Inner-City Private Elementary Schools: A Study* (Milwaukee: Marquette University Press, 1982), p. 19.

[9]Joan Davis Ratteray, "One System is Not Enough: A Free Market Alternative for The Education of Minorities," *Lincoln Review* 4 (Spring 1984): 27.

in every academic sector: reading, vocabulary, mathematics, science, civics, and writing. Far more aspire to and actually do attend college. As Professor James Coleman concluded after a comprehensive investigation of the results of public versus private schooling, "when family background factors that predict achievement are controlled, students in . . . private schools are shown to achieve at a higher level than students in public schools."[10] This is particularly meaningful in the case of minority children, who are all too frequently held hostage to a public educational system that reinforces the vicious cycle of under-achievement, poverty, and despair.

Private schools produce additional positive effects as well. Studies reveal that students in private schools demonstate higher levels of social and educational aspirations and generally feel a stronger sense of self-esteem and control over their destinies.[11] Private sector students give higher ratings to their schools for academic quality and responsiveness to individual concerns, as well as for the fairness and effectiveness of discipline. Indeed, discipline is the single greatest distinction in the operation of private and public schools. Absenteeism, cutting class, physical conflict, vandalism, drugs, verbal abuse, and violent crimes are all twice or more as prevalent in public schools. Most parents report disciplinary improvements at home after enrolling their children in a private school. It is thus little wonder that many parents, particularly minority parents, seek more wholesome educational alternatives than are available in the public sector.

But perhaps most importantly, private schools appear to enhance upward social mobility. As sociologist Andrew Greeley observed in his study of Catholic schools and minority students, such schools tend "to eliminate . . . the effect of parental social class on academic achievement, a finding as rare in educational research as it is striking."[12] Thus, increased access to private educational alternatives could dramatically increase prospects for poor and minority

[10]James Coleman, Thomas Hoffer, and Sally Kilgore, *High School Achievement* (New York: Basic Books, Inc., 1982).

[11]For statistical documentation relating to private versus public education throughout this chapter, see generally ibid.; Cibulka, O'Brien, and Zewe; and Andrew Greeley, *Catholic High Schools and Minority Students* (New Brunswick, N.J.: Transaction, Inc., 1982).

[12]Greeley, p. 88.

children to achieve to the limits of their individual abilities and participate in the mainstream of American life.

Finally, private schools are more efficient than their public counterparts. Because of the need to compete, not only with each other but with subsidized public schools as well, private schools produce their superior results for only 50 to 75 percent of the per-pupil cost in the public sector.

Many families that would benefit enormously from the efficiency and productivity of private schools simply cannot afford them. Indeed, many poor families presently opting for private education at great sacrifice are themselves in a precarious position—fully one-fourth of the parents with children in urban private schools would be forced to remove them if faced with a $15 monthly tuition increase.[13]

The most tragic by-product of the monopoly public school system is its frustration of the aspirations of many capable youngsters. Generations of Americans have made tremendous strides by shrewdly exploiting educational opportunities, but those at the bottom of today's socio-economic spectrum too often lack similar opportunities. Instead, they are trapped in schools devoid of intellectual challenges and individual opportunities, typified by mediocre teachers, disruptive influences, and social experimentations. These failures are attributable to the monopoly system itself. It is time, therefore, to turn to free enterprise.

Removing the Barriers: Education Tax Credits

A comparison of public and private education leads inevitably to the conclusion that increased competition and choice between the sectors is of critical importance. Any policies designed to expand educational alternatives and the opportunity to utilize them, such as legalizing home schooling, relaxing private school regulations, and eliminating teacher certification requirements, would constitute positive steps. Since it is abundantly clear that parents who have relied on their own judgment and sought alternatives to public schools have by and large been more successful in securing positive results than have educational bureaucrats, present restrictions serve no apparent purpose other than to preserve an unsatisfactory status quo.

But policies erasing impediments of this type do little to remove

---

[13]Cibulka, O'Brien, and Zewe, p. 212.

the greatest barrier of all: lack of money. Alternatives to the monopoly system are meaningless without the ability to pursue them.

The solution to the money problem, however, is *not* greater subsidies for public (or private) education, as suggested by the presidential commission and sundry teachers' unions. To the contrary, the money problem can be solved by returning to taxpayers a substantial part of their mandatory financial investment in public schools, thereby allowing them to purchase the education of their choice or voluntarily provide it to others. This policy, typically referred to as "education tax credits," can be implemented at the federal, state, or local levels, as well as at some combination of these through federal revenue sharing. A comprehensive tax credit program should include the following elements:

1. *Tax credits should apply against tax liability dollar for dollar and provide meaningful tax relief.* Credits should reduce taxes by the amount of educational dollars spent. In order to have any real impact, a sufficient credit should be made available to present a real option—it should amount to the actual cost of average private school tuition.

The $250 tax credit proposed by the Reagan administration would provide little substantive gain for those who could most benefit from expanded educational options. Only a comprehensive, full-tuition credit would truly equalize the ability to choose between public and private schools. Anything less comprehensive would reduce existing tuition burdens, but would not likely increase competition in any meaningful sense.

To ensure that the amount of tax forgiveness for those claiming it does not exceed the amount of money presently allocated to public education, the maximum per-pupil credit could be limited to 50 to 75 percent of present public school expenditures, since private schools typically provide education for that fraction of the public sector cost. Accordingly, subsidies for public schools should be reduced for each student opting for the private sector.

For parents with sufficient tax liabilities, an education tax credit of this type would render private schools affordable. The credits would also eliminate or reduce the inequity inflicted upon private school parents who pay taxes for public schools from which they derive no benefits.

2. *Tax credits should be available for scholarships.* A tax program would provide only limited benefits if it aided just those families with sufficient tax liabilities. Thus, a critical component of the

program would be the availability of tax credits not only to parents but to all taxpayers, including those desiring to provide scholarships to low-income students. Interested relatives could in this way provide tuition for family members, and corporations could invest in an educated citizenry. Given a choice between general tax liability and educational scholarships, it is likely that many taxpayers would choose the latter, making private sector alternatives plentiful for needy students.

3. *Regulation of school policies should be prohibited.* An enhanced private educational sector would surely inspire a frenzy to regulate it. But private schools have been successful precisely because they are usually somewhat removed from the stifling regulatory reach of government. The marketplace has proven far superior to the state as a guarantor of educational quality. To preserve diversity, in addition, private schools must be free from regulations that would detract from their unique academic, cultural, and religious characteristics. Regulations relating to any aspect of the conduct of school policies should therefore be forbidden. Crucial to this provision is the understanding that tax credits are *not* government subsidies; they are simply a mechanism through which taxpayers may retain some of their own funds for a socially desirable purpose. Thus, tax credits should not be construed as furnishing an independent basis for private school regulation.

4. *The public sector should be deregulated.* Public schools that are capable of producing quality education should be free to respond to the new competitive challenge. Because such public schools might turn to market techniques such as user fees, tax credits should be available for parental expenses incurred in the public sector as well. In this way, tax credits would encourage the transition of these schools to a quasi-private status.

The comprehensive tuition tax credit system envisioned here would open the doors to expanded educational opportunity. Chairman Pendleton of the Civil Rights Commission agrees that tax credits are "the only alternative that will begin to establish the quality education we need, especially for minority youngsters."[14] Professor Walter Williams adds that a "tuition tax credit system would give poor people at least some of the powers that higher

---

[14]Pendleton, p. 75.

income people enjoy with respect to education, that is the freedom to choose."[15]

Critics of educational choice are nonetheless quick to assail tuition tax credits on a number of grounds, all of them flawed. First, they charge that tax credits would destroy public education. This argument, however, ignores the competitive advantages that public schools would continue to enjoy over the expanding private sector, such as existing physical plants, prime neighborhood locations, and direct public subsidization. Only those public schools of demonstrably inferior quality in highly competitive markets would be likely to go out of business—and that is precisely the fate such schools deserve. The more probable effect of increased competition is that many public schools would begin to shake off generations of acquired lethargy to concentrate once again on providing education efficiently and effectively. In any event, concern over the fate of public education as an institution is misplaced if alternatives prove better at fulfilling the goal of universal education.

Second, critics claim that enhanced choice would result in "skimming" the top students from public schools, leaving the residue in a virtual "dumping ground." But as Professor Williams emphasizes, "it's the absence of 'skimming' and . . . effective 'dumping grounds' which is precisely part of the problem in the public school system."[16] An invigorated private sector would doubtlessly inspire the creation of specialty schools for students running the gamut from gifted to physically handicapped to those with discipline problems. Moreover, the supposition that serious students would leave others behind if given the option to do so is certainly no argument in favor of depriving them of such opportunities and incarcerating them in schools that fail to educate them.

Third, opponents argue that low-income students whose parents have insufficient tax liabilities would not benefit from tuition tax credits. The scholarship provision of the tax credit proposal outlined here should remedy that concern. Some critics, however, find fault with the scholarship provision. Professor John Coons of Berkeley complains, for example, that he does not "see any great advance in preferring a hamburger king or a bank president over some bureaucrat in Sacramento" in deciding how educational

[15]Williams, p. 13.
[16]Ibid., p. 12.

investments shall be made.[17] What eludes such critics is the fact that unlike the present system, the scholarships provided by corporate taxpayers would provide some measure of choice to those who would most benefit by it. It is also clear that every incremental increase in choice expands the overall opportunities available for America's children. Further, it is difficult to comprehend that the remote, isolated decisions of a single bureaucratic agency are preferable to any degree of decentralization.

Coons himself favors a voucher system in which parents would be given certificates redeemable in public or private schools. While representing an improvement over the status quo, vouchers involve direct transfers of money to schools, and in most proposals are accompanied by a host of regulations. In addition to excluding schools that could not or would not accept vouchers under a more burdensome regulatory scheme, such regulations have the propensity to turn private schools into quasi-public institutions, instead of the reverse.

Finally, critics charge that private schools promote segregation. In actuality the converse may be true, however, since blacks and whites are far more segregated in the public than in the private sector. Moreover, the degree of internal economic segregation is less in private schools. Professor James Coleman concludes that "the public schools of the United States constitute a rather highly stratified and differentiated set of schools, not the common school envisioned by Horace Mann."[18] The more integrated private sector demonstrates that in a system of voluntary interaction in which educational excellence is the primary goal, irrational notions of racial prejudice tend to disappear.

The various criticisms of choice in education through tuition tax credits are easily seen to be self-serving and largely without foundation. To the extent they are valid, however, they merely expose potential shortfalls in a system that is certainly a vast improvement over the present one. Apart from preserving the status of those with a vested interest in the status quo, there is little substance to arguments against competition and choice.

[17]John E. Coons, "The Voucher Alternative," *Journal of Social, Political and Economic Studies* 9 (Spring 1984): 99.

[18]Coleman, Hoffer, and Kilgore, p. 48.

The Legal Climate

Until recently, tax credit opponents also asserted that any tax credit program is unconstitutional as an establishment of religion in violation of the First Amendment. For the time being, at least, this argument has been laid to rest.

Traditionally, the Supreme Court has recognized a certain degree of educational freedom. In a 1925 decision striking down a state prohibition against private schools, Justice McReynolds declared in *Pierce* v. *Society of Sisters* that

> the fundamental theory of liberty upon which all governments in this Union repose excludes any general power of the state to standardize its children by forcing them to accept instruction from public teachers only. The child is not the mere creature of the state; those who nurture him and direct his destiny have the right, coupled with the high duty, to recognize and prepare him for additional obligations.[19]

Half a century later, Justice Lewis Powell observed in *Wolman* v. *Walter* that private schools

> have provided an educational alternative for millions of young Americans; they often afford wholesome competition with our public schools; and in some states they relieve substantially the tax burden incident to the operation of public schools. The State has, moreover, a legitimate interest in facilitating education of the highest quality for all children within its boundaries, whatever school their parents have chosen for them.[20]

But in a series of cases in the last decade, the Court invalidated a variety of measures designed to assist private schools and their patrons, holding that since many of the benefits ultimately flowed to religiously sponsored institutions, the "primary effect" of such benefits was invariably the advancement of religion. The Court failed to comprehend that such institutions are themselves principally educational rather than religious in emphasis, and that the real primary effect of programs designed to aid access to such schools is the expansion of educational opportunities.

Indeed, religiously affiliated schools appear to influence the

---

[19]*Pierce* v. *Society of Sisters*, 268 U.S. 510, 535 (1925).

[20]*Wolman* v. *Walter*, 433 U.S. 229, 262 (1977) (Powell, J., concurring in part, concurring in judgment in part, and dissenting in part).

academic success of students far more than their religiosity. More than half of inner-city parochial school students are Protestant, and fewer than 15 percent of the students in such schools consider themselves "very religious." Even in parochial schools with mandatory religion classes, students still spend more time in secular academic classes than do public school students. Thomas Sowell concludes that

> if some . . . religiously oriented groups are willing to conduct good schools in order to be able to put in a word for their beliefs, that is not unreasonable in a pluralistic society. Indeed, [such schools] are partly carrying out a public responsibility at private expense.[21]

A more sensible approach than that advocated by the Court over the past ten years produced the *Mueller* v. *Allen* decision in 1983. By a 5–4 vote, the Court upheld a Minnesota statute providing tax deductions for primary and secondary school expenses. Although available for both private and public school parents, most of the deductions were claimed for expenses in religiously affiliated schools. Speaking for the Court, Justice Rehnquist nonetheless concluded that the First Amendment prohibition against the establishment of religion "simply [does] not encompass the sort of attenuated financial benefit, ultimately controlled by the private choices of individual parents, that eventually flows to parochial schools."[22]

Mueller suggests that tax credits may survive constitutional scrutiny if they (1) are not restricted to religiously affiliated schools and (2) are conferred directly upon the parents rather than upon religiously affiliated schools. The precise parameters must be determined in future cases, but the Court's decision makes it clear for the first time that tax credits are not invalid per se.[23]

The *Mueller* majority, however, is a fragile one, resting on a single vote. The administration can thus make an enormous contribution to educational opportunity not only by fostering education tax credits,

---

[21]Thomas Sowell, *Black Education: Myths and Tragedies* (New York: David McKay Co., Inc., 1972), p. 249.

[22]*Mueller* v. *Allen*, 77 L. Ed.2d at 731.

[23]For a full explanation of the impact of the *Mueller* decision, see Clint Bolick, "Private Sector Educational Alternatives and the *Mueller* Decision," *Journal of Social, Political and Economic Studies* 9 (Spring 1984): 79; and "A Crack in the Wall: The Supreme Court Paves the Way for Private School Tax Relief," *Cogitations on Law and Government* (Winter 1983): 46.

but by appointing to the Supreme Court justices who will apply and expand the *Mueller* precedent and the vital liberties it recognizes.

A Moral Imperative

The foregoing discussion demonstrates that expanded educational choice through tuition tax credits constitutes sound, pragmatic public policy. But additionally, choice in education is consistent with cherished American notions of individual liberty.

The present monopoly public school system is not only inefficient and ineffective, but coercive as well. One observer notes that parents

> cannot simply boycott this institution. Private schools are beyond the reach of most families. . . . Yet some parents are now saying that deliberate withdrawal of their children from compulsory schooling—an illegal act in most states—is not unlike draft resisting in an immoral war.[24]

It is indeed tragic when parents desiring to educate their children in the best possible manner feel impelled to reject the system altogether. Freeing the market to provide for individual needs would increase choice while serving the goal of a well-educated society.

Competition, voluntarism, opportunity, and choice are the hallmarks of the free enterprise system. America's educational crisis can be solved only by freeing the market for education.

[24]Marilyn Ferguson, *The Aquarian Conspiracy* (Los Angeles: J. P. Tarcher, Inc., 1980), p. 280.

XII. Deregulating the Poor

Joan Kennedy Taylor

It was widely assumed that the spending cuts of the Reagan administration would tell us something concrete about government social policy: Either they would inspire a supply-side boost to economic growth that would become a rising tide to lift the boats of the poor (particularly the inner-city black poor), or they would increase the number of poor in the United States in a way that would provide unambiguous proof that the Republican administration was reversing years of progress toward eradicating poverty in order to help the rich at the poor's expense. As it turns out, despite the rhetoric of some Democratic politicians, the figures, when they became available, did not substantiate partisan claims on either side.

In the summer of 1983, a private research group, the Washington-based Center for the Study of Social Policy, issued a report on the economic status of black Americans. Entitled "A Dream Deferred," it was the first comprehensive report on the subject since the 1980 census. The headline news was that, although both black and white families were better off at the time of the study than they had been in 1960, the gap between their average incomes was virtually the same. In 1960, the income of the average black family was 55 percent of the income of the average white family; "today," it was 56 percent. Since most of the data for the report had been collected before President Reagan took office in 1981, the report said nothing about the effects of his administration's policies. But it did provide an unsettling benchmark to measure the supposed gains of previous, more liberal administrations.[1]

Actually, this seemingly static figure reflects a polarization in the black community. On the one hand, black families with two working parents, the report showed, had 84 percent of the income of white families with two working parents, and they increased their

---

[1]John Herbers, "Income Gap Between Races Wide as in 1960, Study Finds," *The New York Times*, July 18, 1983.

earnings at a faster rate. On the other hand, the percentage of black families headed by women with children under 18 had increased from 21 percent to a startling 47 percent. And over the same period, the proportion of black men over 16 who were employed had decreased from 74 percent to 55 percent. That figure undoubtedly masked an even worse situation because an estimated 15 to 20 percent of black men aged 20 to 40 "could not be found by the Census Bureau and are presumed to have neither jobs nor permanent residences."[2]

In August of 1983, the census bureau issued its long-awaited figures on 1982. Newspaper headlines told us that 1982 witnessed the highest poverty rate—15 percent—since the mid-sixties (the previous high was 17.3 percent in 1965). But this dramatic figure was not the clear-cut indictment of Reagan policy changes that it might have seemed. The small print went on to say that the poverty rate "had increased in each of the last four years after hovering just above 11 percent in the mid-1970's."[3]

Administration spokesmen pointed out that 1982 had been a recession year. They argued that the increase in the poverty rate, besides being part of a continuum that included the Carter years, represented an unusually bad general economic situation that had since changed. By November, David Stockman of the Office of Management and Budget was telling a congressional committee, "I am absolutely confident that the poverty rate is going to decline dramatically for 1983."[4] And he was not alone in that prediction. Sheldon Danziger of the non-partisan University of Wisconsin Institute for Research on Poverty told a reporter from the *Christian Science Monitor* in December 1983 that he expected "the 1983 poverty rate to come in at 14.6 percent and stay around that level during 1984."[5]

But if the figures proved no easy consolation for the Democrats, they were not destined to help the Republicans either. In February 1984 the census bureau issued a report requested by the administration on the effect of counting non-cash benefits as income on the

[2]Ibid.

[3]Robert Pear, "Poverty Rate Rose to 15% in '82, Highest Level Since Mid-1960's," *The New York Times*, August 3, 1983.

[4]Robert Pear, "Rate of Poverty Found to Persist in Face of Gains," *The New York Times*, August 3, 1984.

[5]David T. Cook, "It's still not an economic recovery for everyone in US," *The Christian Science Monitor*, December 12, 1983.

poverty rate. The report found that poverty had risen over the previous four years, whether non-cash benefits were considered income or not.[6] The following April, the Congressional Budget Office issued "the first detailed study showing the effects of the recent tax and budget cuts on households at different income levels" since 1981.[7] It found that the widely held assumption that the poor had lost out overall as a result of the tax and budget programs was absolutely correct. "Those in the lowest income category lose more in cash benefits than they gain from the tax changes in every year."[8] Then in August came the census bureau report on the 1983 poverty level, which dashed the administration's hopes for positive policy results by showing not a decline in poverty in the face of general gains in the economy, but a non-statistically significant *increase* from 15 to 15.2 percent. But that was not all. In the same month the Urban Institute issued a new study critical of the effects of Reagan's policies. According to one of the co-authors of the report, Isabel V. Sawhill, while the top segments of the population had gained from the tax cuts, the middle- and lower-income groups had not. "The average income of the poorest one-fifth of all families declined from $6,913 to $6,391, or by nearly 8 percent."[9]

These figures tell us that we are doing something very wrong about the poor—or, at the very least, that we are not doing something right. As Robert Pear wrote in the *New York Times* in August 1984, "Poverty normally declines when family income goes up. But that did not happen last year."[10]

From Poor Law to Great Society

How have past generations of Americans tried to care for the poor? Essentially with variations on a tradition that was, like most of our basic legal-cultural traditions, imported from England.

In feudal society, one was born into a complicated system of privileges and obligations that organized society into a hierarchy

[6]Robert Pear, "Rise in Poverty From '79 to '82 Is Found in U.S.," *The New York Times*, February 24, 1984.

[7]Robert Pear, "Budget Study Finds Cuts Cost the Poor As the Rich Gained," *The New York Times*, April 4, 1984.

[8]Ibid.

[9]Robert Pear, "Study of Reagan Domestic Policy Finds Good and Bad News," *The New York Times*, August 16, 1984.

[10]Pear, "Rate of Poverty."

within which each level performed duties owed to and received protection from the next higher level. The indigent were legally attached to their birthplaces and cared for by noble or church. The dissolution of feudalism left charity to the church poor box, and later the expropriation of the monasteries during the Reformation secularized it. Gradually, charitable contributions became obligatory and were collected and administered by local officials.

These officials were to see to it that the funds they collected were not wasted. As early as 1349, the Ordinance of Labourers had required that every British subject "not living in merchandize, nor exercising any craft, nor having of his own whereof he may live" be compelled to work at such wages as "were accustomed to be given in the places where he oweth to serve," or be imprisoned.[11] In 1531 an Act of Parliament provided for the registration of those unable to work, who would then be authorized to beg. "As for those who sought alms without authorization, the penalty was whipping till the blood ran."[12] With the passage of the Elizabethan Poor Law in 1601, a tax—the "poor rate"—was assessed to care for paupers, while at the same time justices of the peace were required to put paupers to work.

Basically then, the idea embodied in the Elizabethan Poor Law was that the poor were attached to their communities of residence, where they were required to work if they could. If they could not, they would be cared for in some minimal way—but the community could set stringent requirements in return for such care. One requirement became popular and was established by law in England in 1723: the poorhouse, in which the indigent had to live and work in order to receive aid. These ideas were transferred to the American colonies by the British settlers, both in the institutions transplanted directly from England and in the British common law, which became the fundamental legal underpinning of all the original colonies and was either assumed or adopted by new states (with the exception of Louisiana) as they were formed and added to the Union.

For the poor in a small community, a poorhouse (or poor farm, as it was often called in rural areas) was not always available. To cite a 1983 study of nineteenth-century rural poor relief in Massachusetts:

---

[11]Ordinance of Labourers, 23 Edw. 3 (1349), chapter 1.

[12]R. H. Tawney, *Religion and the Rise of Capitalism* (New York: Harcourt, Brace & World, Inc., 1954).

By 1655, each town took responsibility for its own poor and had authority to forbid entrance to strangers. Towns often quarreled over vagrants and who was responsible for them. In the cities and large towns, almshouses or poor farms were established as early as 1660 in Boston and 1702 in Hatfield, a large and prosperous rural town . . . in Western Massachusetts. However, most small communities continued the established practice of auctioning off the poor to the lowest bidder at town meeting, usually once or twice a year, and the town would then pay the citizen-bidder to keep a pauper or two at home.[13]

This "bidding out the poor," as it was called, was a system with great potential for cruelty—paupers were literally sold at auction to the lowest bidder, that is, to the person who required the least amount of taxpayer contribution to feed, house, and clothe a pauper for the indicated period. In return, of course, the bidder had the right to the pauper's labor. Orphans were often apprenticed in a similar fashion.

In 1820 an official survey indicated that there were four current ways of providing for the poor in Massachusetts: (1) selling each pauper separately at auction to the lowest bidder among the town families; (2) selling all the poor at auction to one bidder; (3) "outdoor relief," that is, giving the poor enough to sustain them in their own houses; (4) putting the poor in poorhouses or poor farms.[14] The survey considered the last alternative the best for both pauper and taxpayer.

Although the bidding out of paupers and the apprenticing of orphans continued to be practiced in some localities, poorhouses continued to spread. By the time of the Great Depression, according to Frances Fox Piven and Richard Cloward, "the main legal arrangement for the care of the destitute was incarceration in almshouses or workhouses."[15]

The establishment of poorhouses didn't lessen the incidence of poverty. After the Civil War, cities suddenly expanded as a result of migration from rural areas and the flocking of immigrants to the United States to seek their fortunes. Cities were centers of jobs in

[13]Louise Minks, "From Auction to Poor Farm: A Case Study of 19th Century Rural Poor Relief," *The ALSA Forum* 7, no. 1 (1983): 52–53.

[14]Ibid., p. 56.

[15]Frances Fox Piven and Richard A. Cloward, *Poor People's Movements* (New York: Random House, 1979).

manufacturing, which, low-paying and wretched as they were, were preferable to either the exigencies of rural life or the conditions of starvation and repression in Europe. But the new urbanites were poor. One writer recounts that in the late nineteenth century, in New York, Chicago, San Francisco, Detroit, and Cleveland, "three-fourths of the population were immigrants or the children of immigrants. Many of the immigrants came from impoverished rural communities, and most of them came to find better jobs and make more money."[16] Not all succeeded.

Robert Hunter, a former social worker at Jane Addams's Hull House in Chicago, defined poverty in a 1904 book as an income for a family of five of $460 a year in northern industrial areas—less in the rural South.[17] However, many people above this "poverty line" were in fact living in abject poverty by today's standards. To quote a contemporary authority:

> Urban families with three children and earnings of $500–$800 in 1900 typically owned little furniture and no real estate. They rented two- or three-room flats without hot or even running water and without indoor flush toilets. They subsisted on bread and potatoes. Illness or loss of a job quickly wiped out whatever savings the provident were able to amass. There was no unemployment insurance, little public welfare, virtually no old-age pensions.[18]

Still, most Americans at the time assumed that the poor could overcome poverty with enough effort. The majority of the immigrants who came to seek their fortunes did indeed see their children rise out of the poverty they experienced. Thus, they too felt that those who spent entire lives in destitution did so for lack of enterprise, or were "intemperate" or even criminal. This idea persisted almost unquestioned, except by a few reformers like Robert Hunter, despite severe business cycles and depressions, until the worldwide calamity of the Great Depression with its massive unemployment—and the coincidental droughts that produced the Dust Bowl—shook it to its roots.

It seemed clear that local communities and even counties could

---

[16]Robert W. Smuts, *Women and Work in America* (New York: Schocken Books, 1971), pp. 47–48.

[17]James T. Patterson, *America's Struggle Against Poverty, 1900–1980* (Cambridge, Mass.: Harvard University Press, 1981), p. 7.

[18]Ibid., pp. 6–7.

not handle the need for assistance that these nationwide catastrophes presented. For the first time in our history "outdoor relief," a term soon shortened simply to "relief," became the standard way of dealing with those in immediate need. The first statewide relief authority, New York's Temporary Relief Administration, was established in the winter of 1931–32. It was followed almost immediately by the first federal relief legislation, the Emergency Relief and Construction Act in July 1932.

With the election of Franklin Delano Roosevelt that fall, the way was paved for the New Deal measures that initiated the contemporary welfare state. But by today's standards the welfare state of the thirties was modest. It was generally assumed that the dole was demoralizing and that the solution to the problem of poverty would be social insurance—social security—rather than welfare. The assistance instituted by the New Deal was a four-part system of general relief (still funded primarily by state and local governments); public jobs (federally supported under the Work Projects Administration); federal assistance for the blind, the elderly, and dependent children; and social insurance, which included unemployment insurance.[19]

With the coming of World War II, prosperity and full employment returned to the economy. But the social insurance programs were, along with AFDC, retained, as well as the idea that help for the dependent was ultimately a federal responsibility. The seeds of the welfare state and the welfare bureaucracy had been sown.

Victims of the War on Poverty?

The story after World War II is more familiar to most of us. A period of self-congratulation at having put poverty behind us (the fifties) was succeeded by a period of soul searching that rediscovered poverty and then initiated the Great Society programs to put an end to it once and for all.

Today in the eighties, after billions of dollars have been spent on the poor, we are realizing that our inner cities are in worse shape than they were before. We now have a multigenerational dependency on welfare that seems to be forming an almost unreachable underclass; and we find that the ranks of the unemployable, certainly among poor blacks, seem to be swelling. It would be bad enough if all that money had gone to create a New Class of poverty

[19]Ibid., p. 60.

229

bureaucrats, leaving the problems of the poor untouched. The reality seems to be even worse.

The question we are now confronting is this: What invisible hand, what combination of forces, is responsible for these unintended results of the War on Poverty that Lyndon Johnson announced 20 years ago? Pieces of the answer have been presented by various social critics, most of them conservative. The short answer, which seems uncompassionate and even unreasonable to liberals, is that the welfare system provides an incentive for people to give up and be dependent. Liberal critics reply with some plausibility that the unreformed welfare system is harsh, unfeeling, intrusive, niggardly, and demeaning. In a rich society like ours, they charge, the basic necessities of life should be available to all as a matter of right. Many agree with the conclusions of Frances Fox Piven and Richard Cloward in their very influential book, *Regulating the Poor*, that welfare systems have always been instituted to control the poor. The purpose of welfare and relief in the past, write Piven and Cloward, was never to help the poor, but rather to defuse discontent and potential rebellion. Another purpose was to enforce work by setting up such unpleasant conditions for relief that they would be all but unacceptable. A proper society would provide for all its members.

But in 1984 there appeared *Losing Ground: American Social Policy, 1950–1980*, a book by Charles Murray, a professional evaluator of social programs with seven years' experience at the nonprofit American Institutes for Research.[20] In this work Murray presents a comprehensive and persuasive case for the view that we have indeed, with the best will in the world, created a welfare system in which incentives have been disastrously undercut.

The book sets forth the thesis that the social policies implemented in the Great Society programs and thereafter have been wrong in two ways. First, they have not worked, that is, they have not attained their stated goals. Second, they have been morally wrong, victimizing precisely those people who least deserve it and can least afford it—those of the poor who are struggling to be self-sufficient and perhaps even to better their lot. "It was wrong," writes Murray,

> to take from the most industrious, most responsible poor—take safety, education, justice, status—so that we could cater to the

[20]Charles Murray, *Losing Ground: American Social Policy, 1950–1980* (New York: Basic Books, 1984).

least industrious, least responsible poor. It was wrong to impose rules that made it rational for adolescents to behave in ways that destroy their futures. The changes we made were not just policy errors, not just inexpedient, but unjust.[21]

Why did these policies have such an effect? The reason is simple: because of their assumption that the purpose of welfare is the eradication of poverty, rather than the care of the destitute who have no other recourse. This well-intentioned and even visionary goal set forces in motion that not only changed the economic incentive structure that had previously encouraged the poor to better themselves (mainly, as the author points out, through negative incentives to avoid the consequences of learning nothing in school or being unwilling to seek and hold a job), but also altered status relationships among the poor.

Up until this century most Americans were poor or had grown up in poor households. "Forty-two percent of the population lived on farms in 1900, and most of them were cash poor."[22] Considering also that "as many as 40 percent of wage earners were poor by the standards of the day in 1900,"[23] one can see that, although we have always had a social policy of care for the helpless and destitute in this country, ending poverty as such could only be, until relatively recently, an unthought of and unthinkable goal of social programs.

Instead, there were important distinctions among the poor. Murray points out that farmers, though poor, were proud of their status as the backbone of the nation.

> A person might work hard and be poor; that was the way of the world. Poverty had nothing to do with dignity. A person might be out of a job once in a while because of hard times. That too was the way of the world, and a temporary situation. But a person who was chronically unable to hold onto a job, who neglected children and spouse, was a bum and a no good, consigned to the lowest circle of status.[24]

Paradoxically, as economic growth pulled more and more people

[21]Ibid., p. 219.

[22]Ibid., p. 180.

[23]John Ryan, *A Living Wage* (1906; reprint, New York: Arno, 1971), quoted in ibid., note 2, p. 295.

[24]Ibid., p. 180.

out of poverty, the goal of eradicating *all* poverty began to seem possible. All we had to do was change what were seen as the inequities of the system. Welfare must be cleansed of its stigma, said the reformers; half of the people eligible for help were not applying for it. The system was broadened to cover the working poor, and recipients were told that help was theirs by right. Thus the differences of dignity and pride between the working poor who stressed not taking charity and those who did take it were erased by these and similar government policies (pertaining not only to welfare, but to crime and education) aimed at helping all the poor and holding them blameless for their condition.

But if the delinquent is not to blame for his delinquency, then the youngster who holds a menial job while going to school does not deserve praise, either—in fact, he's a chump. By making all the poor, whether working or nonworking, eligible for welfare supplements, food stamps, and Medicaid, the previous stigma associated with welfare was indeed removed (as the reformers intended). At the same time, however, status was withdrawn from the working poor family and, what is more, from the behaviors that engender escape from poverty—all the difficult investments of time, energy, work, and penny-pinching in the hope of a far-distant payoff that are almost impossible to make without both faith that they will pay off and encouragement, praise, admiration along the way.

Instead, the reformed policies insisted on treating the poor as if they were a homogeneous group. In fact, they made it useful to behave in counterproductive ways—to be delinquent, addicted, or unemployed—in which cases one got help and special programs tailored to ensure success. By contrast, "the ambitious and hardworking students were passed along with A's and with the teacher's gratitude for not contributing to the discipline problem, but without an education that enabled them to compete in a good university."[25]

We are just beginning to realize how profoundly these social programs have failed, especially in the case of inner-city blacks. Blacks who have been part of the middle class and older blacks whose work norms were formed before the welfare programs came into effect have prospered with the decline of official racism and segregation. But more and more young, poor blacks have dropped out of the labor force and have had illegitimate children in ever

[25]Ibid., p. 188.

232

increasing numbers, thus sealing themselves into a borderline existence.

The overwhelming impact of Murray's data may, unfortunately, distract attention from his overall purpose. This purpose is not just to show that the particular programs whose effects he is analyzing have been misconceived; it is to show why there is generally an inverse relationship between the goals of social programs and their effects.

Murray illustrates his point with an extended theoretical example. Describing a hypothetical Comprehensive Anti-Smoking Act with a budget of a billion dollars a year to reduce net smoking, he shows that there is no way to design it that will not actually *increase* net smoking. This example, he cautions, applies not only to "remedial" social programs that try to change behavior, but to all transfer programs. All such programs seek to diminish the number of people in some undesired condition—poverty, unwed motherhood, unemployment—and, by making that condition more valuable as an object of the program, they increase the number of people in that condition. There are, he suggests, three general laws that will predict such a result for social programs in a democracy:

> # 1. The Law of Imperfect Selection. Any objective rule that defines eligibility for a social transfer program will irrationally exclude some persons.
>
> # 2. The Law of Unintended Rewards. Any social transfer increases the net value of being in the condition that prompted the transfer.
>
> # 3. The Law of Net Harm. The less likely it is that the unwanted behavior will change voluntarily, the more likely it is that a program to induce change will cause net harm.[26]

These laws should be the subject of a book in themselves. One can see that all three imply a constant growth in the number of people covered by a program, independent of both population growth and the condition of the economy. The Law of Imperfect Selection leads to a constant redefinition of the rules in order to include those who have been identified as irrationally excluded. The Law of Unintended Rewards means that the target population broadens as people find it either more rewarding or less punitive to be in the specified condition. The Law of Net Harm finds that

[26]Ibid., pp. 211–16.

the more tenacious the undesired behavior, the more likely that a program will be powerful enough to induce it, but not powerful enough to change it.

In this light, should it be surprising that all our transfer programs are growing so fast that modest attempts to slow down their rate of growth can be rightly seen as causing real deprivation to new candidates unable to get coverage?

If one couples the tendency of automatic growth with the understanding that the effects of the programs are unjust—and that what is actually involved is nonmonetary transfers of "safety, education, justice, status" from the working poor to the irresponsible poor—one can see that a proper social policy is advocated neither by present-day Democrats nor their Republican counterparts. More of the same, as the Democrats propose, clearly will not suffice if "the same" is unfair. On the other hand, keeping our present programs and merely slowing them down will not change things enough to provide real alternatives to those trapped in the present set of disincentives to economic self-sufficiency.

All the important data referred to here are generally available, and Murray is not alone in seeing that our social policies have unintended effects. Some black leaders, notably Eleanor Holmes Norton, former head of the Equal Employment Opportunity Commission and now a professor at the Georgetown University Law School, have come to the conclusion that the feminization of poverty—the growing majority of poor families headed by women, especially teenage unwed mothers dependent on welfare—requires us to take a radical look at the welfare system. While being interviewed for an article in *New York* magazine about the number of young blacks on welfare, Norton said,

> We are now into the second and third generation of this cycle of hopelessness, and one way to break it is to change the system that funds it. We're just beginning to think about how exactly the welfare system needs to be changed, but one thing is clear: The assumption that it is a permanent form of maintenance has to be eliminated. People who go on welfare have to be made to understand that it's just temporary, a way to get by while they're being trained for productive work.[27]

[27]Joe Klein, "Babies Having Babies: The Appalling Social Cost of Teenage Pregnancy," *New York*, February 6, 1984, p. 52.

234

In an article about the transformation of American cities from manufacturing centers to administrative and information centers, sociologist John D. Kasarda describes a "seemingly dysfunctional growth of underprivileged populations in our urban centers at a time when these centers are experiencing serious contractions in lower-skill jobs."[28] Kasarda asks, "What is it that continues to attract and hold underprivileged persons in inner-city areas of distress? How are the underprivileged able to stay economically afloat? What, in short, has replaced traditional urban jobs as a means of economic subsistence for the underclass?"[29] The answers are the welfare economy and the underground economy—both functioning to limit options rather than expand them as did previous manufacturing economies—keeping the underclass dependent on "place-oriented" assistance as employment declines further.

The Paradox of Coerced Good Intentions

But the conclusion that many poverty experts come to when contemplating the growth of the underclass is that morality requires us to do even more in the way of government programs. In his introduction to the fourth edition of *The Affluent Society* in the fall of 1984, economist John Kenneth Galbraith devotes himself to an analysis of how society is growing heartless as people become more affluent, thus seemingly equating compassion with the support of more government transfer programs.[30]

Galbraith is one of the most influential advocates of the view that the very structure of our economy requires some people to be poor. Poverty, according to this view, cannot be cured by economic growth, but must be attacked either by radical changes in our economic structure or by redistributive social programs. The general argument of such structuralists as Galbraith goes something like this: (1) industrial society leaves people at the bottom who cannot better themselves; (2) since industrial society is based on self-interest (competition is a war), the poor will continue to suffer unless the government does something about it; (3) even coercion is better than this sort of suffering.

---

[28]John D. Kasarda, "Caught in the Web of Change," *Society* 21, no. 1 (November/ December 1983): 47.

[29]Ibid.

[30]John Kenneth Galbraith, adapted in "The Heartless Society," *The New York Times Magazine*, September 2, 1984.

A good example of the coercion routinely advocated today is the suggested solution to the plight of the homeless visible on the streets of our largest cities. Many of these people have obviously been released from mental institutions under court rulings that those not dangerous to themselves or others may not be confined against their will. There is a mounting feeling, however, especially when such people endanger health by insisting on staying out-of-doors in cold weather, that they should be involuntarily committed to mental institutions or hospitals once more.

Even more commonplace than advocating the coercion of the objects of charity is the idea that charity itself must be coerced. Economist Barbara R. Bergmann's 1981 article in the *New York Times*, "Charity Needs Coercion," set forth a number of arguments for replacing voluntary philanthropy with government programs and drew a fiery response from a number of executives of charitable organizations.[31] A year earlier, Samuel Brittan had argued a similar point in the British magazine *Encounter:*

> The libertarians are not necessarily lacking in personal compassion, but their system is. Redistribution in any democratic society depends on altruism or solidarity on the part of the more fortunate citizens. But whether one thinks of the relief of poverty or (more ambitiously) of income redistribution, personal charity is not enough—for reasons of economic logic. Redistribution is, like defense, a "public good." This means that there is little incentive for the individual to provide it. I might be—indeed would be—willing to pay a voluntary contribution to transfer some of my income to the poor as part of a compact with millions of others. But it would not be rational for me to do so, to the same extent, on my own. The benefit to the income of the poor would be negligible, and the loss of my own income and welfare substantial.[32]

The history of caring for the destitute is threaded with varying amounts of coercion for all concerned. But any coercion, even for a seemingly good cause, is troubling in a society supposedly based on rights. The question inevitably arises: Since people who are free to make choices may make bad or improvident choices (as well as

[31]*The New York Times*, December 13, 1981.

[32]Samuel Brittan, "Hayek, the New Right, & the Crisis of Social Democracy," *Encounter* 316 (January 1980): 35.

anti-social choices), is it in fact possible to have at the same time a society that provides for all its citizens and a society that is free? Feudal society stated the intention to care for all its members, but was limited by its poverty. When the centralized power of feudal society declined and poverty persisted, it seemed to some that the freedom gained by the poor came only at a great price.

The distinguished economic historian and British Labour Party theorist, R. H. Tawney, noted in his famous account of the separation of religion and economic thought, *Religion and the Rise of Capitalism,* that "Bishop Berkeley, with the conditions of Ireland before his eyes, suggested that 'sturdy beggars should . . . be seized and made slaves to the public for a certain term of years.' "[33] Tawney considered this early nineteenth-century suggestion a sign of the deterioration of religious morality that occurred in the transition from a feudal to an industrial society. Shocking as it sounds, however, there is little practical difference between that suggestion and the English workhouse system as it existed for some time after Berkeley's day. This is how a later nineteenth-century writer, Edmund Ruffin, described it:

> The pauper ceases to be a free agent in any respect. If at work far from the place of his birth, (in England,) he is remanded and transported to his own or native parish, there to obtain support. If either this forced exile from his long previous place of residence and labor, or other reasons of expediency require it, husband and wife, and parents and children, are separated, and severally disposed of at the will of the overseers of the poor. The able-bodied laborer, who at his agricultural or other work can earn but six shillings a week, and cannot support his family for less than ten, may, indeed, obtain the deficient four shillings from the parish. But to do so, he is subject to be forced to take any service that the authorities may direct. And as the employer receives the pauper laborer against his will, and only because he thereby pays so much of his share of the poor-tax, he not only has the pauper as an involuntary slave, but he has not even the inducement of self-interest to treat the pauper slave well, or to care to preserve his health or life. The death of the pauper laborer is no loss to his temporary employer, and is a clear gain to the parish.[34]

[33]Tawney, p. 224.

[34]Edmund Ruffin, "The Political Economy of Slavery," in *Slavery Defended: The View of the Old South,* ed. Eric L. McKitrick (Englewood Cliffs, N.J.: Prentice-Hall, 1963), p. 79.

Other critics of early capitalism have decried the replacement of feudal-religious society, which stressed charity and brotherhood, with the labor competition of early industrialism. But not all of them felt, as R. H. Tawney did, that slavery suffered in the comparison. In an early work on sociology, nineteenth-century American writer George Fitzhugh (1806–1881) defended what he saw as the only logical alternative to the chaos he found in Northern cities.

> The competition among laborers to get employment begets an intestine war, more destructive than the war from above. There is but one remedy for this evil, so inherent in free society, and that is, to identify the interests of the weak and the strong, the poor and the rich. Domestic Slavery does this far better than any other institution. Feudalism only answered the purpose in so far as Feudalism retained the features of slavery. To it (slavery) Greece and Rome, Egypt and Judea, and all the other distinguished States of antiquity, were indebted for their great prosperity and high civilization.[35]

Mr. Fitzhugh defended the system of slavery as an institution that allowed different races to relate, and he also recommended its extension to the workers in the Northern states and in other countries, especially those where want was widespread.

> A half million died of hunger in one year in Ireland—they died because in the eye of the law they were the equals, and liberty had made them the enemies, of their landlords and employers. Had they been vassals or serfs, they would have been beloved, cherished and taken care of by those same landlords and employers. Slaves never die of hunger, scarcely ever feel want.[36]

The critic of the British workhouse, Edmund Ruffin (1794–1865), was also a defender of slavery in the American South. Less sanguine than Fitzhugh, however, he held that the only reason contemporary capitalists would not allow the reintroduction of slavery was that free labor was more profitable. "Slaves," he wrote, "could not be subjected to such extreme privation and misery, because they must be fed and clothed, and cannot generally be greatly over-worked, (and never to the profit of the master,) as is caused continually by

---

[35]George Fitzhugh, "Sociology for the South," in McKitrick, p. 43.
[36]Ibid., p. 38.

the pressure of extreme want, and through competition, on free laborers."[37]

In other words, said these defenders of slavery, if what you are concerned about is the care and security of those of the working class who cannot work, we know a system that makes better provision for the young and the old than does the growing industrial system. Slaves may not be free, but where is the freedom of the inhabitant of the workhouse? To the extent that the feudal-medieval-Elizabethan view of society was that of an organic whole out of which one could not fall, it retained many elements of coercion from the social organization that preceded feudalism—slavery.

The point is, it is hard to devise a system in which people are coercively linked together economically that does not have at least some elements of slavery in it. This applies even in our seemingly enlightened age. Rules are made to ensure the orderly distribution of benefits, and then gradually these rules become more stringent. Government funding often starts out under the guise of filling the needs of citizens. These needs progress to the status of economic "rights." Then it is discovered that the so-called rights entail obligations that the funded citizen owes society in return.

We have seen this happen with welfare in contemporary America. First we were told that the community—that is, the government—has a moral obligation to feed and shelter the destitute. Then we were told that all the poor have a right to receive funds that will maintain them on a level with the economic standards of the rest of the community. And then, as it became apparent that there was a budget crunch, the government's fundamental obligation revealed itself as not so fundamental after all. We discovered that welfare recipients could be required to work for the government—even, in many instances, to replace public sector union workers at jobs paying well below the legal minimum wage.

There are indications that a similar thought process is being applied to whole classes of people. Eighteen-year-old men are, of course, subject to registration for the draft and subsequent military service in case of emergency. It is argued that they owe this service in return for, among other things, free public education. And now it may soon be the turn of the elderly as well. Having done much through tax and monetary policies to destroy savings, having encouraged people to think of social security taxes as providing

[37]Ruffin, p. 78.

239

funded retirement annuities (a misrepresentation that would be considered fraudulent on the part of a private company), and having provided elderly retirees with social security pensions and medical support that the federal budget cannot long afford, supporters of big government have begun to suggest that the elderly have obligations in return. An article in a journal published by the American Psychiatric Association in 1982 suggested that all able-bodied Americans over sixty should be conscripted for two years to do public service work in "urban ghettos, hospitals, nursing homes, parks, and forests." According to a UPI dispatch, the article called it "particularly appropriate" that "the effort involve our most experienced citizens" because "responding to society's needs is in the highest interest."[38]

One can see that such an argument leads to the slippery slope of a more and more coercive society and, ultimately, to the kind of totalitarian planning that solves the problems of poverty and crime by regulating the lives of all citizens. If charity is not only a good thing to do voluntarily, but is such a good thing that the government must enforce it—first through escalating taxation, next through forced service, and finally through a planning of safeguards and activities so thorough that no one can fall through the safety net— the secure society becomes indistinguishable from the slave society. In such a case perhaps we need to reassess our assumptions about charity and welfare.

One of the reasons for this slippery slope of coercion in charity is the fact that government *is* coercion. Because it exists to enforce rules, the more that the various operations of society become government operations, the more coercion will rule our lives. What we all want in this country is a compassionate society that will restore the progress toward the elimination of poverty that we were making in the first two-thirds of this century—liberals and conservatives can agree on that. But the compassionate society is the personal society, not the bureaucratized and regulated society. Americans used to be very nosy about the poor: they used to call on them, lecture them, be missionaries to them, bring them food, and establish community schools that poor children were expected to attend. That a surprising number of people still do the equivalent was shown by a Gallup poll in 1981 that found that 31 percent of all

---

[38]"Public jobs draft sought for elderly," UPI, February 7, 1982.

Americans volunteer their services on a regular basis.[39] But much of what used to be done by individuals and associations has been delegated to the bureaucracy. Private charitable organizations have been preempted by welfare and have turned to other areas—they no longer visit poor homes.

In 1980, the then Secretary of the Department of Social and Health Services in the state of Washington, Gerald J. Thompson, said in a speech that Americans had developed a dangerous reliance on government services to handle social problems:

> We're a society of government service junkies. And I use the pronoun "we" deliberately. It's not the recipients of services who are the real users. It's not the deaf, the blind, the mentally retarded or the physically handicapped. . . They're the recipients, not the real users. The real users are the rest of us, who use government services as a substitute for individual and collective action on a direct and personal scale.[40]

We have allowed ourselves to become "users" in this sense partly because of the outmoded assumption that government is the largest and most comprehensive institution in society. Today, however, we know that private organizations can outperform governments. Indeed, multinational corporations and independently owned news services have been under attack precisely because they distribute goods and information more effectively than governments can. As an article in *Time* magazine put it, "Some Third World newsmen cannot telephone outside their own capitals; in contrast, the *Wall Street Journal* can publish simultaneously in twelve locations across the American continent, with a printing plant in Hong Kong offering same-day publication."[41]

One should remember that, for all the rhetoric of social service indulged in by supporters of government programs, the incentives for bureaucrats do not reward efficient delivery of services. Rather, bureaucrats are rewarded for expanding the size of their organization. Not only does more spending mean more appropriations, but, as C. Northcote Parkinson pointed out in *Parkinson's Law*, a larger

---

[39]"31% in Poll Say They Engage in Volunteerism," *The New York Times*, October 18, 1981.

[40]Quoted on "The Editor's Page," *U.S. News & World Report*, June 23, 1980.

[41]Curtis Prendergast, "The Global First Amendment War," *Time*, October 6, 1980, p. 62.

staff of subordinates means a step up in rank and an increase in salary. Bureaucrats are also rewarded for postponing decisions and going through channels. To paraphrase Parkinson again, the bureaucrat says no not because he is mean, but because if he said yes he might be asked to explain his enthusiasm. Economist Thomas Sowell put it this way:

> For a bureaucrat assigned a given task (result), the incentive is to require as many people and as much money as possible to achieve that result. What is politically possible depends upon how *visible* his costs are, not their magnitude in relation to the value of the result. Moreover, the bureaucracy can expand the demand for its services by simply pricing them below cost. There is no such thing as an objective quantifiable "need" for anything. When the price is lower, a larger quantity is demanded. . . . A government bureaucracy . . . can always demonstrate a large "need" for its output, and therefore a "justification" for a large staff and budget.[42]

Steps Toward a More Compassionate Society

If, then, we are faced with the very real possibility that government welfare programs are working in a direction opposite to that intended; if, as Charles Murray is persuasively arguing, almost any other replacement programs would similarly make worse the conditions they were designed to ameliorate; if the history of welfare reveals a universal tension between perfect security and freedom, with the balance always tipping toward coercion as programs become more expansive; and if governments are inherently inefficient economically—if all this, then what alternatives are left? What concrete steps can we take to restore a more personal, compassionate society?

One thing we can do immediately as a matter of government policy is to revise our tax code so that we no longer collect taxes from families below the official poverty level. It makes no sense at all for us to be taking with one hand and giving benefits with the other. If it is government policy to help these people, the least we can do is not take from them what little money they have.

When David Stockman testified before the House Ways and Means Committee on September 22, 1984 about the effects of President

---

[42]Thomas Sowell, *Knowledge and Decisions* (New York: Basic Books, 1980), pp. 142–43.

Reagan's policies on the poor, he was asked what needed to be done for the poor people. He replied, "More economic growth."[43] But as Jane Jacobs has pointed out in great detail, especially in her recent *Cities and the Wealth of Nations*,[44] economic growth is not the homogeneous monolith that statistics sometimes make it seem, any more than is "the poor." Economic growth comes from the individual decisions of individual entrepreneurs, especially those who are small. In order to foster the decisions that lead to growth, there is a great deal government can do to get out of the way. Economists such as Walter Williams have detailed how such government policies as minimum wage and licensing laws make it harder for the poor to better themselves.[45] Williams has documented the fact that in 1948, before minimum wage laws became widespread, "black youths aged 16 to 17 experienced less unemployment than their white counterparts."[46] The laws restricting pushcarts and peddlers—to say nothing of the laws requiring complex examinations or licensing fees for such occupations as barber, carpenter, or taxi driver—put a disproportionate burden on the poor. We are driving economic opportunity from our inner-cities with our tax policies and economic regulations and, again, we are victimizing the most productive, most responsible, and most ambitious of the poor.

Charles Murray points out that "American society is very good at reinforcing the investment of an individual in himself," but that we no longer allow such mechanisms to work for the poor. "I begin," he writes,

> with the proposition that it is within our resources to do enormous good for some people quickly. We have available to us a program that would convert a large proportion of the younger generation of hardcore unemployed into steady workers making a living wage. The same program would drastically reduce births to single teenage girls. It would reverse the trendline in the breakup of poor families. It would measurably increase the upward socioeconomic mobility of poor families. These improvements would affect some millions of persons. . . . A wide variety of persuasive evidence from our own culture and around the world, from

[43]David E. Rosenbaum, "Stockman Denies Fueling Poverty," *The New York Times,* September 23, 1984.

[44]Jane Jacobs, *Cities and the Wealth of Nations* (New York: Random House, 1984).

[45]Walter E. Williams, *The State Against Blacks* (New York: McGraw-Hill, 1982).

[46]Walter E. Williams, "Race and Economics," *The Public Interest* 53 (Fall 1978): 148.

experimental data and longitudinal studies, from theory and practice, suggest that the program would achieve such results.

The proposed program . . . consists of scrapping the entire federal welfare and income-support structure for working-aged persons, including AFDC, Medicaid, Food Stamps, Unemployment Insurance, Worker's Compensation, subsidized housing, disability insurance, and the rest. It would leave the working-aged person with no recourse whatsoever except the job market, family members, friends, and public or private locally funded services.[47]

What would happen if we did as Murray suggests? Murray points out that one of the main reasons we do not is that we, the voters, want to think of ourselves as trying to provide for the needs of everyone. Disbanding the present system would clearly help many people immediately, but it would also leave some in distress. Unfortunately, we cannot specify exactly what options would arise in a free society if the current government-regulated welfare system were abandoned. We can be sure that there would still be family ties, many kinds of associations (Tocqueville said that the genius of America was its formation of associations to get various things done), and a wider range of optional decisions. But we can also be sure that problems would be solved in ways we cannot now foresee. To quote Thomas Sowell again:

> Both the friends and foes of economic decision-making processes refer to "the market" as if it were an institution parallel with, and alternative to, the government as an institution. The government is indeed an institution, but "the market" is nothing more than an *option* for each individual to choose among numerous existing institutions, or to fashion new arrangements suited to his own situation and taste.
>
> The government establishes an army or a post office as *the* answer to a given problem. "The market" is simply the freedom to choose among many existing or still-to-be-created possibilities.[48]

Let us go back to an earlier and crucial question: Is it possible for us to have a society that takes care of everyone and yet, at the same time, is free? Are the elements of coercion that creep in against both donor and donee (in every society that has tried to be comprehensive about social services) organically related to the attempt?

[47]Murray, pp. 227–28.
[48]Sowell, p. 41.

Communist societies pride themselves on having no beggars on the streets, but they do not have personal freedom either. Is this a necessary relationship, or an accidental one?

We do not yet have answers to these questions, but in seeking to restructure the failed policies of the immediate past we would do well to keep them in mind.

XIII. Reforming Resource Policy: Toward Free Market Environmentalism

Terry L. Anderson

No other field of economic inquiry, with the possible exception of antitrust, has focused more on market failure and its implications than has natural resource economics. In a leading textbook on the subject, Alan Randall states that

> resource economics . . . raises questions about the effectiveness of existing market and institutional structures in allocating resources, in adjudicating among the claims of individuals in the present generation, and adjudicating among the claims of present and future generations.[1]

In general, resource economists have focused on problems of third-party effects and public goods. Solutions requiring governmental intervention have been proposed and analyzed to determine what taxes, subsidies, and regulations will improve efficiency.

Most economic research on environmental and natural resource issues focuses on why "efficient" or "optimum" allocation will not or cannot be achieved through the market process. The market failure arguments center on the divergence of private and social discount rates or private and social costs. Economists have tended to see third-party effects, or externalities, as pervasive cases of market failure calling for governmental intervention. In the textbook that dominated college courses during the 1960s and 1970s, Paul Samuelson states that

> *Wherever there are externalities, a strong case can be made for supplanting complete individualism by some kind of group action. . . .* The reader can think of countless . . . externalities where sound economics

Special thanks is given to the Political Economy Research Center for its support of this research effort and to Gale Ann Norton for her useful comments on an earlier draft.

[1]Alan Randall, *Resource Economics* (Columbus, Ohio: Grid Publishing, 1981), p. 42.

would suggest some limitations on individual freedom in the interest of all.[2]

In a major college natural resource economics text, Charles Howe uncovers what he believes to be a "number of reasons why even well informed competitive markets may fail to allocate resources in the socially most desirable way over time." His list includes the failure of markets to account for environmental values, the divergence between private and social discount rates, the shortsightedness of markets, and the problem of monopoly.[3] From this perspective it has been easy to justify governmental intervention in the allocation of almost all natural resources, including land, air, energy, timber, water, and agriculture.

More recently, this traditional approach has been criticized and challenged by economists who have begun to incorporate property rights and transaction costs into their analysis of market process. Particularly in the fields of industrial organization, public choice, and economic history, this new brand of institutional economics is generating a body of literature that is changing the way we think about government and its role in a market system.

In this chapter we will expand that list of fields to include natural resource economics. Economists are beginning to recognize the importance of property rights and institutions in the study of natural resources, and the result is an emerging "new resource economics" paradigm.[4] The first part of the chapter briefly states the elements of the new paradigm, and the second examines the history of governmental resource policies. The third part provides examples of how new institutional economics can be applied to resource problems, suggests alternatives to the intervention solutions, and presents evidence that market processes can provide environmental amenities.

The New Resource Economics

In examining what he calls the "myth of social costs," Steven Cheung concludes:

[2]Paul A. Samuelson, *Economics*, 11th ed. (New York: McGraw-Hill, 1980), p. 450.

[3]Charles W. Howe, *Natural Resource Economics* (New York: John Wiley and Sons, 1979), p. 103.

[4]See Terry L. Anderson, "The New Resource Economics: Old Ideas and New Applications," *American Journal of Agricultural Economics* 64 (December 1982): 928–34.

The question is . . . why public policies exist in the way they do and why they vary in different economic systems. The answer to this question of the economic interpretation of political behavior requires an understanding of the real-world constraints relative to government decision-making. A recent shift of interest in that direction and a growing recognition of the importance of the analysis of government behavior in the theory of public choice, the economics of politics, presage a new momentum in the development of economics, particularly in industrial organization, public choice and economic history.[5]

In these fields, emphasis is being placed on property rights and transaction costs. As a result, economists are rethinking the concept of monopoly, reconsidering the behavior of bureaucracies, and asking how and why institutions change over time.

Natural resource economists have also begun to apply the transaction costs/property rights analysis. Anthony Fisher captures the essence of the change:

We have already abandoned the assumption of a complete set of competitive markets . . . but if we now similarly abandon the notion of a perfect planner, it is not clear, in my judgment, that the government will do any better. Apart from the question of the planner's motivation to behave in the way assumed in our models, to allocate resources efficiently, there is the question of the ability to do so.[6]

The new resource economics approach is giving the kind of rigorous, theoretical, and empirical attention to governmental failure in natural resource allocation that previous efforts have given to market failure. Using this approach, it is clear that

it is not sufficient to compare the performance of either the market or a nonmarket mechanism against an "ideal," "optimum," or "theoretical" standard and conclude that it is inappropriate for policy purposes. Market "failure" in some abstract sense does not mean that a nonmarket alternative will not also fail in the same or in some other abstract sense.[7]

[5]Steven N. S. Cheung, *The Myth of Social Cost* (London: Institute for Economic Affairs, 1978), pp. 67–68.

[6]Anthony C. Fisher, *Resource and Environmental Economics* (Cambridge: Cambridge University Press, 1981), p. 54.

[7]Emery N. Castle, "The Market Mechanism, Externalities, and Land Economics," *Journal of Farm Economics* 47 (August 1965): 552.

The new resource economics begins with the individual, especially the entrepreneur, and asks whether the opportunities he discovers and the actions he undertakes increase wealth for society or simply redistribute existing wealth. The answer to this question depends entirely on transaction costs and the resulting contracts. For entrepreneurs to face the full opportunity costs and reap the full benefits of their actions, there must be explicit or implicit contractual terms covering all relevant costs and benefits. It is the structure of property rights and the costs of specifying, measuring, and enforcing contractual terms that determine resource allocation.

It is also important to recognize that as the values of resources change and new technologies are developed, different costs and benefits are specified in contracts. Higher resource values induce entrepreneurs to accept contracting costs that had been too high given previous values. Similarly, new technologies can reduce the costs of specifying, measuring, and enforcing contractual terms. Both phenomena were at work in the evolution of property rights in the American West,[8] and both are influencing the provision of environmental amenities through the market process.

When property rights are not well-defined, enforced, and transferable, or when transaction costs are high, the entrepreneur has at least two opportunities for increasing his wealth. First, consider the economics of a common pool. Cheung has shown how entrepreneurs faced with a common pool resource compete for the valuable resource until all returns are dissipated. Because of high transaction costs or lack of property rights, certain marginal impacts are not contracted for.[9] For example, when one farmer pumps from a groundwater basin, he may increase the lift for others. Since no one owns the water, however, they cannot contract with the first pumper to make him pay the higher cost. Too much pumping too fast can occur. Exploiting a resource under these conditions benefits the individual at the expense of the rest of society.

Entrepreneurs also adversely affect society when they engage in activities that use the coercive power of government to increase personal wealth at the expense of others.[10] Such transfer activity

[8]See Terry L. Anderson and Peter J. Hill, "The Evolution of Property Rights: A Study of the American West," *Journal of Law and Economics* 18 (April 1975): 163–80.

[9]Steven N. S. Cheung, "The Structure of a Contract and the Theory of Non-Exclusive Resource," *Journal of Law and Economics* 13 (April 1970): 49–70.

[10]Terry L. Anderson and Peter J. Hill, *The Birth of a Transfer Society* (Stanford: Hoover Institution Press, 1980).

consumes time and money, and therefore is costly. But it only redistributes the existing pie; pie slicing becomes a substitute for pie enlarging. In the context of the new institutional economics, transfer activity means that entrepreneurs engage in efforts to raise transaction costs for their competitors or to *redefine* property rights in their favor. Both these actions require governmental action. With so many decisions on natural resource use placed in the hands of state and federal bureaucrats, the transfer game is important for coal company executives as well as environmental leaders. Both types of entrepreneurs recognize that their wealth and the wealth of their principals are affected by bureaucratic decisions. Hence, interest groups spend large amounts of money and other resources trying to influence those decisions. It is not surprising that the percentage of chief executive officers from the Fortune 500 companies visiting Washington, D.C., every two weeks rose from 15 percent in 1970 to 65 percent in 1980.

While such entrepreneurial efforts explain the demand for transfer activity, the activities of politicians and bureaucrats explain the supply. Just as entrepreneurs in the marketplace recognize and fill demands for goods and services, politicians and bureaucrats discover opportunities to meet the demands of their constituencies. The constraints on each, however, are very different. With well-specified contracts, private entrepreneurs provide new goods and services only when they expect the benefits from those goods and services to exceed the opportunity cost of inputs used in their production. Politicians and bureaucrats providing goods and services to interest groups, however, do not have to pay the full opportunity cost of expended resources. They can increase their own utility by increasing budgetary discretion, power, and wealth.

The principal/agent relationship between politicians and bureaucrats on the one hand and voters on the other is weakened as a result of several factors. First, voters are faced with a relatively high cost and low return for becoming well informed on most issues. On the basis of this calculus, it is rational for voters to remain ignorant ("rationally ignorant") on most issues. The exception is those issues that most directly involve the voter. For example, farmers may remain rationally ignorant on defense issues but will be quite well informed on agricultural policy. This results in a special-interest effect, which is a second factor influencing the political process. People who are directly affected by policies find it in their interest to spend time and money trying to influence decision makers. Because the costs of policies are often diffused and the benefits concentrated, special-interest groups will be well organized in the political arena. This combination of rational voter ignorance and the special-interest effect increases the role of government in our society. In short, these factors raise the transaction costs of fully specifying contracts between governmental agents and citizen principals. By explicitly incorporating these costs into our models, we can better understand which situations are likely to result in governmental failure.

Natural resource economists who follow the transaction costs/property rights approach question whether allocation problems can be solved simply by asking government decision makers to maximize net benefits. As Friedrich Hayek states,

> The problem is thus in no way solved if we can show that all the facts, *if* they were known to a single mind . . . would uniquely determine the solution; instead we must show how a solution is produced by the interaction of people each of whom possesses only partial knowledge.[11]

The new paradigm is certainly having an impact on natural resource economics and policy, but developing a new theory is not enough. The notion that pervasive externality and public-good problems exist in the natural resource and environmental areas now appears to have been "based on armchair theorizing, rather than empirical investigation."[12] The new resource economics is causing us to rethink such theories and reexamine the facts. In this light, it is time to develop new policies.

What Went Wrong

The traditional policy approach to natural resource and environmental problems has been to counter perceived market failure with governmental allocation. While there are many different ways of categorizing governmental involvement in these areas, the remainder of this chapter will focus on land, water, and environmental quality. Though these resources involve many different federal agencies, there are many unique aspects to each that make them

---

[11]Friedrich A. Hayek, "The Use of Knowledge in Society," *American Economic Review* 35 (1945), reprinted in *Individualism and Economic Order*, Friedrich A. Hayek (Chicago: Henry Regnery Co., 1972), p. 91.

[12]John Burton, "Epilog," in Cheung (1978), p. 72.

candidates for policy reform. To fully understand these potential reforms it is useful, first, to review briefly their policy histories. In each case, concern over monopoly, speculation, third-party effects, and free-rider problems have led to the substitution of governmental for market allocation. The net result is that neither fiscal responsibility nor environmental quality have been achieved.

Public Lands

Government ownership of land has been with us since the founding of the country, but the size and uses of these holdings have expanded vastly. A land ownership map of the United States reveals the changes that have occurred. Though one-third of the nation's land is owned by the federal government, the percentage varies greatly from east to west. In such states as New York (0.8 percent), Massachusetts (1.4 percent), Georgia (5.6 percent), and Minnesota (6.7 percent), federal ownership is low compared with that in Alaska (95.3 percent), California (44.3 percent), Nevada (86.4 percent), and Arizona (44.6 percent). With the beginning of the conservation movement in the late nineteenth century, vast tracts of land were reserved for the federal government. As a result, the Department of the Interior and the U.S. Forest Service control over 95 percent of all federal holdings, or 32 percent of the entire United States.

As the new resource economics paradigm discussed above predicts, problems of government failure have been pervasive in public land management. Ronald Johnson has shown that actions of the Forest Service "appear more consistent with the budget maximization hypothesis than with the espoused conservation objectives of protecting the forests from the ravages that would allegedly occur under private ownership."[13] Perhaps the best example of this is the harvesting of timber in areas of the Rocky Mountain region where such harvesting cannot be "justified by a free timber market."[14] Though the U.S. Forest Service could increase timber production and provide watershed protection and general recreation at a lower cost by not managing its holdings according to the principles of multiple use and sustained yield, it has not chosen to do so. The

---

[13]Ronald N. Johnson, "Budget Maximization and Agenda Control: The Case of the U.S. Forest Service," in *Forestlands: Public and Private*, ed. Robert Deacon and M. Bruce Johnson (San Francisco: Pacific Institute, forthcoming).

[14]William F. Hyde, "Compounding Clear-Cuts: The Social Failures of Public Timber Management in the Rockies," in *Bureaucracy vs. Environment*, ed. John Baden and Richard Stroup (Ann Arbor: University of Michigan Press, 1981), p. 200.

agency has been subject to many different interest groups that have actively engaged in transfer activity.

Examples from the Bureau of Land Management are also indicative of the problems of governmental failure. Gary Libecap's careful study of the BLM concluded that existing arrangements for managing federal rangelands rely "on bureaucratically assigned use rights which encourage inefficient land use."[15] The reasons for such inefficiencies are that (1) bureaucrats ignore market signals because they neither bear the costs nor receive the benefits of their decisions, and (2) grazing leases are tenuous, thus reducing the incentive for ranchers to improve the land. A nation-wide assessment of BLM range conditions in 1974 concluded that 17 percent of the rangelands were in good or excellent condition, 50 percent were in fair condition, and 33 percent were in poor or bad condition.

If governmental agencies such as the Forest Service and the Bureau of Land Management have difficulty managing lands for the production of timber and grazing, for which market signals are available, it is not surprising that they have even more difficulty managing wilderness lands. Growing pressures from environmental groups throughout the 1970s and 1980s have brought millions of acres into the wilderness system. Unfortunately, under this designation important economic tradeoffs have been ignored because the bureaucratic structure does not encourage decision makers to weigh costs and benefits. When this incentive structure is combined with rigid legislation, important opportunity costs are not taken into account and transfer activity is encouraged.

Water

When pioneers settled our western frontier, they found resource constraints that necessitated changing the institutions that had developed in the east. This was particularly evident with respect to water, which was so much more scarce west of the 100th meridian. The institutions that the frontiersmen developed laid the foundation for an effective water market. Following the doctrine of prior appropriation, water rights were defined and enforced and made transferable. In part, it was a sense of justice that led the early settlers to allocate water rights on the basis of "first in time, first in right." With secure water rights, individuals had the necessary

[15]Gary D. Libecap, *Locking Up the Range* (Cambridge, Mass.: Ballinger Publishing Company and the Pacific Institute, 1981), p. 100.

tenure security to stimulate private investment in water projects that delivered water where it was demanded. A variety of organizational structures were used to mobilize the necessary capital for building dams to store water and constructing aqueducts to deliver it. Thousands of miles of ditches were dug and millions of acres blossomed as a result of entrepreneurial efforts to use water.

Because of changing state regulation and federal intervention with the Reclamation Act of 1902, these private efforts were greatly diminished. State regulations reduced the security and transferability of water rights and hence reduced the efficacy of markets. Large-scale federal involvement in reclamation has provided subsidized water and has promoted excessive consumption and inefficiency. Without proper information and incentives, alternatives to large-scale reclamation have not been considered carefully. For example, Randolph Ulrich estimated that the costs of bringing desert land in the semi-arid West into agricultural production were 5 to 14 times greater than the costs of clearing, fertilizing, and irrigating lands in the humid Southeast.[16] Noted historian Benjamin Hibbard concluded that

> had we really been concerned over the future food supply as we pretended to be, or being so concerned, had we calmly asked how to increase it in the cheapest and easiest manner, certain of the reclamation projects would still be undeveloped.[17]

The problem is that we have a system of water institutions that "runs strongly against the development of a system of water law based on individual choice and the market mechanism."[18]

Massive federal reclamation projects have made "the desert bloom like a rose," but there is little economic justification for the blossoms. Huge subsidies have been made available to relatively few farmers. With water delivered at a tiny fraction of its actual cost, farmers are encouraged to apply the water to low-valued uses. Such projects as the Garrison Diversion in North Dakota are the epitome of what can happen. Billions of dollars have been spent in that

[16]Randolph Ulrich, "Relative Costs and Benefits of Land Reclamation in the Humid Southeast and Semi-Arid West," *Journal of Farm Economics* 30 (1953): 62–73.

[17]Benjamin H. Hibbard, *A History of the Public Land Policies* (Madison: University of Wisconsin Press, 1965), p. 449.

[18]Jack Hirshleifer, James C. DeHaven, and Jerome W. Milliman, *Water Supply: Economics, Technology, Policy* (Chicago: University of Chicago Press, 1960), p. 249.

project to irrigate only hundreds of acres on fewer than 1,500 farms. In the process, thousands of acres of environmentally sensitive wetlands have been destroyed. Again, our water policy has brought neither fiscal responsibility nor environmental quality.

Environmental Quality

The fact that property rights, which are the basis of market transactions, are more likely to be produced as their potential value rises is especially important to remember when considering environmental quality. During the nineteenth century, clean air and water were abundant in all places except the very densely populated cities. Essentially, environmental quality was a free good. Under these conditions there was little concern about pollution.

When environmental quality began to become more scarce, the common law attempted to provide remedies through property rights or liability rules. However, the cost of defining rights to such things as clean air was often very high. As a result, many environmental resources were left in a common pool where individual decision makers could overexploit them. The solution to this problem has been more governmental intervention through legislative action coming mainly in the form of standards, prohibitions, and fines. All these tools have been aimed at reducing pollution levels in the air, water, and ground.

At the same time, these regulatory measures have generated a huge bureaucracy and encouraged more transfer activity; the recent experience with Superfund at the Environmental Protection Agency is indicative of the problems that can occur. There is little question that environmental regulations have slowed economic progress. Where such progress was occurring at the expense of common pool resources, efficiency would perhaps dictate that the progress should have been slowed. At the same time, however, the regulatory process has given tremendous power to bureaucrats in the form of either the carrot or the stick. Given this bureaucratic power, it is no wonder that entrepreneurs have focused on influencing the political process. Environmental groups are pitted against business and consumer interests in never-ending conflicts over who shall "own the environment." Both groups, therefore, are forced to spend huge amounts of time and money in transfer activity. Whatever gains have been made in environmental quality have thus come at a tremendously high cost.

Free Market Environmentalism

Those who follow the traditional approach to natural resource economics are willing to acknowledge a property rights solution to some problems, but they generally argue that such a solution could not work for wilderness, water, and amenity allocation.

> With respect to bodies of land and water, extension of property rights may effectively internalize what would otherwise remain externalities. But the possibilities of protecting the citizen against such common environmental blights as filth, fume, stench, noise, visual distraction, etc. by a market and property rights are too remote to be taken seriously.[19]

But voluntary, contractual solutions to many natural resource and environmental problems can and do evolve. When they do not, transaction costs can be blamed for the failure. These costs, however, may not be those associated with standard market transactions only; they can be the result of governmental action designed to correct alleged market failure. The federal government can go a long way toward improving natural resource and environmental allocation by removing restrictions and encouraging a system of private property rights to land, water, and environmental quality.

Reforming Land Policy

There are two main categories of goods currently being produced from federal lands. The first includes commodities such as timber and forage which are readily marketed in the private sector. The other category includes amenities such as wilderness experiences, free-flowing rivers, endangered-species protection, and general environmental values. It is generally accepted that this latter category either cannot be produced by the private sector, or that when it is produced by the private sector it is priced so high that low-income individuals are not able to afford it.

Before discussing policy options, let us consider this last point. Certainly, markets will not necessarily provide goods at low prices for low-income individuals. If one accepts that an unequal distribution of income necessitates redistribution, there is no logical reason why it should follow that such redistribution should occur through public-land policy. If the problem is that the poor do not

[19]E. J. Mishan, "A Reply to Professor Worcester," *Journal of Economic Literature* 10 (March 1972): 62.

have sufficient income to purchase goods and services, it should be solved by allowing them to expand their income potential. Furthermore, even if amenity values from public lands could be produced only at relatively high prices, that would not mean that poor individuals could not purchase such amenities. People at the lower end of the income spectrum frequently do compete for goods with people at the upper end. There is no reason to believe that their demand for some form of amenity or recreational goods would not be met. Finally, the data do not show that the poor are the people who enjoy the amenity value of public lands under current policy anyway. In fact, for national parks the opposite is true: the average income level of park visitors is higher than the national average. The bottom line is that the redistribution argument does not provide a sound basis for public land policy.

Any land policy must trade off the land uses described earlier against one another. Federal laws such as the Federal Land Policy and Management Act and the National Forest Management Act require that this be done by managing for multiple use. It is a simple matter to use economic theory to show that maximization of the value of land resources necessitates that the additional value resulting from a certain use in relation to another be equal to or greater than that resulting from any other use. It is quite another matter, however, to implement this "equi-marginal" principle. To do so requires that decision makers have information on the value of all the various uses. For a rancher trading off wheat production against barley production, the task is not too complex. It is simply a matter of determining the additional value of wheat versus barley and how much additional wheat versus barley can be produced from the land. In the absence of market information, however, making such tradeoffs is impossible. If we cannot determine the relative values of amenities and commodities, there is no way of knowing whether more of one or the other should be provided. Hence, while the various federal legislation requiring multiple use management sounds good, it is impractical as long as market information is not being generated.

Therefore, all future federal land policy, short- or long-term, should be aimed at generating as much information as possible about competing land use values. It should be emphasized that this does not mean more studies. Surveys designed to solicit opinions from individuals about how much amenities are worth do not, in general, provide reliable information. As long as individuals are not faced with a tradeoff between various goods, there is no way of knowing how accurate their survey responses might be. A great deal of economic literature has been aimed at problems in this area.

The call for more information about competing values is a call for policies that focus on market mechanisms. The first of these mechanisms is, of course, the pricing of goods produced from public lands. Although a price (commonly referred to as a "user fee") is already charged for many outputs from public lands, in most cases they are clearly below market clearing levels. For everything from grazing rights to hunting-camp privileges, user fees are extremely low. As a result, people are required to compete for resources in ways other than through price competition. For many public campgrounds, for example, this means long queues or reservations far in advance. Low prices may also mean that politicians and bureaucrats have favors to distribute when they allow individuals to obtain these under-priced goods and this, in turn, provides the potential for corruption. Furthermore, as long as prices are set too low, overuse of resources is encouraged. Today there is a great deal of concern about the overuse of national parks, wilderness areas, and free-flowing rivers. In the absence of market prices, other rationing devices are implemented, but these promote neither efficiency nor equity.

Perhaps the best example where user fees could be applied is the case of national parks. The entrance fee to Yellowstone is currently two dollars for seven days. Compare this price to the cost of a movie, a ski lift ticket, or a day at the waterslide. It is obvious that the price of a visit to Yellowstone is far below any sensible market clearing level. If higher user fees were collected and left in the budget for Yellowstone, people not valuing a visit as worth the higher price would be deterred from visiting the park, while others would provide revenues to improve the quality of the resource. In the case of snowmobile visits during the winter, for example, user fees could be applied to road and trail maintenance. A few years ago the National Park Service threatened to close Yellowstone to snowmobiling because it cost so much to maintain trails. Although raising the snowmobile fee to five dollars per day would have generated sufficient revenue to cover the cost, that proposal was not considered; rather, the Park Service lobbied along with snowmobilers for additional budget for trail maintenance.

This latter point illustrates how difficult it is to raise user fees as long as land resources are in the public domain, and therefore suggests that user fees are only an imperfect first step toward market allocation. There are significant problems with raising user fees because consumers always want lower prices for the things they consume. And even if prices could be set near the market clearing level at one point in time, it would be very difficult to adjust those prices with changing levels of scarcity. People will use the political process to fight adjustments upward and to implement adjustments downward in their favor. Finally, without the competition and profits that provide discipline in the private sector, there is no way of really knowing if prices are correct. It may be obvious that a $2.00 fee for visiting Yellowstone is below the market clearing level, but it is not clear whether the daily fee should be $10.00 or even $65.00—the real price in 1910 adjusted to 1980 dollars.

For these reasons, the long-term solution to the problem of determining tradeoffs between multiple uses of public lands is to turn over the management of those lands to the private sector. Some future directions for private management, ranging from large-scale, long-term leasing to disposal to private ownership, have been discussed by noted resource economist Marion Clawson.[20] Leasing is already being used for oil and mineral rights on public lands and could be expanded as an intermediate step toward implementing private management of land resources. Such a proposal must include a requirement for competitive bidding for the leases. Many Bureau of Land Management tracts are already under lease for grazing at prices far below their market value. If leases are to be issued, they should be competed for through market mechanisms rather than through transfer activity.

Complete disposal of some or all public lands is another alternative. For those lands currently producing marketable commodities such as timber and forage, there appears to be no good justification for not following this approach. The only question for such lands is how to dispose of them. One option, of course, is simple auction, while another is to implement some type of homesteading principle. In any case, the important policy implication is that the transfer of public lands to private ownership must be considered.

There are several objections to the disposal proposition. The first is that not everyone would be able to compete equally if the land

[20]See Marion Clawson, *The Federal Lands Revisited* (Baltimore: The Johns Hopkins University Press and Resources for the Future, 1983).

were auctioned. The argument is that the large corporations would prevail. But this argument overlooks the fact that there are many so-called public-interest groups like the Nature Conservancy, the Wilderness Society, and the Audubon Society that do have sufficient revenue to purchase public lands. Furthermore, much public land would not be of value to and hence would not attract the energy, mineral, or timber companies.

A second objection argues that there is no way to put a value on environmental amenities. This, of course, is true only in the absence of a market. If public-interest groups were using their revenue for market competition instead of transfer activity, we would have some very clear ideas of what environmental amenities are worth. There are certainly cases in which the Nature Conservancy has competed in the market process to purchase lands of environmental value. Thus, this argument provides good rhetoric, but not good policy.

The final argument against disposal is that there is a significant free-rider problem associated with many amenity values. For example, if people get satisfaction from simply knowing that a forest exists for grizzly bear habitat, they can get that satisfaction without paying a fee for it. Hence, markets could be expected to under-provide grizzly bear habitat. The logic of this argument cannot be disputed, but the evidence is that people do make significant contributions to public-interest groups when, in fact, they could remain free riders. The membership fees collected by the groups mentioned above are certainly not trivial. In short, the free-rider problem is greatly exaggerated.

Fortunately, there are alternatives for divestiture of public lands that would overcome the objections raised against a simple auction. John Baden and Richard Stroup, for example, have suggested that wilderness endowment boards be established to manage some unique environmental assets. Composed of leaders from established environmental groups, such boards would be charged with promoting the "public interest" by providing wilderness values. Members of the boards would be bound to manage the wilderness lands in a trust capacity that is well established in the common law. Though the boards would, in this proposal, own the wilderness lands, they would have an incentive to more carefully weigh the alternative uses.[21] The now-classic example of the Rainey Preserve owned by

[21]Richard L. Stroup and John Baden, "Endowment Areas: A Clearing in the Policy Wilderness?" *Cato Journal* 2, no.3 (Winter 1982): 691–708.

the Audubon Society suggests that energy values would be traded off against amenity values. This example shows that marginal adjustments to minimize damage to the environment can be made while generating revenues that can be applied to the environmental cause. There is no reason why oil exploration and development could not take place in small, well-controlled parts of existing wilderness areas. A wilderness endowment board would have the incentive to consider what such development is worth and how the revenue from it could be used to purchase additional wilderness lands. This alternative should be seriously considered in all future land policy.[22]

Another proposal for disposing of federal lands has been put forth by Vernon Smith. He has suggested an auction scheme in which all citizens would be given public land share certificates denominated in acres and usable only in the auction. The main components of the proposal are as follows:

1. All public lands would be divested over some reasonable but definite and limited horizon, say 20, 30, or 40 years. . . .
2. All such lands would be partitioned into tracts or primary units (e.g., quarter sections) as seems appropriate to the topography and certain classifications of the land. . . .
3. Corresponding to each tract of land would be a set of distinct, separable, elemental deed rights appropriated for each tract. . . .
4. Once divested these tract deed rights would be freely transferable, individually or in any combination, by bequest, sale, assignment, lease, and so forth, as alienable private property. . . .
5. Any individual with a documented historical claim to rights defined by one or more of these deeds would be assigned the appropriate deed(s). . . .
6. All tracts and deed rights associated with them would be assembled into blocks. . . .
7. Bids would *not be denominated in money* but in public land share certificates, analogous to no par value stock certificates. . . .
8. The auction procedure would correspond to what has been called a "combinatorial" sealed-bid auction.[23]

[22]Richard L. Stroup and John Baden, "Saving the Wilderness: A Radical Proposal," *Reason* (July 1981).

[23]Vernon L. Smith, "On Divestiture and the Creation of Property Rights in Public Lands," *Cato Journal* 2, no.3 (Winter 1982): 672–76.

The importance of Smith's proposal is that it overcomes the distributional questions raised by a money auction. Each individual would have an equal endowment of land shares. Once an individual had his share, it would be his to do with as he pleased. Some might sell their shares to environmental organizations that would, in turn, compete with energy companies. Under this scheme, distribution of lands does not encourage transfer activity and does not discriminate against those with less income. Certainly there are transaction costs associated with this disposal proposition, but it does provide a way of getting the lands into private hands so that the necessary tradeoffs can be made in the private sector.

In conclusion, future federal land policy should be aimed at market management solutions that necessitate some form of disposal to private ownership. The asset management plan proposed by the Reagan administration was a step in the right direction which, unfortunately, did not get far in the political arena. Some of the objections to that plan could be overcome by considering the alternative disposal mechanisms discussed above.

Reforming Water Policy

Water policy at the federal level suffers from two major problems. First, it provides massive subsidies to special-interest groups, and second, it does not allow the establishment of water rights that can be traded in the marketplace. These two problems must be overcome in considering future water policy.

The water crisis that seems so imminent is an institutional crisis caused by rules of the game that have seriously distorted information and incentives on both the demand and the supply sides. To slow the growing demand for water, most policies call for conservation programs that do not include price increases. To correct the supply-side problems, many policies call for major storage and delivery systems which are seen as the technical solution. We can be certain, however, that while these governmentally sponsored technological fixes may relieve the symptoms, they do not eliminate the causes, of water shortages.

Since the potential water crisis is an institutional problem, the solution must also be institutional. Instead of using collective action to find a technological fix, it is more productive to consider adopting alternative rules of the game that will induce water consumers to curtail their demands and private water producers to increase their supplies.

Water policy is the perfect issue on which to bring together a coalition of fiscal conservatives and environmentalists. Nearly all the major federal water projects have difficulty passing the benefit-cost test and are environmentally destructive—the Garrison Diversion project in North Dakota is a prime example. For this reason, the next administration will have an excellent opportunity to change existing water policy in a direction that is both fiscally prudent and environmentally sensitive. The basis for an alliance is there.

The starting point for changing water policy is to consider, again, the prices being charged for federally provided water. In the Central Valley of California, water is supplied to farmers at an average price of $5.00 per acre-foot, at a time when it costs $325.00 to provide an additional acre-foot. Given that it is unlikely that profits from even the most highly valued agricultural crops could justify paying $80.00 per acre-foot of water, it is clear that low prices encourage inefficiency. If water is to be provided through projects like the Central Arizona Project, it should be priced at a market clearing level. The problem with implementing such a policy, however, is identical to that confronting user fees for public lands. The economics of governmental failure suggest that it would be difficult, at best, to raise water prices. Furthermore, the history of federal involvement in water projects suggests that the water pork barrel remains full.

A good example of the difficulty faced by environmentalists and fiscal conservatives is the recent debate over what price to charge for electricity and water from the Hoover Dam. In testimony that opposed subsidizing power from the dam, Thomas Graff, senior attorney for the Environmental Defense Fund (EDF), argued that power subsidies would encourage electricity and water waste and deprive the Treasury of $3.5 billion (1984 dollars) for the first ten years of the proposed power contract. The fact that such an enormous subsidy was passed by Congress attests to the power of the water lobby and the difficulty of encouraging water markets.

The long-term solution to the water crisis is to encourage water markets by establishing secure water rights that can be traded in the marketplace. Two recent Supreme Court decisions suggest that courts are recognizing the importance of transferability. In *Sporhase* v. *Nebraska*, the Supreme Court ruled that the commerce clause of the Constitution prohibits Nebraska from preventing the transfer of water into uses in Colorado. Following this decision, the Supreme Court ruled in *El Paso* v. *Reynolds* that New Mexico could not restrict the export of 296,000 acre-feet of ground water out of New Mexico into Texas. More strict adherence to the commerce clause should further enhance the market process for water and improve water allocation.

Another recent decision, *Colorado* v. *New Mexico*, however, works in opposition to water markets. In this case, a lower court found that a late claimant on the Vermejo River, which flows from Colorado into New Mexico, could withdraw 4,000 acre-feet per year even though the river was fully appropriated in New Mexico. The special water master in the case found that an irrigation district in New Mexico was not using its water efficiently and therefore was not "materially affected" by the Colorado diversion. But this is a perfect example of an allocation problem to which water markets could have provided the solution—if the Colorado firm had valued the water highly enough, it could have purchased it from downstream users. By allowing the doctrine of prior appropriation to rule, the court could have encouraged market allocation. Instead, the potential for more political conflicts was increased through an effort by the court to apportion the water equitably between the states. This doctrine of equitable apportionment interferes with prior appropriation rules and encourages transfer activity rather than efficient water allocation. Further application of a strict interpretation of the commerce clause is called for.

The federal government can also improve water allocation by allowing recipients of federally subsidized water to sell that water. In most cases the water has been paid for through higher prices for land to which the water is being delivered. To individuals who have paid these higher land prices, there is no real subsidy. Hence, every recipient of federally subsidized water should be granted the right to that water and allowed to sell it if he so wishes, thus encouraging more efficient allocation. When the diversion and use of water are prevented from changing, highly valued alternatives are foregone at a cost to both the water owner and society. H. Stuart Burness and James P. Quirk assert that "often what appears to be a shortage of water is actually the manifestation of restrictions on water rights transfer."[24]

An excellent example of how restrictions on the transfer of federal water discourage efficiency and encourage environmental degradation is provided by the Metropolitan Water District in southern

[24]H. Stuart Burness and James P. Quirk, "Water Laws, Water Transfers and Economic Efficiency," *Journal of Law and Economics* 23 (April 1980): 133.

California. Because the MWD stands to lose large quantities of water due to its low priority rights to the Colorado River, the MWD and southern California in general have been motivated to support the construction of the Peripheral Canal. If water rights were transferable, however, much of this shortfall for the MWD could be made up by conservation measures in the Imperial Irrigation District (IID). The problem is that "existing California statutes preclude a transfer of water outside irrigation districts; one would hope enabling legislation would be quickly forthcoming."[25]

Pressure for such transfers is now being applied by the MWD and the EDF. A study by the latter has shown that water efficiency in the IID can be increased so that approximately 450,000 acre-feet of water per year can be conserved. The conservation techniques would include the construction of more efficient irrigation facilities and the implementation of different irrigation management practices. The physical improvements would include lining canals, expanding seepage recovery systems, constructing more regulatory reservoirs, expanding electronic control, and providing more flexible deliveries. On-farm improvements would include expanding the use of tailwater recovery systems and improving irrigation techniques regarding leech water. The EDF study shows that the MWD could finance the improvements in return for the water.[26]

The main impediment to this transfer is likely to be policy at the Bureau of Reclamation. The IID's contract with the Department of the Interior states that "water shall be delivered as ordered by the district, and reasonably required for potable and irrigation purposes within the boundaries of the district," making any transfer out of the district an abrogation of the contract. Therefore, such a transfer must be approved by the Bureau of Reclamation. In the past, such transfers have been opposed on the grounds that they allow farmers to profit from the sale of water delivered from federal irrigation projects. But Secretary of the Interior William Clark has suggested that he would not object to such "profiting," and there is evidence that the Bureau is considering a relaxation of its transfer restrictions.

The combination of a reduction in subsidies and more reliance on market transfers would improve the efficiency of water allocation, reduce the fiscal drain on the Treasury, and encourage

[25]Ibid.

[26]Robert Stavins, *Trading Conservation Investments for Water* (Berkeley: The Environmental Defense Fund, Inc., March 1983), p. xix.

environmentally sound conservation. President Carter came into office with a "hit list" of water projects which quickly disappeared in the political process. The Reagan administration has eliminated some water projects simply because of the fiscal constraints forced on it by the large deficit. Included in these cutbacks was the Garrison Diversion in North Dakota, a project which never made fiscal or environmental sense. The time has come, however, to change "politics as usual." Work by the EDF in California and by other conservation organizations in water policy suggests that the time is right for a coalition of fiscal conservatives and environmentalists to oppose the water pork barrel. Here is an excellent place to encourage free market environmentalism.

Reforming Environmental Regulation

The problems associated with natural resource allocation are unique because so many natural resources appear destined to remain in the common pool. As stated earlier, it is accepted that "the possibilities of protecting the citizen against such common environmental blights as filth, fume, stench, noise, visual distraction, etc. by a market and property rights are too remote to be taken seriously."[27] Air and water are treated as resources belonging to everyone and hence to no one, and the result is often a physical deterioration of these resources. But we should not be so quick to accept a common pool status of natural resources as a static, unchangeable state.

The common pool must be recognized as resulting from a special case in which something economists call "transaction costs" prevent property rights from being established. Transaction costs are the expenditure of valuable inputs necessary to define, enforce, and transfer property rights. Such costs can be broken down into two categories. First, transaction costs may be due to collective legal restrictions on the establishment of property rights. In this case, laws or court interpretations may simply prohibit or make it difficult for individuals to claim rights. Of course, such restrictions can be overcome by investing in the political process, but the cost of doing so is high. Second, transaction costs may be due to the fact that "real" costs are incurred in defining and enforcing rights. For example, land ownership depends on surveys, recordation, and in some cases, fences. These can be thought of as inputs into the production of property rights. As the potential value of rights and technology

[27]Mishan, p. 62.

changes, property rights evolve as individuals invest more resources in their production.[28]

Air, water, and land pollution, or environmental degradation in general, are classic examples of how both kinds of transaction costs affect the establishment of private property rights. In the environmental area legal restrictions come in two forms. First, there are simply prohibitions on private claims. In most states in the West, for example, it is illegal for individuals to claim water in its natural course for environmental or recreational purposes. Ownership depends on diversion of the water from the natural stream bed so that instream flows are reduced.[29] Such restrictions make it impossible for markets to provide instream flows.

The second legal restriction on property rights is the limiting of liability. If a person uses his property in a way that harms another person's property, the principle of private property requires that the one doing the harm be held liable for his actions. Whenever this liability is limited, property rights are attenuated. For example, legislation that restricts the liability of nuclear-power producers in the event of radiation damages or the liability of oil transporters in the event of oil spills increases the likelihood of environmental degradation. If strict liability were applied in these two cases, environmental quality could be expected to improve.

There are also examples of pollution resulting from the fact that it is simply "too expensive" to define and enforce property rights. Prior to the rise in energy prices, it did not make economic sense to establish solar collection rights. This, however, is obviously changing as such rights become more valuable. Similarly, the cost of determining who is polluting a stream may not be worth undertaking if fishing rights to the stream have a low value. Both these examples are, of course, situations where property rights are evolving.

Within this context the federal government can play a role in promoting environmental quality either by eliminating legal restrictions on the establishment of property rights or by helping to lower transaction costs. Legal restrictions on liability are a logical place to begin. Consider the Love Canal example of toxic waste. In this famous case, toxic wastes were placed beneath privately owned

[28]See Anderson and Hill (1975).

[29]See Terry L. Anderson, *Water Crisis: Ending the Policy Drought* (Baltimore: The Johns Hopkins University Press, 1983).

property in a clay canal which was sealed using the best technology available. Strict liability rules should have forced the owner to take precautions to limit seepage. Unfortunately, the chemical company responsible for placing these wastes in the ground was forced, under threat of condemnation procedures, to sell the land to Niagara Falls. The city and its officials, however, were not fully liable for their actions regarding the canal. As a result, when the city disrupted the landfill, chemicals seeped out and caused damage. The lack of strict liability thus promoted irresponsible actions on the part of the local government.[30] Such problems could be reduced if federal, state, and local courts would enforce strict liability rules regarding pollution and environmental degradation. At the federal level, legislation that limits liability in the case of nuclear power accidents or oil spills must be removed. If individuals are to be made responsible for their actions, liability rules must be enforced.

The goal of lowering transaction costs presents another opportunity for government to promote environmental quality through a property rights-market approach. A first step in this direction would be to rely more on emission charges and transferable emission permits. Emissions charges are basically rights to pollute that are purchased from some governmental agency. Transferable emission permits, on the other hand, are rights granted to polluters that can then be traded in a standard market process. The Environmental Protection Agency has experimented with transferable permits in the form of bubbles, offsets, and banks,[31] and these offer a move in the direction of encouraging markets. Emission charges and transferable emission permits fall short of relying totally on a free market solution to pollution, but they do provide a form of property rights that can be traded.

A second possibility for reducing transaction costs in cases where liability may be extremely difficult or impossible to prove was offered by the Superfund legislation. Unfortunately, as Richard Epstein has pointed out, the existing Superfund legislation went too far. "The objections to the statute lie not in its insistence that pollution is a tort, but in its choice of remedies and its unwarranted expansion

[30]See Eric Zuesse, "Love Canal: The Truth Seeps Out," *Reason* (February 1981).
[31]See Jerome W. Milliman, "Can Water Pollution Policy Be Efficient?" *Cato Journal* 2, no.1 (Spring 1982): 165–96.

of governmental power."[32] Epstein goes on to say that

> the Superfund legislation, it seems clear, suffers from overambi-
> tion, which blocks the way to a more modest, but more effective,
> governmental policy. Three elements are central to a sound policy:
> 1. The government should be allowed to maintain an action for
>   the destruction or damage to unowned natural resources. . . .
> 2. The government should operate a permit system that allows
>   it to identify the individual defendant responsible for the
>   release of a chemical substance into the environment. . . .
> 3. The government should be given broad and immediate pow-
>   ers to clean up and regulate existing dumps.[33]

In this sticky area of pollution, it seems difficult to completely
eliminate a role for government. But we can hope for a much more
limited role that relies on strict liability.

The ultimate goal of federal involvement in promoting environmental quality should be to establish property rights to common
pool resources. While this may be extremely costly under present
conditions, we should recognize that property rights are continually
evolving. The role of the government should be to reduce the
transaction costs in this evolutionary process. As J. H. Dales has
pointed out,

> It is time . . . that we took air and water out of the category of
> unrestricted common property and begin to establish some spe-
> cific rules about their use or, to put it in another way, to establish
> something more sophisticated in the way of property rights to
> their use than the rule that "anything goes."[34]

The traditional approach to natural resource economics has led
to more and more governmental intervention and less reliance on
markets. Such an approach implies that market failure is pervasive
and therefore must be replaced by collective action. The evidence,
however, suggests that governmental failure is pervasive at least
as much, if not more.

The new resource economics approach suggests alternative ways
of solving natural resource and environmental problems. Cheung

[32]Richard Epstein, "The Principles of Environmental Protection: The Case of
Superfund," *Cato Journal* 2, no.1 (Spring 1982): 23.

[33]Ibid., pp. 33–34.

[34]J. H. Dales, *Pollution, Property and Prices* (Toronto: University of Toronto Press,
1968), p. 65.

270

has pointed out that this changing view leads to important questions:

> Why do market contracts not exist for certain effects of actions? Because of the absence of exclusive rights, or because transaction costs are prohibitive? Why do exclusive rights not exist for certain actions? Because of legal institutions, or because policing costs are prohibitive?[35]

Answers to questions such as these can help formulate new land, water, and environmental policies that will have the support of environmentalists and fiscal conservatives. The potential for a coalition of fiscal conservatives, environmentalists, and those who value freedom is beginning to manifest itself as a force to be reckoned with. The efforts of the EDF cited above, for example, were influential in challenging established government water policy. Research by the Wilderness Society attacking deficit timber sales by the Forest Service is also beginning to influence congressional thinking. Some environmentalists see that the deregulation of natural gas prices, which is supported by natural gas producers, would actually help the environment by removing the pressure to search for gas in remote areas. Other examples can be found in nuclear energy and synthetic fuels production. In summary, this coalition can help reform natural resource policy and move us toward free market environmentalism.

[35]Cheung (1970), p. 58.

XIV. The Supreme Court: The Final Arbiter

Bernard H. Siegan

How well is the Supreme Court doing its job? The question frequently arouses mixed, and on occasion strong, emotions. At times the Court appears to be guided strictly by the Constitution, as when it struck down the legislative veto despite its use by Congress for a lengthy period. At other times, however, the Court seems to act independently of the original, intended understanding of the Constitution. This is particularly true for its decisions in the economic area. Thus, the Court recently read the important public use limitation virtually out of the Fifth Amendment's eminent domain clause. Or consider abortion. The Constitution's silence on the the subject has not deterred the Court from vigorously protecting abortion by overruling, in whole or in part, abortion statutes of every state in the Union.

This chapter will consider these and other cases to evaluate the Court's record over the years. In a society committed to the rule of law, the Court's performance must be measured by determining whether it has observed its constitutional mandate. The first part of this chapter will define the purpose of judicial review, and the second will consider the record of the Court from that perspective. The third part will offer suggestions for the future.

Judicial Review and the Liberties of the People

From the beginning of our constitutional system, there has never been a consensus on the role of the Supreme Court. The Constitution specifies little about the powers of the judiciary; it is much more revealing about the other branches of government. Generally, it is assumed that the Supreme Court has authority to review, that is, to consider and annul, legislative acts of Congress, although this power nowhere appears in the Constitution. The charge for such authority is much clearer with respect to state legislation affecting the Constitution, but there is considerable room to conjecture here as well.

My view is that in the absence of constitutional direction, we must look at the history and background of judicial review in order to understand its powers and limitations. Considered from this perspective, the purpose of judicial review is to guarantee two distinct parts of the American plan of government: first, the structure of government established by the Constitution, and second, the liberties of the people.

Structural matters include the organization, composition, powers, and limitations of the various branches of the federal government and their relationship to state governments. The judiciary should implement structure and organization strictly in accordance with the intent of the Framers of the Constitution unless there is a strong and compelling justification for doing otherwise.

The same should be true for its second responsibility, the protection of liberty; however, here the problem of interpretation is different. The original Constitution set forth the structure and organization of government, but protected few liberties and contained no Bill of Rights. Yet throughout the ratification debates, supporters of the Constitution (the Federalists) maintained that the national government—being one of limited and enumerated powers—had no authority to diminish fundamental liberties. Therefore, they argued, there was no need for a Bill of Rights. Moreover, specification of a series of rights might imply that the federal government has power to diminish others not specified, with the result that it would come to possess more powers than intended.

Pursuant to the position taken by the Federalists, the judiciary, as the interpreter of the Constitution, would be obligated to enforce liberties of the people by annulling laws that violated them, even though those liberties might not be specified. How would the Supreme Court know which liberties to protect and to what extent? As with much of our rather short Constitution, the Court would have to invoke the common law, which then and now, in England and America, consists of judge-made law. The Constitution was drafted within the context of the common law, as the celebrated chancellor James Kent of New York explained in his authoritative *Commentaries on American Law:*

> It was not to be doubted that the constitution and laws of the United States were made in reference to the existence of the

common law. . . . In many cases, the language of the constitution and laws would be inexplicable without reference to the common law; and the existence of the common law is not only supposed by the Constitution, but it is appealed to for the construction and interpretation of its powers.[1]

The ratification arguments over the protection of press freedom provide an illustration of the role the judiciary would have in securing liberties. In *The Federalist Papers* (which were published during the ratification debates), Alexander Hamilton wrote that there was no need to be concerned about press freedom inasmuch as the Constitution does not grant the government any power to restrain it.[2] Does this mean, then, that as far as the national government is concerned, freedom of the press is absolute? James Wilson, a delegate to the Constitutional Convention from Pennsylvania and later a Supreme Court justice, explained during the ratification debates that freedom of the press was still subject to the powers of government under the common law, which were then considerable.[3] In other words, the national government had no power to diminish freedom of speech or of the press as those terms were then defined under the common law.

From this example, it is apparent that the judiciary would have a large role in defining and protecting freedom, a not unusual role for judges at the time of the framing of the Constitution. In that period, common law tradition espoused the progressive enlargement of the people's liberties. In applying the common law, the judges changed it continually, pursuant to new understandings and conditions.

The common law was dedicated to the rule of "right and reason." From the earliest years of the English state, judges and Parliament created and steadily expanded common law protections; while at one time only the meager rudiments of criminal procedure were required, by Blackstone's day "absolute rights" to life, liberty, and property were acknowledged. When the Constitution was framed, the system was highly regarded as a guardian of individual rights,

[1] 1 James Kent, *Commentaries on American Law* (New York: Da Capo Press, 1971), pp. 315–16.

[2] *The Federalist Papers* no. 84 (New York and Scarborough, Ont.: Mentor, 1961), pp. 513–14.

[3] John Bach McMaster and Frederick D. Stone, eds., *Pennsylvania and the Federal Constitution 1787–1788* (Philadelphia, 1888), pp. 308–9.

and many Americans equated common law with natural law. For them, the unwritten English Constitution, which consisted principally of common law rights, provided the greatest measure of human freedom. As historian Gordon S. Wood has put it, "what made their revolution so unusual [was that] they revolted, not against the English Constitution, but on behalf of it."[4] Thus, although few liberties were enumerated in the original U.S. Constitution, a large measure of freedom was retained by the people, to be safeguarded by the judiciary.

Essentially then, the Supreme Court's role was to protect those liberties necessary to maintain and enhance the form of government that was created. The Framers' generation viewed the judiciary as another means of achieving the libertarian objectives of government. Thus, in the economic area, the Framers believed the judiciary would protect ownership and thereby help perpetuate a system based on freedom of enterprise. The Framers surely would never have accepted judicial review if they had thought it would be used to advance government authority and regulation.

To assure adoption of the Constitution, the Federalists promised that they would amend it after ratification to include a Bill of Rights. Accordingly, James Madison, on June 8, 1789, introduced in the House of Representatives a series of amendments protecting the exercise of certain rights for the most part already protected under common law. Because he, like other Federalists, believed the national government was limited in its powers to curtail rights, he proposed a general provision that would maintain the then existing restraints on it. Later, in modified form, this provision became the Ninth Amendment.

> The exceptions here or elsewhere in the Constitution, made in favor of particular rights, shall not be so construed as to diminish the just importance of other rights retained by the people, or as to enlarge the powers delegated by the Constitution; but either as actual limitations of such powers, or as inserted merely for greater caution.[5]

By this language, Madison sought to make certain that the enumeration of certain rights would not confer any greater powers on

---

[4]Gordon S. Wood, *The Creation of the American Republic 1776–1787* (Chapel Hill, N.C.: University of North Carolina Press, 1969), p. 10.

[5]1 *Annals of Congress* 436 (1789–90).

the federal government, a fear he had previously expressed. The final form of the Ninth Amendment is consistent with that purpose:

> The enumeration in the Constitution of certain rights shall not be construed to deny or disparage others retained by the people.

As this amendment indicates, the Bill of Rights did not affect the common law rights that the people already possessed under the Constitution. Thus, the First Amendment's guarantee of free expression ("Congress shall make no law . . . abridging the freedom of speech, or of the press") did not expand or limit this freedom since the provision was likewise definable under the common law.

The foregoing discussion concerns only the constitutional limitations on the national government's powers to restrain the people's liberties. It also has a relationship to the powers of the state governments. The early courts accepted the idea that legislatures are inherently limited in power. In *Calder* v. *Bull* (1798),[6] Justice Chase asserted that the federal and state legislatures were without power to overrule certain vital principles of free republican government. It would have been senseless, he argued, for the people to entrust a legislature with such powers; they will therefore not be presumed to have done so unless it were so specified. To maintain that the federal or state legislatures possess such powers unless they are expressly restrained from them would be political heresy, altogether indefensible in free republican government. Consequently, in *Wilkinson* v. *Leland* (1829),[7] Justice Story concluded that no court of justice would be warranted in assuming that the power to curtail or disregard the rights of personal liberties and private property lurked under or might be implied from any general grant of legislative authority.

In *Fletcher* v. *Peck* (1810),[8] per Chief Justice Marshall, and *Terrett* v. *Taylor* (1815),[9] per Justice Story, the United States Supreme Court struck down state legislation in part or in whole on the basis that the nature of the society itself restrains the legislative power even in matters on which the federal and state constitutions are silent. In these two cases the state legislatures had enacted retrospective

---

[6] 3 U.S. (3 Dall.) 386 (1798).
[7] 27 U.S. (2 Pet.) 627 (1829).
[8] 10 U.S. (6 Cranch) 87 (1810).
[9] 13 U.S. (9 Cranch) 43 (1815).

legislation divesting owners of property they had acquired in good faith. Both justices invoked the natural law principle that forbade the legislature from appropriating property without compensating the owner.

In the years following the above-mentioned decisions, the Supreme Court declined to apply natural law to annul state statutes, and in 1833 it held that the Bill of Rights affected only the federal government.[10] The states were consequently largely immune from federal judicial review to protect liberties. This period came to a close in 1868, with the adoption of the Fourteenth Amendment. Three clauses of its Section 1 constitute broad protection against violation of liberties by the states:

> No state shall make or enforce any law which shall abridge the privileges or immunities of citizens of the United States; nor shall any state deprive any person of life, liberty or property, without due process of law; nor deny to any person within its jurisdiction the equal protection of the law.

Although the adoption of this language was motivated principally by the desire to protect the rights of emancipated slaves, it was also intended to be a guarantee of fundamental and natural rights generally, including those set forth in the first eight amendments to the Constitution. Privileges and immunities, due process, and equal protection were catch-terms used in that period to denote protection against government oppression with respect to race or otherwise.

Thus the original Constitution, together with the Bill of Rights and the Fourteenth Amendment, created a broad sphere of security for citizens and other persons against government impositions and oppressions. Section 1 of the Fourteenth Amendment provided protection against abuses by the states that the original Constitution and Bill of Rights had accorded against abuses by the national government.

However, the amendment's safeguards were exclusively against governmental infringements on the exercise of fundamental and natural rights, not political rights—an important distinction. Fundamental and natural rights emanate from nature, entitling one to act freely as a human being. Political rights are created by government. The debates of the 1866 Congress that framed the Fourteenth Amendment provide examples of the difference. For those framers—

---

[10]*Barron* v. *Baltimore*, 32 U.S. (7 Pet.) 243 (1833).

and in all likelihood their predecessors as well—life, liberty, and property were natural rights, while rights of suffrage, jury service, and schooling were political in character. These and other political rights relate to the establishment, support, or management of government.

The Supreme Court and the Protection of Liberty

There was another important limitation on the legal protections afforded by the Constitution: the judiciary must function within the confines of a system, separating and limiting the powers of each branch of government. As early judges and authorities asserted, in constitutional matters the function of the judges was strictly and exclusively judicial. The judges were to be interpreters, exercising no more than a veto or negative power over legislation abridging the exercise of liberties even when such a remedy did not provide a complete solution to the problem. They had no authority to exercise powers granted to the legislative and executive branches of the federal government. Examples of matters that are solely legislative in character are taxation and spending; examples of executive authority are the administration of state-created systems and of foreign affairs, and prosecuting wars.

The federal judiciary is, accordingly, the guardian of the Constitution. Its role is to prevent any governmental unit, branch, agency, or official from either usurping the powers of any other governmental authority or denying the people their liberties. Given the broad wording of the Constitution, this is an enormous and difficult responsibility. In the case of liberties the Constitution, as we saw, provides little guidance as to what is or is not secured. On the whole, the document is more specific about structural matters, but even here much remains undefined. Private contracts, which deal with comparatively minor matters, may run dozens of pages; the U.S. Constitution, which, together with its 26 amendments, governs an entire nation, totals only about 15 book-size pages. Many provisions are short, eloquently stated, and sufficiently ambiguous to allow interpretations that were not intended.

Under these circumstances it is understandable that throughout its history the Supreme Court has been a highly controversial institution. Jeffersonians, for example, vigorously condemned the Court over which Chief Justice Marshall presided; and in the twentieth century, liberals in the first half, and conservatives since then, have likewise strenuously criticized the Court. The basic premise of the

Constitution—to limit and disperse governmental powers—has frequently not been observed by justices who either rejected it or refused to be bound by it.

At times a judicial decision affects little more than the interests of the litigants, but often it may also have far-reaching implications for the political, economic, or social character of society. For the balance of this section, I shall discuss decisions that have greatly affected the course of the nation. Although many consider judicial excess to be a recent problem, we shall see that it has actually been with the Court for a very lengthy period. We begin with a consideration of four cases dealing with government structure. In three of them, the Court changed the intended constitutional design. In the fourth, the Court sustained original intention despite the fact that Congress had for quite some time pursued a contrary course.

Article I, Section 8 of the Constitution sets forth the specific powers of Congress. After their enumeration, a clause authorizes Congress to "make all laws which shall be necessary and proper, for carrying into execution the foregoing powers, and all other powers vested by this Constitution in the government of the United States, or any department or officer thereof." While accounts of the Constitutional Convention are silent as to the meaning of "necessary and proper," the Federalists minimized its scope in the ratification debates. The only purpose of this clause, they claimed, was to enable Congress to implement its explicitly stated powers, for otherwise Congress could not fulfill its responsibilities. They argued that essentially the federal government had little more than those powers that were identified in the Constitution.

These representations were very important for the history of our nation. Had the people believed that the necessary and proper clause or any other provision significantly enlarged the federal power beyond what was specifically stated, the Constitution might never have been ratified. While much contemporary opinion preferred a stronger national government than that which the Articles of Confederation conferred, it was not favorable to substituting a powerful government that left the states with limited authority over the populace within their own jurisdictions.

In *McCulloch* v. *Maryland* (1819),[11] Chief Justice Marshall expanded on behalf of a unanimous Court the meaning of the necessary and proper clause in a manner completely contrary to what the

[11]17 U.S. (4 Wheat.) 316 (1819).

Federalists had represented in the ratification debates. At issue was whether Congress had authority to charter a corporation, the United States National Bank, in spite of the fact that no such power appears in the Constitution. In upholding the corporate charter, Marshall asserted that the Constitution allowed Congress to exercise powers vastly greater than those specified in the enumerations. Congress is allowed to adopt legislation that is not specifically prohibited and that is "really calculated to affect any of the objects entrusted to the government." The determination of necessity is largely a matter for Congress to decide, with only a very limited role for the courts. Thus, in this one decision, the Court eliminated a core understanding of the Constitution that held that Congress was limited essentially to the powers enumerated in that document. Commenting on the meaning of the decision, Albert Beveridge, Marshall's laudatory biographer, put it this way: "In effect John Marshall thus rewrote the fundamental law of the Nation."[12]

Veazie Bank v. *Fenno* (1869) and *Juilliard* v. *Greenman* (1884)[13] provide two further illustrations of the judiciary acting to vastly expand the power of Congress. The evidence is most convincing that the delegates to the Constitutional Convention intended to devise a currency based on gold and silver. When an early draft of the Constitution granting Congress the power to borrow funds and issue paper money was presented for debate, Pennsylvania delegate Gouverneur Morris moved to strike the words "to emit bills of credit" which at that time meant printing and circulating paper money without backing in precious metals. He explained that "if the United States had credit, such bills would be unnecessary, if they had not, unjust and useless."[14] Morris's motion passed by a vote of nine states to two. But a ban on paper money was not inserted, and this omission enabled the Supreme Court to conclude that no such prohibition was intended. However, every speaker in the debate had assumed that this authority did not have to be expressly forbidden for it to be denied Congress.

In the *Veazie Bank* case the majority concluded, without citing any supporting decision, that "it is settled by the uniform practice of

[12]Albert J. Beveridge, *The Life of John Marshall*, vol. 4 (Boston and New York: Houghton Mifflin Company, 1916), p. 308.

[13]75 U.S. (8 Wall.) 533 (1869) and 110 U.S. 421 (1884).

[14]Max Farrand, *The Records of the Federal Convention of 1787*, vol. 2 (New Haven, Conn. and London: Yale University Press, 1966), pp. 308–9.

the government, and by repeated decisions, that Congress may constitutionally authorize the emission of bills of credit." Subsequently, in the *Juilliard* case, the Supreme Court held that Congress had unlimited discretion to determine when it was "necessary and proper" to designate paper money as legal tender.

The *Veazie Bank* and *Juilliard* decisions meant in effect that the Framers had wasted their time debating the issue and voting overwhelmingly to strike the emissions power from the Constitution. To be sure, it is possible that there was no consensus to ban the power entirely, but the Framers surely must have wanted substantial limitations, at least to prevent the improper or reckless creation of paper money. Their problem was draftmanship; they did not write their intention carefully enough into the Constitution to prevent the Supreme Court from applying an entirely different interpretation.

Immigration and Naturalization Service v. *Chada* (1983)[15] is a recent decision whose importance lies in part in revealing that at least seven members of the Court, both liberals and conservatives, are still willing to strictly observe the original understanding of the Constitution, even at the expense of long-standing legislative practices. Since 1932, Congress had followed the practice of authorizing, in certain instances, one or both houses to invalidate by resolution the decisions of administrative agencies. Since then, 295 congressional veto-type procedures have been inserted in 196 different statutes. In the *Chada* case, a one-house veto resolution was challenged as violating the presentment and bicameralism provisions of the Constitution (Art. I, Sec. 7, cl. 2 and 3). The presentment sections require that any bill, order, resolution, or vote be presented to the president before becoming law, enabling him to veto it if he so wills. Under the bicameral requirement, no law can take effect without the concurrence of a prescribed majority of the members of both houses. Concluding that it was essentially legislative in purpose and effect, the Court declared the legislative veto unconstitutional. Chief Justice Burger's opinion stressed the importance of preserving constitutional integrity, notwithstanding the change in conditions and attitudes over the course of time.

> The choices we discern as having been made in the Constitutional Convention impose burdens on governmental processes

---

[15]462 U.S. 317 (1983).

282

that often seem clumsy, inefficient, even unworkable, but those hard choices were consciously made by men who had lived under a form of government that permitted arbitrary governmental acts to go unchecked. There is no support in the Constitution or decisions of this Court for the proposition that the cumbersomeness and delays often encountered in complying with explicit constitutional standards may be avoided, either by the Congress or by the President. . . . With all the obvious flaws of delay, untidiness, and potential for abuse, we have not yet found a better way to preserve freedom than by making the exercise of power subject to the carefully crafted restraints spelled out in the Constitution.[16]

These same considerations apply to the Court's protection of liberty, although here the Court can legitimately exercise more discretion. As in cases dealing with government structure, the Court's performance in matters pertaining to liberty has been uneven: much freedom has been preserved, but not enough, and many judicial excesses have occurred. Under the premise that it is protecting liberties, the Court has (1) usurped powers belonging to other governmental bodies and (2) given certain interests preference over others. The harmful consequences of these practices have considerably offset the benefits the nation has obtained from the Court's vigorous protection of some liberties.

The most flagrant example of the first category is the Supreme Court's efforts to integrate the nation's schools. The Court has applied the Fourteenth Amendment's equal protection clause to supervise schools for the purpose not only of racially desegregating, but also of racially integrating, them—subjecting them to what Justice Rehnquist has described as "in practice a federal receivership."[17] It has sustained racially based busing, quotas, and other controls to enforce integration. The pursuit of this policy conflicts with the understanding of the Congress that framed the Fourteenth Amendment, which was that Section 1 safeguards only fundamental and natural rights from violation by the states. There is no fundamental or natural right to education, nor to an integrated education; each is a political right created by government and is accordingly not within the guarantees of the Fourteenth Amendment. (The Supreme Court has never held education to be a fundamental right.) Moreover, the funding and administration of schools

---

[16]462 U.S. at 349–50.

[17]*Keyes* v. *School District No. 1*, 413 U.S. 189, 257 (1973) (Rehnquist, J., dissenting).

are responsibilities belonging to the legislative and executive branches of government; they do not involve the judicial function of interpretation. As Justice Powell once acknowledged in a majority opinion, the justices "lack both the expertise and familiarity with local problems so necessary for the making of wise decisions with respect to the raising and disposition of public revenues."[18] "No taxation without representation" is as sound a proposition today as it was in George III's reign.

Judicial usurpation of legislative and executive powers is not confined to school integration. In *Shapiro* v. *Thompson* (1969)[19] the Court struck down welfare statutes in the states and the District of Columbia that denied assistance to those residing there for less than one year. These jurisdicitions were, as a result, required to fund a large number of indigents from monies that had to be obtained either from other programs or new taxes, thereby invading the spending and taxing prerogatives of legislatures. The Court subsequently recognized the problem. In *San Antonio Independent School District* v. *Rodriquez* (1973)[20] the Court refused to require increased funding for schools in lower-income areas, and in *Maher* v. *Roe* (1977) and *Harris* v. *McRae* (1980)[21] it refused to order funding for the procurement of abortions. In the latter two cases, the Court denied that the constitutional right to an abortion required that government pay for it. "It simply does not follow that a woman's freedom of choice carries with it a constitutional entitlement to the financial resources to avail herself of the full range of protected choices." A decision requiring the funding of abortions would have injected the Supreme Court into the policy question of how public welfare monies should be spent, a matter wholly legislative in character. The Court reasoned similarly in the *Rodriquez* case, in which the plaintiffs had demanded that the Court overrule property tax programs that frequently yielded less funds for lower- than for higher-income area schools.

Unfortunately, the Court did not subsequently maintain its restraint. *Plyer* v. *Doe* (1982)[22] presented the question whether Texas could deny to the children of illegal aliens the free public education

[18]*San Antonio School District* v. *Rodriguez*, 411 U.S. 1, 41 (1973).

[19]394 U.S. 618 (1969).

[20]411 U.S. 1 (1973).

[21]432 U.S. 464 (1977) and 488 U.S. 297 (1980).

[22]457 U.S. 202 (1982).

it provides to the children of citizens or of legally admitted aliens. The Court invalidated Texas law and required the state to fund such education, thus crossing the legislative line it had observed in the school tax and abortion cases.

Judges and commentators who support judicially mandated spending programs insist that such programs are essential to remedy social ills afflicting certain portions of the population. In doing so, they tend to ignore the full societal implications of those decisions that may make them more harmful than helpful. In *Plyer* it is likely that the Court-mandated funding will be acquired, as in *Shapiro,* from other programs or from the taxpayers. In making its decision, the Court did not investigate the importance of existing programs that might, as a result, have to be limited. Nor did it consider the effect of increased taxes on individuals and corporations and on the economic welfare of the state or community. The Court made its decision upon one basis alone—the perceived impact upon certain children of denying them free education—which is but a single facet of a complex problem.

In the absence of a more exhaustive probe of costs and benefits, the Court is not in a position to find that the refusal of Texas to supply additional schooling is unjustified. The issue of justification is, after all, the critical question in deciding whether a particular group's equal protection rights have been violated. Viewing the problem in light of the state's many educational and financial concerns is far different from considering the problem by itself, and thus could yield an entirely different answer. In any event, the inquiry required is far too vast and uncertain to be judicially manageable; yet any determination significantly short of it is unsatisfactory and unsound—it simply does not provide a credible base for overruling a legislature. This is added reason for resolving these matters at the legislative, not the judicial, level.

The Court has shown similar disregard for a gestalt approach in the procedural due process cases that commenced with *Goldberg* v. *Kelly* (1970).[23] In that case, the Court held that a state could not terminate public assistance payments to a recipient without first affording him the opportunity for an extensive evidentiary hearing. The Court was again considering but one facet of a complex problem, which, in this instance, was that of distributing a given amount of welfare funds as efficiently and justly as possible. Extensive

[23]397 U.S. 254 (1970).

evidentiary hearings are costly, and the funds applied to that purpose cannot be used for others that the program's administrators might believe would better serve recipients as a whole.

The *Goldberg* decision led to a flood of suits seeking review of administrative procedures that allegedly operated adversely to the complainants. In time, the Supreme Court recognized that the problem involved in large measure the efficient allocation of a specified amount of appropriated funds and, in *Mathews* v. *Eldridge* (1976),[24] formulated a rule based mostly on a cost-benefit analysis as to what procedural requirements would best serve the public interest. Thus the Court still retains supervision over the administration of governmental programs, hardly a judicial role or one for which judges have any special knowledge or skill.

In its function of protecting personal liberties, the Court has applied the Constitution with a very discriminating hand. Regardless of constitutional language and purpose the Court has its own preferences on liberties, giving some very high, and others very low, priority. A recent case dramatizes the point. The eminent domain clause of the Fifth Amendment states that "private property shall not be taken for public use without just compensation." In *Hawaii Housing Authority* v. *Midkiff* (1984)[25] the Court in an 8-0 opinion held that state legislatures had almost unlimited power to define the clause's public use requirement. The role of the Court in deciding what constitutes public use, the opinion asserted, "is an extremely narrow one," and judicial deference to the legislature's determination in this regard is required "unless the use be palpably without reasonable foundation." Such a view is indeed remarkable for a court entrusted with the responsibility of protecting liberty.

This concern for the will of the legislature contrasts sharply with the position the Court has taken in the abortion cases. Although the Constitution contains no provision relating to sexual privacy or abortion, the Court in *Roe* v. *Wade* (1973)[26] held that a woman's decision whether or not to terminate her pregnancy was protected as a fundamental right under the due process clause of the Fourteenth Amendment. Any limitation on that right adopted by a legislature would be strictly scrutinized and held valid only if it were necessary to achieve a compelling state interest. Yet this right

[24]424 U.S. 319 (1976).
[25]104 S.Ct. 2321 (1984).
[26]410 U.S. 113 (1973).

286

was never contemplated by the framers of the Fourteenth Amendment. According to Justice Rehnquist, when the Fourteenth Amendment was ratified in 1868 there were on the books at least 36 laws enacted by state and territorial legislatures limiting abortion. The amendment might never have been adopted in its present form had the framers or ratifiers thought it would annul these laws. Nevertheless, protection for abortion, which has little basis in original meaning, is given vastly greater priority by the Court than protection under the public use limitation specifically stated in the Fifth Amendment and undoubtedly embodied in Section 1 of the Fourteenth.

As the foregoing examples reveal, the Supreme Court has its own hierarchy of liberties that cannot be explained by reference to constitutional wording or intent. This hierarchy is the most important element in the Court's determination of whether a constitutional transgression may or may not have occurred in a particular case. When a law is challenged as violating a person's liberty, the Court will impose one of four different standards of review depending on the liberty involved:

1. Strict scrutiny is applied to laws limiting the exercise of expression, religion, sexual privacy (including abortion), and travel, and to classifications based on race. For such a statute to survive, the legislature must show that its adoption was necessary to achieve a compelling state interest.
2. High intermediate scrutiny is applied to classifications based on gender.
3. Low intermediate scrutiny governs restraints on the use of private property such as zoning or other land-use regulations.
4. Minimal scrutiny applies to limitations on other economic activity such as the production and distribution of goods and services.

These differences are in practice considerable. Let us suppose that a statute would survive strict scrutiny only if the legislature had had a *very, very good reason* for passing it; high intermediate scrutiny would then demand a *very good reason;* low intermediate scrutiny, a *good reason*; and minimal scrutiny, a *reason*—as it happens, any that will pass a sanity test will do. This means that legislatures have great difficulty in restraining freedom of speech or press, and almost none in curtailing freedom of enterprise.

Constitutional history does not support this dichotomy. The framers of the original Constitution, the Bill of Rights, and the Fourteenth Amendment were committed to securing the material liberties. Consider the many provisions protecting the exercise of economic activity. The Constitution prohibits the federal government and the states from passing ex post facto laws (Art. I, Secs. 9 and 10), which for the framers in all probability comprehended retroactive property and economic laws. The Constitution also forbids the states from impairing the obligation of contracts (Art. I, Sec. 10), a very broad guarantee against the imposition of certain economic regulation. (Chief Justice Marshall believed that this provision forbade the states to engage in virtually any economic regulation.) In fact, a major reason for convening the Constitutional Convention was to protect property and economic rights in the states to secure the functioning of a free economy.

The Bill of Rights contains six provisions directly or indirectly guaranteeing ownership. The Fifth Amendment contains the eminent domain provision already discussed and also states that no person shall be deprived of life, liberty, or property without due process of law. The Second Amendment prohibits the confiscation of arms. The Third Amendment restricts the quartering of troops in any house, even in time of war. The Fourth Amendment forbids unreasonable searches and seizures. The Eighth Amendment prohibits excessive bails and fines.

Section 1 of the Fourteenth Amendment is also a broad protection of property and economic rights. Among other things, it incorporated and "constitutionalized" the Civil Rights Act of 1866. This statute protected against discriminatory treatment the rights of most United States citizens "to make and enforce contracts . . . [and] to inherit, purchase, lease, sell, hold and convey real and personal property."[27] In the congressional debates on this act and the Fourteenth Amendment, leading sponsors frequently cited in support of their proposals the commentaries of Sir William Blackstone and Chancellor James Kent, both of whom strongly emphasized the right of property. For Blackstone the right of property meant the "free use, enjoyment, and disposal [by the owner] of all of his acquisitions, without any control or diminution, save only by the laws of the land."[28] Kent wrote that "the right to acquire and enjoy property [is] natural, inherent and unalienable."[29]

[27]Act of 9 April 1866, ch. 31, 14 Stat. 27.
[28]1 William Blackstone, *Commentaries on the Laws of England*, pp. 134–35.
[29]2 Kent, p. 1.

The most important civil rights for the framers of the original Constitution, the Bill of Rights, and the Fourteenth Amendment were those of life, liberty, and property. Contemporary Supreme Court policy largely ignores this understanding with respect to the last item of this trilogy.

Advancing Liberty

In *Economic Liberties and the Constitution*, I made the following observations:

> The federal judiciary has wandered far from its mission. Persons who should have access to these courts are effectively denied it, and the courts engage in practices belonging to other governmental bodies. Such departures from original design should be of concern to more than strict constructionists. They represent fundamental change in the function of a most powerful institution, brought about by that body itself—the very one which the Framers relied on most to maintain constitutional integrity. To this extent, the trust originally reposed in the judiciary has been compromised.[30]

These statements refer to the Court's role in protecting liberties, a constitutional function that is less complex than what it has undertaken. The Court should apply an even hand in determining whether a statute has denied an individual or corporation the right to engage in a particular activity. If such has occurred, the judicial remedy should go no further than invalidating that law with respect to the activity involved.

In matters affecting the people's freedom, the scope of judicial review should be defined by the general goal of protecting and preserving liberty. A foremost principle for a society that has limited its government in order to maximize freedom is that no one should be needlessly deprived of freedom. Thus, a law of little benefit to society that yet restrains human action has no legitimate purpose or utility. The same holds true for a law that impedes individual choice significantly more than is necessary to achieve a legislative objective.[31]

These principles have long been extant in English and American

---

[30]Bernard H. Siegan, *Economic Liberties and the Constitution* (Chicago and London: University of Chicago Press, 1980), 107–8.

[31]Ibid., pp. 322–26.

jurisprudence. Referring to civil liberty, Sir William Blackstone wrote in 1765 that it

> is no other than natural liberty so far restrained by human laws (and no farther) as is necessary and expedient for the general advantage of the public. Hence we may collect that the law, which restrains a man from doing mischief to his fellow citizens, though it diminishes the natural, increases the civil liberty of mankind: but every wanton and causeless restraint of the will of the subject, whether practiced by a monarch, a nobility, or a popular assembly, is a degree of tyranny. Nay, that even laws themselves, whether made with or without our consent, if they regulate and restrain our conduct in matters of mere indifference, without any good end in view, are laws destructive of liberty. . . . That constitution or frame of government, that system of laws, is alone calculated to maintain civil liberty, which leaves the subject entire master of his own conduct, except in those points wherein the public good requires some direction or restraint.[32]

In constitutional adjudication, Blackstone's exposition takes the form of tests to determine whether the legislative means substantially achieves the legislative ends; whether the means and ends are legitimate; and whether, when restraint is necessary, the one utilized is the least onerous to liberty. Throughout its history the Court has applied such criteria in deciding on the validity of challenged legislation. Thus, the contemporary Court does not countenance measures limiting the exercise of what it designates to be fundamental liberties that cannot be vindicated under a rigorous application of these standards. Unfortunately, it is most arbitrary in selecting which liberties to protect.

When it comes to structure, the Court's responsibility is to maintain the integrity of the constitutional plan devised by the original Framers (and as subsequently amended) without damaging the fabric of society. There is no evidence to suggest that these Framers contemplated a Supreme Court empowered to alter or change the product of their lengthy and considered deliberations.

---

[32]1 Blackstone, pp. 121–22.

Contributors

Terry L. Anderson, professor of economics at Montana State University, is a senior fellow of the Political Economy Research Center and an adjunct scholar of the Cato Institute.

Bruce Bartlett, former executive director of Congress's Joint Economic Committee, is the author of three books.

David Boaz is vice president of the Cato Institute.

Clint Bolick is an attorney at the Mountain States Legal Foundation.

Edward H. Crane is president of the Cato Institute.

James Dale Davidson is chairman of the National Taxpayers Union and author of *The Squeeze.*

Catherine England is senior policy analyst at the Cato Institute.

Peter J. Ferrara, chairman of the advisory committee of the Independent Retirement Alliance, is a former senior staff member with the White House Office of Policy Development and author of *Social Security: The Inherent Contradiction.*

Jule R. Herbert Jr., executive director of Americans for Tax Reform, was formerly president of the National Taxpayers Legal Fund.

Thomas Gale Moore, coordinator of domestic studies at the Hoover Institution, is an adjunct scholar of the Cato Institute and the author of *Freight Transportation Regulation* and other works on regulation.

Milton Mueller, an associate policy analyst of the Cato Institute, is co-author of *Telecommunications in Crisis: The First Amendment, Technology, and Deregulation.*

Earl C. Ravenal, a former Pentagon official, is a professor at the Georgetown University School of Foreign Service and an adjunct scholar of the Cato Institute.

Bernard Siegan, Distinguished Professor of Law at the University of San Diego, is the author of *Economic Liberties and the Constitution* and other works.

Joan Kennedy Taylor is publications director of the Manhattan Institute for Policy Research.

Murray L. Weidenbaum, former chairman of the Council of Economic Advisers, is director of the Center for the Study of American Business at Washington University in St. Louis and the author of *Business, Government, and the Public* and other works.

Cato Institute

Founded in 1977, the Cato Institute is a public policy research foundation dedicated to broadening the parameters of policy debate to allow consideration of more options that are consistent with the traditional American principles of limited government, individual liberty, and peace. Toward that goal, the Institute strives to achieve a greater involvement of the intelligent, concerned lay public in questions of policy and the proper role of government.

The Institute is named for *Cato's Letters*, pamphlets that were widely read in the American Colonies in the early eighteenth century and played a major role in laying the philosophical foundation for the revolution that followed. Since that revolution, civil and economic liberties have been eroded as the number and complexity of social problems have grown. Today virtually no aspect of human life is free from the domination of a governing class of politico-economic interests. A pervasive intolerance for individual rights is shown by government's arbitrary intrusions into private economic transactions and its disregard for civil liberties.

To counter this trend the Cato Institute undertakes an extensive publications program dealing with the complete spectrum of policy issues. Books, monographs, and shorter studies are commissioned to examine the federal budget, social security, regulation, NATO, international trade, and a myriad of other issues. Major policy conferences are held throughout the year from which papers are published thrice yearly in the *Cato Journal*. The Institute maintains an informal joint publishing arrangement with the Johns Hopkins University Press.

In order to maintain an independent posture, the Cato Institute accepts no government funding. Contributions are received from foundations, corporations, and individuals, and other revenue is generated from the sale of publications. The Institute is a non-profit, tax-exempt, educational foundation under Section 501(c)3 of the Internal Revenue Code.

CATO INSTITUTE
224 Second St., S.E.
Washington, D.C. 20003